MW01036874

Gender and Political Theory

Gender and Political Theory

Feminist Reckonings

Mary Hawkesworth

polity

First published in 2019 by Polity Press

Polity Press
65 Bridge Street
Cambridge CB2 1UR, UK

Polity Press
101 Station Landing
Suite 300
Medford, MA 02155, USA

ISBN-13: 978-1-5095-2581-2
ISBN-13: 978-1-5095-2582-9 (pb)

A catalogue record for this book is available from the British Library.

Library of Congress Cataloging-in-Publication Data
Names: Hawkesworth, M. E., 1952- author.
Title: Gender and political theory : feminist reckonings / Mary Hawkesworth.
Description: Cambridge, UK : Medford, MA, USA : Polity Press, 2019. | Series: And political theory | Includes bibliographical references and index.
Identifiers: LCCN 2018025183 (print) | LCCN 2018042205 (ebook) | ISBN 9781509525850 (Epub) | ISBN 9781509525812 | ISBN 9781509525829 (pb)
Subjects: LCSH: Sex role--Political aspects. | Political science--Philosophy. | Feminist theory--Political aspects.
Classification: LCC HQ1075 (ebook) | LCC HQ1075 .H396 2019 (print) | DDC 305.42--dc23
LC record available at https://lccn.loc.gov/2018025183

Typeset in 11 on 13 pt Monotype Bembo by Servis Filmsetting Ltd, Stockport, Cheshire
Printed and bound in the UK by CPI Group (UK) Ltd, Croydon

The publisher has used its best endeavours to ensure that the URLs for external websites referred to in this book are correct and active at the time of going to press. However, the publisher has no responsibility for the websites and can make no guarantee that a site will remain live or that the content is or will remain appropriate.

Every effort has been made to trace all copyright holders, but if any have been inadvertently overlooked the publisher will be pleased to include any necessary credits in any subsequent reprint or edition.

For further information on Polity, visit our website: politybooks.com

Contents

1

Sexed Bodies: Provocations

The referent, "woman," has no prior unity, no bundle of easily recognized characteristics, traits, dispositions. (Hartman 1997: 99)

In August 1995, Kimberly Nixon responded to a recruitment ad placed by the Vancouver Rape Relief Society. A feminist nonprofit collective that provided a hotline, counseling services, and a small shelter for women who had suffered sexual violence, Vancouver Rape Relief was seeking volunteers to be trained as unpaid peer counselors. To qualify for the training, volunteers had to stipulate that they agreed with four core beliefs: (1) violence is never a woman's fault; (2) women have the right to choose to have an abortion; (3) women have a right to choose who their sexual partners are; and (4) volunteers must work on an ongoing basis on their existing prejudices, including racism. Nixon shared these beliefs. In addition, she was a survivor of sexual assault as well as physical and emotional violence inflicted by her male partner. After receiving personal counseling from Battered Women Support Services in Vancouver, Nixon had volunteered both at Battered Women Support Services and at a halfway house for women in crisis. She wanted to help women who had experienced the trauma of sexual violence and she felt well qualified to undertake the training offered by Vancouver Rape Relief, so she applied for the program. Following a telephone interview and a face-to-face interview, she was invited to join the training program. During a break in the training session, however, Nixon was taken aside by the training facilitator Danielle Cormier, who asked if she had been a woman since birth. Nixon responded: "I've been who I am since I was born. I am a woman. I was just born wrong." She acknowledged that she had completed sex confirmation surgery in 1990. At that point, Cormier asked Nixon to leave, saying "a woman had to be oppressed since birth to be a volunteer at Rape Relief. Because Nixon had lived as a man she could not participate . . . men were not allowed in the training group" (Wall 2007).

The day after her exclusion from the training, Nixon filed a complaint with the British Columbia (BC) Human Rights Tribunal, which had been created by the provincial government to resolve discrimination cases involving race, color, sex, sexual orientation, religion, disability, and age. Due to its backlog of cases, the Tribunal did not hold hearings on the complaint until December 2000. In the intervening years, Vancouver Rape Relief offered to make a formal apology to Nixon and pay $500 in compensation for "hurt feelings." It also offered to allow Nixon to participate in the Society's work by joining the fundraising committee, but it refused to reconsider its decision to exclude her from the training program. Following hearings that lasted twenty-one days, and an additional eleven months of deliberations, the BC Human Rights Tribunal ruled that Vancouver Rape Relief had discriminated against Nixon and imposed a fine of $7,500—the highest damage award in the Tribunal's history—as compensation for the injury to Nixon's self-respect and dignity. The Tribunal concluded "that the actions of Rape Relief impacted on the dignity of Ms. Nixon and denied her the opportunity to participate fully and freely in the economic, social and cultural life of British Columbia" (*Vancouver Rape Relief* v. *Nixon et al.*, 2003 BCSC 1936 [150]; here and hereafter, numbers in square brackets refer to the paragraph in the court decision).

Vancouver Rape Relief appealed the Tribunal decision to

the British Columbia Supreme Court, arguing that its action did not constitute discrimination for several reasons: the BC Human Rights Code did not include protections for "gender identity, including transsexualism," hence the Tribunal had exceeded its jurisdiction; "discrimination," according to the Code, occurred only in the context of "employment" or "service provision" and did not cover volunteer activities; Nixon's exclusion was not discrimination because it was due to her lack of a *bona fide* qualification for the training—having the life experience of being raised as a woman; and finally, the BC Human Rights Code included a special exemption (Section 41) that allowed historically disadvantaged groups to organize among themselves to promote their interests—as a matter of freedom of association (Namaste and Sitara 2013: 214–15).

In the first decade of the twenty-first century, Canadian courts were asked to resolve a host of complex questions about sex as a classificatory scheme, a legal status, a personal qualification, a subjective identification, and an object of knowledge. The ruling in *Vancouver Rape Relief* v. *Nixon et al.* (2003), crafted by the Honorable Mr. Justice E.R.A. Edwards, indicates the sweeping power of the state to regulate bodies and the questionable criteria it deploys to determine sex. Although Kimberly Nixon was anatomically female and held a birth certificate granted by the government of British Columbia indicating that she was legally female, the provincial Supreme Court ruled that anatomy and legal status were insufficient to establish her womanhood: "The presence or absence of a birth certificate indicating Ms. Nixon is female cannot determine the outcome of this case" [44].

To support this remarkable position, Justice Edwards suggested that there was an omission in the law passed by the British Columbia legislature (Section 27 of the Vital Statistics Act) which authorized the issuance of revised birth certificates to those who had sex confirmation surgery. The provincial law pertained only to those born in British Columbia. Because the provincial legislature did not claim the power to control birth certificates from geographic sites beyond its borders, the court concluded that BC birth certificates were both geographically limited and temporally constrained. Birth certificates register name, parentage, sex and date of birth, but in the case of transsexuals, the court claimed they identified sex only *after* sex confirmation surgery. The court's logic accords the provincial legislature a power it does not have—to make laws governing citizens in other political jurisdictions. It suggests that birth certificates convey information they do not contain—sex before and sex after body modification. In addition, the court decision makes the objective status of a legal document— the birth certificate—conditional on the subjective appraisal of those who view it: "It did not provide that such proof *must be accepted by all persons* as determinative of the sex of a person whose birth certificate has been changed" [50, emphasis added].

According to Justice Edwards, Kimberly Nixon's sex was neither a matter of physical embodiment nor a legal status documented by an official birth certificate; it was a matter of subjective deter- mination by the Vancouver Rape Relief Society, which holds a "political belief . . . as an article of faith that persons who have not lived their lives entirely as girls and women are unsuitable as peer counsellors" [54]. Rather than considering that Kimberly Nixon's experience of sexual violence might count as a special qualifi- cation for a peer counselor, the court accredited Rape Relief's transphobic judgment that transwomen are *not* women: "There is a significant danger that a male counsellor, someone who may still have some male characteristics though dressed as a female or a man disguised as a woman will be disturbing to someone already extremely disturbed or afraid" [29]. Because Rape Relief "pro- motes the interests and welfare of women as an 'identifiable group' pursuant to s. 41 of the Code," the court accorded them a special status in determining who is a woman [84].

"Identifiable group" has a particular meaning in the context of the Canadian Constitution, which includes three equality pro- visions mandating nondiscrimination against Canadian citizens. Yet Canadian law also makes special provision for "identifiable groups" such as First Nations, who have been subjected to systemic disadvantage since the arrival of European settlers. By invoking section 41 of the BC Human Rights Code, the court suggested that any possible discrimination against Kimberly Nixon must be considered in relation to the competing rights of historically disadvantaged groups to organize to promote their interests:

> In this respect Rape Relief is in the same position as any other non-profit organization under s. 41 of the Code, making the inevitably fine distinctions necessary to determine which persons are within an "identifiable group" defined by race, religion, ancestry, color and so on. What distinguishes this case is the fact that "sex" has been conventionally viewed as a binary concept but is no longer, whereas race, religion, ancestry and certainly color have subgroups, sects, combinations and hues which are long established or more or less obvious. [93]

The court struggles with language as it tries to grapple with the possibility that an "identifiable group" is not readily identifiable. In the past, the court suggests, a binary classification seemed to facilitate sex identification, but this is no longer the case. How then is the court to know what the defining characteristics of a woman (or man) might be and which individuals possesses them? In the absence of binary constructions of sex that had governed social conventions in earlier eras, the court deferred to Vancouver Rape Relief to define "women." It accepted Rape Relief's basic claims "that 'women', defined as those persons who have lived their whole lives as females, constitute an 'identifiable group' and that Ms. Nixon can be identified as a person who is not part of that group" [88]. Thus the court held that Kimberly Nixon's exclusion did not count as discrimination.

To shore up this logic, the court turned to a decision by the Canadian Supreme Court, *R. v. Powley* (2003 SCC 43), which attempted to define historically disadvantaged groups subject to special protection under the Canadian Constitution. *Powley* involved the *Métis* people, descendants of First Nations people and European colonial settlers. Justice Edwards suggested that, like the *Métis*, "women" were members of "an identifiable group" whose characteristics were not well established [94]. *Powley* established a three-part test to determine identity: "self-identification, ancestral connection, and community acceptance" [96]. In applying this test, however, the court did not give equal weight to each criterion.

Justice Edwards rejected Kimberly Nixon's self-identification, claiming it was contradictory: "In this case with respect to the first criterion, Rape Relief acknowledges Ms. Nixon self-identifies as a female, but the evidence shows she also identified herself to Ms. Cormier as someone who had not always lived exclusively as a female" [97].

Ancestral connection has a fraught history in settler colonial societies, where it was frequently used by courts to dispossess Indigenous peoples and sever ties to "white" forebears. In an attempt to avoid these racist legacies, in *Powley*, the Canadian Supreme Court asserted that claimants must "have a real link to the historic community whose practices ground the right being claimed. We would not require a minimum 'blood quantum', but we would require some proof that the claimant's ancestors belonged to the historic *Métis*" [32]. In drawing an analogy between the *Métis* and women, Justice Edwards reinterpreted the meaning of ancestral connection to move "sex" back toward a biological ground:

> The Court rejected "blood" or genetics as the *sole* basis for meeting the ancestral connection criterion, by acknowledging ancestral adoption or "other means", but left undecided what might be an alternative objective requirement. If genetic characteristics are a legitimate criterion which must be objectively proved, it would seem that absence of pre-transsexual surgery male characteristics is at least arguably an objective basis for determining membership in an "identifiable group" of women. [99]

Justice Edwards aligned the views of Vancouver Rape Relief not only with biological determinism, but with long-standing misogynist constructions of women as "male-minus," as those who lack certain male characteristics—whether those characteristics are framed in terms of rationality, strength, courage, or physical properties (a penis, testes, facial hair)—a view that feminists had repudiated for centuries.

In discussing women as an identifiable group, Justice Edwards accorded the greatest weight to "community acceptance," suggesting that this provides the most objective legal foundation for membership in an identifiable group. "The core of community acceptance is past and ongoing participation in a shared culture, in the customs and traditions that constitute a . . . community's identity and distinguish it from other groups" [102]. In *Powley*, the Canadian Supreme Court recognized the *Métis* community in Sault Ste. Marie as the legitimate group to determine membership. By contrast, Justice Edwards designated the Rape Relief collective, one of the litigants in the case, rather than the women of Vancouver or the transfeminine community of British Columbia, as the community with the power to determine who is accepted as a woman and who is not: "If the Rape Relief collective is analogous to a community, quite clearly Ms. Nixon did not meet Rape Relief's community membership criterion" [103].

In overturning the decision of the BC Human Rights Tribunal, the BC Supreme Court allowed Vancouver Rape Relief, which it characterized as "a small relatively obscure self-defining private organization" [145], to do what the legislature of British Columbia could not do—define "women." Contrary to the explicit language of Section 27 of BC's Vital Statistics Act, Vancouver Rape Relief defined women as "those who have always lived exclusively as girls and women" and used that definition to exclude Kimberly Nixon from its training program. Ironically, the court claimed that this small group of feminist activists could exercise this power precisely because it was a private organization. Indeed, the court insisted that exclusion from a small self-defining group could not rise to the level of discrimination: "Exclusion from a self-defining 'identifiable group' is in no objective sense equivalent to legislated exclusion from a public program of benefit entitlement" [155]. According to Justice Edwards, "Exclusion by state action has a potential impact on human dignity which exclusion by a self-defining organization like Rape Relief never could have. Legislated exclusion is there for all to see. Rape Relief's exclusion of Ms. Nixon was private . . . it was not a public indignity" [147].

Contrary to the findings of the BC Human Rights Tribunal that Rape Relief had injured Kimberly Nixon's dignity and denied her the opportunity to participate fully and freely in economic, social, and cultural life, the BC Supreme Court stated:

Rape Relief provides access to only a tiny part of the economic, social and cultural life of the province. By reason of Rape Relief's self-definition, perhaps reflected in its small number of members, exclusion from its programs is quite evidently exclusion from a backwater, not from the mainstream of the economic, social and cultural life of the province. It may be an important backwater to its members and to Ms. Nixon, but that is a subjective assessment. [154]

The final sections of Justice Edwards' decision suggest that any public affront associated with exclusion from the Rape Relief training was due to Kimberly Nixon's own action:

Rape Relief's exclusion of Ms. Nixon from its club-like sisterhood cannot be equated with legislated exclusion from entitlement to public benefits ... in terms of its objective impact on human dignity. It attracted publicity and took on political significance outside the private relationship between Rape Relief and Ms. Nixon, only because Ms. Nixon chose to initiate a complaint under the Code. [161]

Resonating with victim-blaming logics, Justice Edwards suggests that any public harm stemming from Rape Relief's exclusion was of Kimberly Nixon's own doing; she had no one but herself to blame.

In his final salvo, Justice Edwards criticized the Human Rights Tribunal for lending an "aura of objectivity to Ms. Nixon's subjective sense that her dignity had been compromised" [162]. He chided both Vancouver Rape Relief and Kimberly Nixon for airing their private squabbles in public:

It is not the function of the Code to provide a referee with authority to impose state-sanctioned penalties in political disputes between private organizations established to promote the interests of self-defined "identifiable groups" and their members or prospective members. It took several years and must have cost the parties and public purse dearly to attempt to resolve this dispute. This case illustrates how ill-suited the Code is for resolution of such disputes. [157]

Kimberly Nixon had turned to the Human Rights Tribunal and subsequently the courts to remedy injustice. Speaking for the BC Supreme Court, Justice Edwards refigured her complaint as a personal dispute among competing private interests that fell well below the threshold of injustice—and as such, beyond remedy or redress.

Despite Justice Edwards' depiction of the case as broaching abuse of judicial process, two additional Canadian courts weighed in on the matter. Nixon appealed the BC Supreme Court ruling to the BC Court of Appeals. In 2005, Appeals Court Justice Mary E. Saunders sustained the Supreme Court's ruling, although she noted that in her view, the behavior of the Rape Relief Society did indeed constitute discrimination under the Human Rights Code. But she recognized that the injury to Kimberly Nixon had to be measured against competing rights, most notably the free association of "identifiable groups" who grant preference to a certain class of persons in the promotion of their interests and welfare (Wall 2007). Nixon turned to the Supreme Court of Canada for a final appeal, but in 2007 it declined to hear the case without providing any reason. Given the demands on its time, the Supreme Court of Canada declines to hear 89 percent of the cases brought before it (Flemming 2004: 30). But in dismissing this case without a hearing, the Canadian Supreme Court chose to assign court costs estimated to exceed $100,000 to Kimberly Nixon.

Although Kimberly Nixon received no justice from the Canadian courts, the Canadian Parliament subsequently intervened to shore up the rights of transwomen, transmen, and gender variant people in Canada. In response to sustained pressure from diverse Canadian social justice activists, Parliament updated the Canadian Human Rights Act and the Criminal Code to grant protections on the basis of gender identity and gender expression. Bill C-16 passed the House of Commons and the Senate with strong majorities and received Royal Assent on June 19, 2017. These legal changes are in keeping with the Yogyakarta Principles on the Application of Human Rights Law that have been endorsed by fifty-four nations across the world. Designed to provide guidelines on the obligations of states to respect, protect, and fulfill the human rights of all persons, Principle #3 stipulates that:

Everyone has the right to recognition everywhere as a person before the law. Persons of diverse sexual orientations and gender identities shall enjoy the legal capacity in all aspects of life. Each person's self-defined sexual orientation and gender identity is integral to their personality and is one of the most basic aspects of self-determination, dignity and freedom. No one will be forced to undergo medical procedures, including sex reassignment surgery, sterilization, or hormonal therapy as a requirement of legal recognition of their gender identity. No status, such as marriage or parenthood, may be invoked as such to prevent the legal recognition of a person's gender identity. No one shall be subjected to pressure to conceal, suppress, or deny their sexual orientation or gender identity. (Shrage 2012: 230)

Legal recognition by the Canadian federal government is designed to prevent the flawed logic embedded in the BC Supreme Court decision from affecting future cases, but it does not eliminate the role of jurists in *interpreting* provisions of the law or the meanings of words pertaining to sex and gender in specific cases. As the epigraph to this chapter emphasizes, interpretation is required because "the referent, 'woman,' has no prior unity, no bundle of easily recognized characteristics, traits, dispositions" (Hartman 1997: 99).

Kimberly Nixon's encounter with Vancouver Rape Relief and the judicial system in Canada raises a host of thorny issues. What is a woman? What is a man? How do biology, psychology, socialization, interpersonal relations, law, sexual violence, public expectations, power, and political theory figure in answering those questions? Is the man/woman binary the best way to understand sexed embodiment? Do certain characteristics determine who "qualifies" as a woman or a man? How does the presumed naturalness of heterosexuality structure accredited notions of sex and gender? When and under what conditions can a person be subjected to sex verification? Who has a right to demand such proof of sex and who decides the standards that constitute proof? Is gender identity a personal matter rightly subsumed under privacy protections or a public matter involving status issues of legitimate state concern? Are sex and gender political? Are sex-based and gender-based

oppressions palpable forms of injustice subject to redress? Can the
state be trusted as the guardian of sexual citizenship?

These vexing questions find no ready answers in the Western
tradition of political theory, which routinely depicts sex and gender
as natural and pre-political. By exploring operations of state power
typically omitted from canonical accounts, *Gender and Political
Theory: Feminist Reckonings* will demonstrate that embodiment
is profoundly political. The following chapters will show how
popular conceptions of human nature, public and private, citizenship, liberty, the state, and injustice relegate women, people of
color, sexual minorities, and gender variant people to an inferior
status despite constitutional guarantees of equality before the law.
They will also suggest that by masking the state's role in the creation of subordinated and stigmatized subjects, traditional political
theory has contributed to pernicious forms of injustice. Drawing
insights from critical race, feminist, postcolonial, queer, and trans*
theory, this book questions the scope of popular theories of justice
and expands the conceptualization of injustice in ways that make
pernicious state action and omission visible and actionable.

To lay the groundwork for these arguments, it is necessary
to challenge certain key assumptions about sex that have permeated canonical political theory—most notably, the notion that
sex is hierarchically ordered, whether biologically determined or
ordained by God.

Interpreting Sex

As Justice Edwards' arguments in *Vancouver Rape Relief* v. *Nixon
et al.* make clear, the meaning of sex is anything but obvious.
Yet, many people assume that "man, woman, male, female are
. . . ontologically given and stable across cultures" (Stryker and
Aizura 2013: 9). So pervasive are these assumptions that sociologist
Harold Garfinkel (1967) characterized beliefs about the fixity of
sex as the "natural attitude"—a series of "unquestionable" axioms
that tie gender irrevocably to sex. These axioms include the belief

that there are two and only two sexes/genders; the belief that sex/
gender is invariant; the belief that genitals are the essential sign of
sex/gender; the belief that the male/female dichotomy is natural;
the belief that being masculine or feminine is natural and not a
matter of choice; and the belief that all individuals can (and must)
be classified as either male or female—any deviation from such
a classification being either a joke or a pathology. Garfinkel also
noted that for most people the beliefs constituting the natural attitude are "incorrigible": they are held with such conviction that it is
near impossible to challenge their validity (Garfinkel 1967: 122–8).
     Western political theory is rife with examples of the natural
attitude. Although theorists have actively constructed putative sex
differences, they have characterized the attributes they assign to
men and women as natural and altogether beyond the reach of the
state. Aristotle (c. 384–322 BCE) was among the first to deploy
the language of sexual difference. In the *Metaphysics* (1058a30), he
asserted that "female and male are contrary and their difference is
a contrariety." Conceptualizing the female as the "privation" of
the male, Aristotle suggested that women differ from men in their
requirements for nutrition (i.e., they eat less); in their "deficient
desire" (as evidenced by their "passive" role in copulation); in their
"defective rationality" (their deliberative capacity exists but lacks
"authority"); and in the generation of life, "the female provides
the material, which the male fashions" (738b20). In recognition
of these significant defects, Aristotle dubbed women "impotent
males" (728a17–21).
     Aquinas (1225–74) adapted Aristotle's ideas to fit the demands
of Christian theology. In *Summa Theologica* (I 92 I ad 1; I 99 2
ad 1), Aquinas preserved the view of women as "defective" or
"misbegotten males," and as "helpmeets particularly in the work of
generation." Yet in tying women to the body and to reproduction,
Aquinas subtly shifted corporeality toward a more sinful view of
carnality. Among Catholic theologians, who dominated Western
political thought for close to a thousand years, men's sensual desires
were taken as proof that women are inveterate seductresses. Prone
to lust, greed, sloth, and guile, women's weak character and carnal
nature necessitated and legitimated male control.

   Modern political theorists were also unkind in their construction
of women's "nature," equivocating between claims about human
equality and women's natural subordination. Although John Locke
(1632–1704) in his *Second Treatise on Government* (1690 [1980])
repudiated patriarchal power as the basis of political authority and
asserted that all humans are equal, rational, and governed by principles of fairness and reciprocity, he also insisted that women "owed
subjection" to their husbands and consented to conjugal inequality
by consenting to marry (38). Indeed, Locke took women's agreement to subordinate their will to their husbands' as evidence of a
somewhat defective rationality, which warranted their husbands'
control (150).

   Jean-Jacques Rousseau (1712–78) also posited human beings
as equal, independent, innocent, and perfectible in "the state of
nature." Yet, he suggested that in the ideal democratic society,
governed by liberty and equality, women "must be trained to bear
the yoke from the first, so that they may not feel it, to master their
own caprices and to submit themselves to the will of others" (1762
[1955]: 332). Rousseau deployed the language of "natural law" to
insist that men and women ought to be different:

> In answering to the different ends for which nature has designed them
> . . . a perfect man and a complete woman should no more resemble
> each other in mind than in feature, nor is their perfection reducible
> to any common standard . . . The one should be active and strong,
> the other passive and weak: it is necessary that one should have both
> the power and will, and the other should make little resistance. This
> principle being established, it follows that woman is expressly formed
> to please the man. (322)

   Building on Rousseau's notion that women and men should
be socialized to sexual difference, Immanuel Kant (1724–1804)
defined women as "the fair sex" and men as "the noble sex." In his
essay, "Of the Difference of the Sublime and the Beautiful in the
Counterrelation of Both Sexes" (1764 [1964]: 76–7), Kant argued
that the full force of convention ought to be used to produce
women who instantiate the principles of beauty and understand

themselves as creatures of sentiment, feeling, and emotion. By contrast, all the resources available to society should be used to produce men who typify the principles of fairness, intellect, judgment, and duty. Appealing to an invisible soul, divine mandate, or nature's intent, Western thinkers have freely invented sex differences, accredited mystifications and distortions, and deduced from these "natural" endowments lessons for political organization. Whether imagined as deficient, defective, devious, or devilish, women were to be subordinated, controlled, and excluded from full participation in social, cultural, economic, and political life. Within the Western philosophical tradition, interpretations of sex routinely rely on binary constructions that afford power and rights to men while denying them to women. Theorists in the ancient world were explicit about their exclusions: women along with "barbarians" and "natural slaves" were barred from the polis. Modern political theorists have been far more duplicitous. They invoke the language of equality and liberty, yet their "inclusionary pretensions" give way in practice to "exclusionary effects" (Mehta 1997: 59). As Carole Pateman pointed out in *The Sexual Contract*, "the difference between the sexes is presented as the quintessentially natural difference. Men's patriarchal right over women is presented as reflecting the proper order of nature" (1988: 16). Characterized as naturally subordinate, women were not only excluded from political participation, their inferiority was placed beyond interrogation. "The classic theorists have left a legacy within which the complex, varied dealings and relations between the sexes are ruled outside critical inquiry" (Pateman 1988: 222).

Denaturalizing Sex

Like jurists in the courts, theorists in the Western canon often advance claims about the "universal subject," failing to note that their claims mistake particular historical experiences for the human condition. In the words of Simone de Beauvoir (1908–86),

"Men define the world from their own point of view, which they confuse with absolute truth" (1949 [1974]: 162). Yet as these brief examples drawn from ancient and modern political thought indicate, political theorists are often so ensnared within the "natural attitude" that they fail to notice that their contradictory assertions about women and gender undermine the internal consistency of their claims about human nature. They routinely fail to notice that the hypotheses they advance about gendered embodiment are inadequately warranted (Okin 1979; Osborne 1979). Operating within the tenets of the natural attitude, they assume it is easy to differentiate women from men.

Gender and Political Theory: Feminist Reckonings seeks to disrupt the natural attitude and the dichotomous constructions of sex and gender that it sanctions. Following Donna Haraway, the book "contests the naturalization of sex differences in multiple arenas of struggle" (1991b: 131). Toward that end, I draw upon feminist theory, critical race theory, postcolonial theory, queer theory, and trans* theory to interrogate unexamined assumptions about sex, sex difference, sexuality, gender, gender identity, gender expression, embodiment, and the meaning of biological materiality itself. Each of these theoretical traditions is rich and varied and there are numerous and important points of disagreement among them. But taken together, they make a compelling case that binary categorizations fail to do justice to the complexity, fluidity, and historically specific possibilities of human embodiment.

The following chapters offer a novel approach to feminist theory. Many works devoted to feminist theory organize their subject matter as a fixed body of work structured in relation to the history of Western political thought. Within this framework, liberal-feminist theory is conceptualized and compared with Marxist-feminist and socialist-feminist theory, psychoanalytic-feminist theory, radical-feminist theory, black-feminist theory, postcolonial-feminist theory, poststructuralist-feminist theory and posthuman-feminist theory (Jaggar and Rothenberg 1993; McCann and Kim 2003; Tong 2014). As Carole Pateman noted long ago, however, "The classification of feminists into radical, liberal, socialist suggests that feminism is always secondary, a supplement to other doctrines"

(1988: x). Rather than replicate this approach, I use feminist theory capaciously to interrogate categories of political analysis and illuminate specific dimensions of political life in concrete historical circumstances.

The feminist theorization of *intersectionality* advanced by black feminist theorists, for example, provides compelling reasons to reject the notion that gender can be studied in isolation from race, class, ethnicity, nationality, or sexuality (Crenshaw 1989, 1991; Hancock 2016; Cooper 2016). Unqualified claims about "women" may convey the mistaken notion that an organic relationship exists among women independent of time, space, culture, class, race, sexuality or nationality, masking critical power dynamics. To avoid generalizations that hide oppressive relations among women, an intersectional approach requires careful attention to the *politics of identity*—the intricate ways that processes of exclusion and marginalization create hierarchies of difference among women and among men. Gender is a facet of complex structures of domination, but intersectional analysis makes clear that gender is always constituted in relation to race, class, ethnicity, nationality, sexuality, and presumptions about ability and disability.

Black feminist theorists have theorized intersectionality to challenge the presumption of "sexual dimorphism" (the belief that there are two and only two sexes), the notion that race is a biological phenomenon, and the view that sexual desire follows automatically from possession of particular genitalia. Rather than acquiescing in the normalization of a political order stratified by race, sex, heterosexuality and the geopolitics of North/South, intersectionality scholars conceptualize racialization and gendering as political processes that create and sustain divisions of labor, social stratifications, modes of subjection, and structures of desire. Moreover, they trace the historical emergence of—and the political work done by—beliefs concerning biological determinism to European political theories that were themselves intricately tied to practices of enslavement, colonization and the invention of "modernity." Rather than accepting the naturalization of race, sex, and sexuality, intersectionality thoroughly "denaturalizes" embodiment, demonstrating how racialized notions of maleness and femaleness were constructed in relation to conquest, slavery, waged, unwaged and coerced labor, legal constraints, and political status—and then consolidated into national orders and international regimes of finely honed hierarchies of difference. Intersectional analyses demonstrate how, far from reflecting a "natural condition," biological determinist accounts of race and sex are themselves mechanisms of racialization and gendering that mask violent modes of domination (Crenshaw 1989, 1991; Roberts 1997, 2011; Hancock 2007a, 2007b, 2011, 2016; Simien 2007; Alexander-Floyd 2012; Cooper 2016).

Postcolonial and decolonial theories offer a second important approach to the denaturalization of sex and gender. Theorists in the global South have challenged accounts of modernity that originated in Europe and North America, contesting narratives of progress and civilization that legitimated European colonialism and imperialism. By insisting on historical specificity, they challenge "two founding myths of Eurocentrism: (1) the history of human civilization as a trajectory from *state of nature to liberal democratic* Europe (present in evolution and modernization); and that (2) *differences between Europe and non-Europe are biological*, not a consequence of a particular history of power" (Quijano 2000: 542, emphasis in original). As technologies of power, race and sex involve far more than mechanisms of social classification. As Quijano notes, "In America, the idea of race was a way of granting legitimacy to relations of domination imposed by conquest" (534). A particular theorization of race situated the conquered in a "natural" position of inferiority and distributed the human population by gender, ranks, places, and roles. It produced new social identities as it justified "extraction of wealth, and suppression of Indigenous knowledge production, systems of meaning making, cultural life, symbolic systems, and modes of self-understanding" (541). Rather than treating race and sex as natural characteristics or physical attributes, postcolonial theorists analyze racialization and gendering as practices of domination.

Racialization was gendered in the colonial era—Indigenous and enslaved men and women suffered different modes of subordination at the hands of colonizers. And gendering was racialized—norms of masculinity and femininity varied markedly across "races." Indeed, as Sally Markowitz has shown, "strong sex/gender dimorphism," which is associated with contemporary versions of biological determinism, was conceived as an achievement of civilization, perfected only by the European bourgeoisie. "Sex/gender difference [wa]s imagined to increase as various races 'advance' . . . the ideology of the sex/gender difference itself turns out to rest not on a simple binary opposition between male and female but rather on a scale of racially coded degrees of sex/gender difference culminating in the manly European man and the feminine European woman" (2001: 391). Colonized women and men were racialized, gendered, and sexualized by the conquistadors. Gendering provided a powerful means to destroy the more egalitarian social relations of Indigenous men and women, as men were feminized and sexually abused and women were appropriated for sexual and reproductive labor (Lugones 2007: 2010). Europeans introduced sexual hierarchies that broke down solidarity among men and women that had been grounded in norms of complementarity and reciprocity.

> In place of harmonious collaboration, European colonizers positioned [Indigenous] men and women as antagonists. Through sexual violence, exploitation, and systems of concubinage, the colonizers used gender to break the will of Indigenous men and women, imposing new hierarchies that were institutionalized with colonialism. The bodies of women became the terrain on which Indigenous men negotiated survival under new colonial conditions. Sacrificing Indigenous women to the lust of the conquerors, perversely, became the only means of cultural survival. (Mendoza 2016: 30)

Postcolonial theorizing shares with theorizations of intersectionality a deep commitment to analyzing the operations of power in purportedly natural relations.

Queer theory builds upon the poststructuralist insight that "gender essentialism gets the world wrong. Men are linked to masculinity and women to femininity by discourse, social expectations, social constraints and social power rather than by natural inclination or biological programming" (Sjoberg 2016: 7). Once the formative power of discourse is recognized, "the notion that there is an inherent, 'pre-social' human being and all the attendant biological determinisms" become untenable (Buff 2013: 68). Queer theorists conceptualize the body as more varied, open-ended, plural and malleable even as they investigate the power of social norms to discipline bodies, desires, and erotic practices. In particular, they analyze the social construction of sexuality through sexual categories and discourses that privilege and promote heterosexuality. Michael Warner coined the term *heteronormativity* to capture the multiple fields involved in the normalization of procreative sexuality, including "gender, the family, notions of individual freedom, the state, public speech, consumption and desire, nature and culture, maturation, reproductive politics, racial and national fantasy, class identity, truth and trust, censorship, intimate life and social display, terror and violence, health care, and deep cultural norms about the bearing of the body" (1993: xiii). Lisa Duggan demonstrated that heteronormativity has even permeated gay and lesbian activism and life, conceptualizing *homonormativity* as "a politics that does not contest dominant heteronormative assumptions and institutions, but upholds and sustains them, while promising the possibility of a demobilized gay constituency and a privatized, depoliticized gay culture anchored in domesticity and consumption" (2003: 50). By making visible the political dimensions of established sexual orders, queer theorists seek to disrupt sexual hierarchies and binarisms, and "dismantle not merely the family structure itself . . . but sexual identities (lesbian, gay, straight) and heteronormative familial roles (mother, father, parent, child)" (Thomas 2017: 403–4). By investigating "the relationships between stigmatized erotic populations and the social forces which regulate them," queer theory expands the understanding of "*sexual politics* in terms of such phenomena as populations, neighborhoods, settlement patterns, migration, urban conflict, epidemiology, and police technology" (Rubin 2011: 147). Queer theorists enlarge conceptions of justice to encompass sexual variation and they think creatively about strategies to redress marginalization, stigmatization, and exclusion.

Trans* theory emerged in the context of a growing activist movement that seeks to unite all possible oppressed gender minorities . . . transsexuals, drag queens, butch lesbians, cross dressers, feminine men, masculine women, female to male (FTM), male to female (MTF), gender queer, trans woman, trans man, butch queen, fem queen, transy, drag king, bi-gender, pan-gender, femme, butch, stud, two spirit, people with intersex conditions, androgynous, gender fluid, gender euphoric, third gender, and man and woman. (Enke 2012: 4)

Trans* theory brings vital insights to discussions of sex, gender, and embodiment, grounded in the experiences of those who "move away from the culturally specific expectations associated with the sex one is assigned at birth . . . toward gender self-determination" (5). Trans* theorists challenge the assumption that transwomen are categorically different from cis women (those whose gender identification conforms to the sex assigned at birth), as well as the assumption that all transwomen are the same (Heaney 2017: 196). They conceptualize *transmisogyny* as a "particular denigration directed at transwomen that combines the force of misogyny, grounded in sexual violence, devaluing of feminized work, and biologizing of intellectual inferiority, with a charge of artificial or inadequate womanhood and the imperative to prove one's womanhood" (Heaney 2017: xiii). Debunking the notion that there are only two configurations of human bodies (male/female) and the belief that sex is fixed from birth, trans* theorists have coined the term *cissexism* to refer to the "presumption that assigned sex and identified sex always align and the rejection of all evidence that this is not a universal condition" (xiii). Trans* theorists emphasize that "many humans—in their gender identities and gender expressions—do not conform to conventional gender expectations and moral judgments about what kinds of gender 'go with' what kind of body," and they note that "gender variation itself is intensely valuable as one facet of the creative diversities essential for wise and flourishing societies" (Enke 2012: 4–5). Extending Beauvoir's insight that "one is not born, but rather becomes, a woman," trans* theory demonstrates that "there is no natural process by which *any*one becomes woman [or man] . . . *every*one's gender is made" (1). Moreover, it illuminates the coercive aspects of gendering: "binary gender norms and gender hierarchies are established and maintained through violence against those who visibly deviate from them" (4). In this way, trans* theory makes visible "the political processes [that] are seen and felt in the realities of the flesh" (Cameron, Dickenson and Smith 2013: 3).

In addition to their importance in analyzing contentious presuppositions about embodiment, insights grounded in feminist, critical race, postcolonial, queer, and trans* theories help explain how multiple people can look at the same things, but perceive them differently. The approach to feminist theory presented in this book advances a cogent account of the *politics of knowledge*, explaining how "facts" can be contentious, and why supposedly neutral accounts of political life are seldom what they seem (Hawkesworth 2006). Tacit assumptions about the nature of men and women, about race, class, sex, and sexuality, about the scope of legitimate state action and the possibilities for social change, shape perceptions of the "facts" every bit as much as they shape specific policy stances. Each of the following chapters uses feminist theory to contest established "facts," to challenge received views, and to map alternative approaches to particular political questions. Whether the topic is the meaning of gender, sex, embodiment, the public/private distinction, the state, or injustice, feminist theory illuminates the theoretical assumptions that shape perceptions and inform arguments. The book deploys feminist theory to analyze traditional political theories, laws, policies, institutional practices and processes in order to enrich understandings of the stakes involved in ongoing controversies and enable perception of the raced and gendered dimensions of political life.

The product of ongoing struggles for social justice, this approach to feminist theory is perhaps best understood "as a form of resistant knowledge developed to unsettle conventional mindsets, challenge oppressive power, think through the full architecture of structural inequalities and asymmetrical life opportunities, and seek a more just world," to borrow the felicitous language of Vivian May (2015: ix). Raising questions that are inconceivable within the constraints of the natural attitude, these chapters seek "to trouble power relations, imagine better worlds, and work to achieve them" (Ferguson 2017: 283).

2

Conceptualizing Gender

> *The Nature you bedevil me with is a lie. Do not trust it to protect you.*
> (Stryker 1994: 240–1)

> *Gender does in fact have a history and a controversial one at that.*
> (Germon 2009: 1)

Although Sigmund Freud (1856–1939) is typically credited with the pronouncement that "anatomy is destiny" (1924: 274), his view echoes the ideas of most canonical thinkers in the Western tradition. Simone de Beauvoir set out to refute that tradition in *The Second Sex*, where she provided a detailed account of the intricate processes that "divide humanity into two classes of individuals whose clothes, faces, bodies, smiles, gaits, interests and occupations are manifestly different" (1949 [1974]: xx). Arguing that these differences are always structured by power, Beauvoir cautioned against romanticizing sexual difference. Indeed, she noted that while claiming freedom for themselves, men have used sexual difference to condemn women to "immanence (*en soi*): a brutish life of subjection to given conditions" (xxxv). Denying contingency and ignoring specificity, male thinkers constructed women's subordination as a "natural condition that seems beyond the possibility of change" (xxiv). Beauvoir was ruthless in her criticisms of scientists who suggested that ovaries, uterus, hormones, chromosomes, menstruation, or pregnancy dictate women's destiny. She was equally scathing of philosophical musings that defined femininity as a "Platonic essence." She characterized these products of the philosophical imagination as dangerous "male fantasies" (xix) that contributed to culture-specific efforts to make women conform to male dictates. "Man defines woman in relation to himself, she is not regarded as an autonomous being; she is what he decrees, 'the sex'. She appears to man as an essentially *sexual* being because he has produced her as such" (xxii). Beauvoir interrogated science, religion, law, philosophy, psychology, literature, culture, and education in order to trace the complex modes of power used by men to produce women as Other. Deploying differential treatment—or "sex discrimination"—as she candidly called it, men "produce in women moral and intellectual effects so profound that they appear to spring from [women's] nature" (xxxii). Comparing the active processes that produce passivity, docility, and subordination in women with the mechanisms that produce the oppression of Blacks and Jews, Beauvoir drew parallels between racialization and feminization. And she noted that the accomplishment of these ends was the work of whole civilizations: "Civilization as a whole produces this creature, intermediate between male and eunuch, which is described as feminine" (267).

Beauvoir brilliantly analyzed the production of sexual difference, but she did not use the language of *gender* to do so. Bernice Hausman (1995) has suggested that gender as a category that denotes masculine and feminine states of subjective being emerged only in the decade after Beauvoir published *The Second Sex*. Related to "new technologies of the body (biotechnologies, surgery, endocrinology) and of representation (photography, film, television, cybernetics) that infiltrated and penetrated everyday life" only after World War II, gender is of fairly recent origin (Preciado 2013: 271).

[As] an interior knowledge about oneself, a sense of the sexual "I" that appears to one's consciousness as emotional evidence of reality . . .

gender (femininity/ masculinity) is not a concept, it is not an ideology, and it is not simply a performance: it is a techno-political ecology. The certainty of being a man or a woman is a somatic-political fiction . . . an operational program of subjectivity through which sensorial perceptions are produced that take the form of affections, desires, actions, beliefs, identities. (272)

Preciado's historically specific conceptualization captures the expansiveness of gender as a phenomenon that links one's sense of self to sex, sexuality, sexual identification, gender roles, gender stereotypes, gender identity, gendered affects and emotions, as well as gendered divisions of labor and power. But exactly how gender aligns these disparate dimensions of human experience is a matter of intense dispute.

As Jennifer Germon notes in the epigraph to this chapter, "gender does in fact have a history and a controversial one at that" (2009: 1). To explore this history, the chapter begins by considering contrasting accounts of the origin and meaning of gender. It then compares sociobiological, feminist, and queer theorizations of sex, sexuality, and gender and analyzes the efforts of several leading theorists to explain the complex relationships that bind sex, sexuality, gender and subjectivity.

Historicizing Gender

David Rubin points out that "gender can be traced back to multiple points of origin" (2012: 897). One popular account ties the understanding of gender to early feminist efforts to explain women's oppression by distinguishing cultural forces from natural proclivities. In *A Vindication of the Rights of Woman* (1792), Mary Wollstonecraft (1759–97) argued that men claim women's character, behavior, and social role are natural when in fact all are products of human artifice, generated by the imposition of severe discipline. Insisting that "the sexual distinction which men have so warmly insisted upon is arbitrary" (1792 [1975]: 193), Wollstonecraft argued that men used physical force to subjugate women, and then devised sophisticated rationalizations to make such subordination appear natural. "Man, from the remotest antiquity, found it convenient to exert his strength to subjugate his companion, and his invention to shew that she ought to have her neck bent under the yoke" (26). In the final decades of the eighteenth century, the rationale for women's subordination was shifting with the emergence of the notion of biological determinism. Philosophers, political revolutionaries, and men of science had begun to claim that women's bodies have such a profound influence upon the operations of their minds that it disqualifies them from participation in public life (Laqueur 1990).

Asserting that men and women have different natures, proponents of the emerging gender ideology insisted that men and women be assigned to sex-segregated social and economic roles for their own happiness, as well as for the good of society. Indeed, French aristocrat, revolutionary, and diplomat Talleyrand (1754–1838), who assisted in writing the *Declaration of the Rights of Man*, persuaded the French National Assembly that women's "share should be uniquely domestic happiness and the duties of the household." In his "Report on Public Instruction" (1791), presented to the Assembly on behalf of the Committee on the Constitution, Talleyrand argued that, "in accordance with the will of nature," women should renounce political rights to ensure their happiness and their long-term protection (Offen 2000: 59). Wollstonecraft railed against this emerging ideology, which associated femininity with aristocratic norms of idleness, loose morals, vacant minds, and sexual intrigues, but she was not able to dissuade republican political theorists and practitioners from creating an exclusively male political assembly, "free from women's corrupting influence" (Anderson 2000: 36). Inspired by anti-aristocratic sentiment that displaced animosity against kings onto women (Landes 1988), proponents of "Liberty, Equality, and Fraternity" failed to notice how little their characterizations corresponded to the lives of the vast majority of women.

In *The Subjection of Women* (1869), British philosopher John Stuart Mill (1806–73) challenged universal claims about women's nature, insisting that women's capabilities could be known only when women were freed from the manifold constraints that curbed their potential. Until that time, "What is now called the nature of women is an eminently artificial thing—the result of forced repression in some directions, unnatural stimulation in others" (Mill 1869 [1970]: 22). Mill suggested that men devoted considerable effort to the production of literature, philosophy, and cultural practices designed to convince women that their greatest satisfaction stemmed from winning the attention and admiration of men.

> All women are brought up from the very earliest years in the belief that their ideal of character is the very opposite to that of men; not self-will, and government by self-control, but submission, and yielding to the control of others. All the moralities tell them that it is the duty of women, and all the current sentimentalities that it is their nature, to live for others; to make complete abnegation of themselves, and to have no life but in their affections. (16)

When laws bar women from education and the professions and preclude their ownership of property, the resulting economic dependence fosters the formation of a "feminine character" that replicates an idealized image of the docile subordinate that men prefer.

Both Wollstonecraft and Mill gestured toward what later feminists would call the sex/gender distinction. They advanced persuasive cases that women's self-understandings and aspirations were structured by cultural norms that channeled them into a narrow set of social roles and responsibilities. They did not question that there were two sexes and only two sexes; nor did they consider that the constructions of femininity, which they denounced as life-constraining, were class and race specific. But they sought to break the hold of philosophical and scientific claims about women's nature in order to afford women greater possibilities for self-determination.

In *Sex, Gender and Society* (1972), British sociologist Ann Oakley foregrounded a nature/culture distinction in her discussion of male domination and female subordination, introducing the term *gender*.

She defined gender as "a matter of culture: it refers to the social classification into 'masculine' and 'feminine'" (1972: 16). Drawing language from the social sciences, she suggested that sexual divisions of labor be understood as "gender roles," which had pronounced effects on "gender identity" and "psychosexual orientation" (159). Familiar claims about inborn differences between women and men involved a category mistake, confusing nature with culture: "Sex differences may be 'natural', but gender differences have their source in culture, not nature . . . The aura of naturalness and inevitability that surrounds gender-differentiation in modern society comes, then, not from biological necessity but simply from the beliefs people hold about it" (189).

Oakley conceptualized gender to break the hold of biological reductionism—the belief that anatomy dictates disposition, ability, and social role—initiating decades of feminist scholarship that revealed the wide variation in cultural constructions of femininity and masculinity and in social roles assigned to men and women historically and cross-culturally. Drawing upon this conceptualization, feminist scholars used gender to analyze the power relations embedded in the organization of social roles and relationships between men and women, to demonstrate how certain valued traits were associated with men and other less valued characteristics attributed to women, and to illuminate how women's bodies came to signify potent desires that required monitoring and control within particular cultures. Gender was also used to make visible unequal distributions of burdens and benefits and micro-techniques of power within specific societies.

As feminists explicated gender as a cultural construct, debates about the nature of gender grew in scope and intensity. Some feminists theorized it as an attribute of individuals, an interpersonal relation, a legal status or a matter of behavioral conformity to social norms; others conceived gender as a structure of consciousness, a triangulated psyche stemming from the Oedipal conflicts of early childhood, an internalized ideology, or an account of individual identity and aspiration. Feminist scholars debated whether gender was better understood as a product of socialization, the effect of normalizing practices, a structural feature of labor, power, and cathexis, a layering of personality, or a "doing" or performance. They also argued about whether gender was a prison house that ought to be abolished, or a radically repressed dimension of human potential that ought to be unleashed as inherently liberating (Hawkesworth 1997).

By grounding their analyses on a nature/culture dichotomy, many feminist scholars advanced a "base/superstructure" model of the sex/gender distinction (Connell 1987: 50; Laqueur 1990: 124). Within this model, the sexed body is assumed to provide the raw material which culture can refine in various ways. For this reason, feminist discussions of gender often did not move far beyond presuppositions concerning inherent sex differences. By accepting that sex is biological and that sex and gender are dimorphic, they replicated core tenets of the natural attitude. Thus Linda Nicholson suggested that many feminist views avoided strict biological determinism only to fall back upon biological foundationalism. Within this frame, "the body is viewed as a type of rack upon which cultural artifacts, specifically those of personality and behavior, can be thrown or superimposed" (Nicholson 1994: 80). Raewyn Connell explained the pervasiveness of this tendency in feminist accounts of gender by noting that in contemporary culture, "the notion of natural sex difference forms a limit beyond which thought cannot go" (1987: 66). Similarly, Holly Devor described biological foundationalism as the dominant cognitive schema in North America—the conceptual structure that organizes social experience on the basis of shared understandings (1989: 45–6). Linking biological foundationalism to developments since the seventeenth century, historian Thomas Laqueur observed that "It is a sign of modernity to ask for a single, consistent biology as the source or foundation for masculinity and femininity" (1990: 61).

Black feminist theorists pointed out that the presumption that natural sex differences structure gender often conflates the experiences of affluent whites in advanced economies with masculinity and femininity. In Scenes of Subjection (1997), Saidiya Hartman noted that the experiences of enslaved women bore no resemblance to bourgeois conceptions of white femininity. Defined as property, denied all rights of self-determination, subjected to brutal physical labor, excluded from contractual relations such as marriage, rights of motherhood, and legal protection against sexual assault, black women's experiences of womanhood did "not divest the slave women of gender, but reveal[ed] the role of property relations—the possession of the enslaved—and racial subjugation in the constitution of gender and sexuality" (Hartman 1997: 100). Noting that the racialization of gender did not end with the abolition of slavery, Patricia Hill Collins demonstrated that Blacks were often penalized for failing to conform to gender norms from which they were intentionally excluded. "Within a Western sex role ideology premised on ideas of strong men and weak women, on active, virile masculinity and passive, dependent femininity, the seeming role reversal among African Americans has been used to stigmatize black people" (Collins 2004: 44). Intersectional analysis, then, with its attention to the mutual constitution of race, class, ethnicity, nationality, and sexuality, raises important challenges to any notion of dimorphic gender.

Lessons from Linguistics

Quite apart from accounts of gender that foreground relations of male domination and women's subordination, some feminist theorists have drawn insights from linguistics, noting that gender initially existed as a grammatical category. Etymologically, gender derives from the Latin, *genus*, via old French, *gendre*, roughly translated as "kind" or "sort." "The most puzzling of grammatical categories, genders are classes of nouns reflected in the behavior of associated words" (Corbett 1991: 1). Gender is puzzling for linguists precisely because it is *not* universal or invariant. In some languages gender is central and pervasive, while in others it is totally absent. Corbett's examination of more than 200 languages revealed that "the number of genders is not limited to three; four is common, and twenty is possible" (5). As the proliferation of genders in specific languages makes clear, gender need not have anything to do with sex. In some languages, "gender marks the distinction masculine/feminine/non-sexed; but in other languages

the divisions animate/inanimate, human/non-human, rational/
non-rational, male human/other, strong/weak, augmentative/
diminutive, male/other, female/other function exactly as does
the division into male/female" (30). As the etymology suggests,
grammatical gender is based on a wide range of "kinds" including "insects, non-flesh food, liquids, canines, hunting weapons,
items whose lustrous surfaces reflect light . . . The worldview of
the speakers determines the categories" (30, 32). Given the enormous variation in grammatical genders, the determining criterion
of gender is agreement: genders are distinguished syntactically by
the agreements they take. In some languages, adjectives and verbs
show agreement; in others, adverbs, numerals and even conjunc-
tions agree; but in all cases agreement is the way in which genders
are reflected in the behavior of associated words (5).

Gender's conceptual appeal for feminists is closely tied to its
versatility in linguistics. As a linguistic construction, the cultural
origins and historical specificity of gender are unmistakable.
Gender's relation to the belief systems of specific peoples frees it
from the specter of biological determinism. Moreover, linguistic
gender is not inherently enmeshed in binary opposition. There
is another facet of gender's linguistic legacy, however, that should
give feminists pause. If feminists were to draw an explicit analogy
with grammatical gender, they would conceive genders as categories of persons constituted in and through the behavior of
associated others, emphasizing that the relevant behavior involves
concord or harmony. Although this aspect of the grammatical her-
itage is seldom acknowledged, notions of agreement, harmony, and
complementarity surface obliquely in numerous feminist accounts
of gender. Indeed, as the final sections of this chapter demonstrate,
a close reading of some of the most sophisticated accounts reveals
that notions of complementarity form the tacit core of multiple explanations of gender, situating it in a functionalist frame.
Within this frame, gender emerges as a cultural construct devised
to promote particular conceptions of social harmony inseparable
from heteronormativity.

Gender and the Regulation of Embodied Difference

Feminist science-studies scholars have traced an alternate lineage in the conceptualization of gender tied to mid-twentieth-century medical research on intersex bodies (Hausman 1995; Germon 2009; Rubin 2012, 2017). While completing his doctoral research on "endocrine functions and psychological states of hermaphroditism . . . John Money coined the term *gender role* as a diagnostic category and treatment protocol for patients whose anatomical configurations were regarded as unintelligible within the dominant frame of dimorphic sex" (Rubin 2012: 892). Claiming his formative role in the conceptualization of gender, Money suggested that in his early work,

> the word *gender* made its first appearance in English as a human attribute, but it was not simply a synonym for *sex*. With specific reference to the genital birth defect of hermaphroditism, it signified the overall degree of masculinity and/or femininity that is privately experienced and publicly manifested in infancy, childhood, and adulthood, and that usually though not invariably correlates with the anatomy of the organs of procreation. (1995: 18–19)

As David Rubin has noted, Money pathologized intersex persons, characterizing their physical embodiment in terms of "birth defects" that required medical intervention (2012: 893). Rather than acknowledging that sexual dimorphism fails to account for the panoply of naturally occurring bodies, Money and his colleagues at Johns Hopkins insisted that the anatomy of intersex infants is "improperly differentiated," or indeed, "sexually unfinished" (Money and Ehrhardt 1972: 5). Yet, in legitimating a role for medical intervention to complete what nature had left unfinished, Money appealed to the necessity of aligning genitalia with "psychosexual orientation—libidinal inclination, sexual outlook and sexual behavior" (5). Moving beyond a strict biological conception of sex, Money defined gender as one of a number of heterogeneous elements constitutive of sex:

The first step was to abandon the unitary definition of sex as male or female, and to formulate a list of five prenatally determined variables of sex that hermaphroditic data had shown could be independent of one another, namely, chromosomal sex, gonadal sex, internal and external morphologic sex, and hormonal sex (prenatal and pubertal), to which was added a sixth postnatal determinant, the sex of assignment and rearing . . . The seventh place at the end of this list was an unnamed blank that craved a name. After several burnings of the midnight oil I arrived at the term, *gender role*, conceptualized jointly as private in imagery and ideation, and public in manifestation and expression. (1995: 21)

According to Money, gender was not simply one of seven elements associated with sex, it was the key to personal identity. "Infants born with ambiguous genitalia could be surgically 'corrected' and then successfully raised as either males or females" as long as gender assignment occurred before the age of eighteen to twenty-four months, parents strictly enforced the gender of rearing, and children were "not confused by knowledge about their intersexed past" (Rosario 2007: 267).

In contrast to the assumption that sex determines gender identity, Money conceives of sex as malleable, open to surgical intervention and social construction (in the form of child rearing). He also suggests that third-person ascribed identity (physician assignment of sex) dictates personal identity (an individual's gendered self-understanding). In all important respects, then, medical authority determines gender identity and surgical and hormonal interventions produce bodies that conform to that designation. Indeed, the Johns Hopkins Gender Identity Clinic's treatment protocol for the intersex insisted that "the sex of assignment and rearing is consistently and conspicuously a more reliable prognosticator of a hermaphrodite's gender role and orientation than is the chromosomal sex, the gonadal sex, the hormonal sex, the accessory internal reproductive morphology, or the ambiguous morphology of the external genitalia" (Money, Hampson, and Hampson 1955: 333). Within this medicalized frame, appropriate gendered subjectivity for the gender variant requires surgical, hormonal, and psychosocial normalization. The biomedical conceptualization of gender is inseparable from "the regulation of embodied difference through biopolitical discourses, practices, and technologies of normalization" (Rubin 2012: 886).

The regulative ideal at the heart of Money's conception of gender was classed and raced. He brought malleable bodies into alignment with stringent notions of masculinity and femininity drawn from white middle-class experience. The guidelines for gender rearing, which were to be strictly enforced by parents, as well as the counseling provided for post-operative patients, were designed to ensure that gender performances matched surgically sexed bodies. Money's patients were expected to conform to "traditional notions of what it meant to be a middle-class, white adolescent in mid-twentieth-century America" (Reis 2009: 120). As Zine Magubane acutely observes: "Even when the idea that the truth of sex is anchored in the body is thrown radically into doubt, race still provides an anchor for the concept of gender . . . masculine and feminine states of being to which the concept referred were already and inherently coded as white and in opposition to blackness" (2014: 778, 782).

Troubling Sexual Dimorphism

Money and his colleagues gave pride of place to sex assignment at birth and gender socialization in determining gender identity and sexual orientation, precisely because the evidence for dimorphic sex is so problematic. Although cloaked in the authority of science, biological determinism—the view that there are fundamental, innate physiological differences among kinds of humans, manifested in the incontrovertible evidence of race and sex—"is also the product of particular, historical, cultural moments" (Laqueur 1990: 13). As an historical artifact, biological determinism is a thoroughly political doctrine.

Since the eighteenth century, sex has typically been understood as the anatomical division of the human species into male and female. As Laqueur (1990) so carefully documented, however, sexual dimorphism is intimately tied to the politics of modernity. As natural science displaced theology in Enlightenment metaphysics, the "one sex" model of embodiment that had dominated European political thought and practice for nearly two millennia gave way to a "two sex" model that posited men and women as incommensurate opposites rather than as embodied "souls" ordered along a continuum on the basis of proximity to the divine. Although corporeal differences carried political and social consequence in earlier eras, the relevant markers of difference prior to the eighteenth century were not lodged in the genitalia or reproductive organs. "Penis/vagina, testicles/ovaries, female menstruation and the absence of monthly bleeding in men" were not taken "as self-evident marks of opposition . . . Instead each element of these was understood as a version of the other in accord with a metaphysically given relationship: women were less perfect men whose respective anatomy and physiology reflected this order" (Laqueur 2012: 803). In the eighteenth century, the emerging "natural philosophy" proposed that human biology should be understood in terms of sexual dimorphism, "a fixed oppositeness, that was somehow foundational and beyond culture," providing a "natural foundation" for differentiated social roles and responsibilities, legal status, as well as divisions of power and opportunity (802).

In the midst of Enlightenment proclamations of universal rights derived from the "self-evident truth" that all men are created equal, political theorists and republican revolutionaries in both the United States and France extrapolated from the new biological dimorphism grounds for excluding women from membership in the political community. Asserting that reproductive physiology determines individual character and political capacity, republican revolutionaries on both sides of the Atlantic adopted the notion that sexual difference dictates proper political status and behavior, insisting that any transgressions of the gendered political order threatened the very basis of society and civilization. To shore up women's supposed biological incapacity for politics, male law makers passed legislation barring women from participation in political clubs, political organizations, political parties and from political office (Landes 1988, 1998; Cody 2001, 2005).

Over the course of the nineteenth century, male law makers in nations across the globe replicated the republican practice of using the law to bar women from politics and restrict them to the private sphere. As Ann Towns (2009) has demonstrated, exclusion was embraced in Europe as an indication of "more advanced civilization," then imposed as a "civilizing" measure on colonies in Africa and Asia as European nations expanded their colonial empires. These colonial impositions displaced earlier Indigenous forms of women's political authority (Okonjo 1994; Oyewumi 1997).

Despite the overt political means by which these exclusions and restrictions were enacted, the growing authority of science afforded them a "natural" justification: disparate male and female anatomies carried "natural" mandates for social roles—mandates implicated in the very survival of the species. As biological determinist frames gained ascendency, the political work involved in the subordination of women was rendered invisible and replaced with fictive pasts accredited by evolutionary theories that posited male dominance as natural and universal.

In the version of biological dimorphism cultivated over the twentieth century, male and female are construed as "natural kinds," distinguished by unique configurations of chromosomes (XY/XX), hormones (androgens/estrogens), gonads (reproductive organs such as testes and ovaries), internal morphology (seminal vesicles and prostate as opposed to vagina, uterus, and fallopian tubes), external genitalia (penis and scrotum/clitoris and labia), as well as secondary sex characteristics (body hair, facial hair, breasts). Feminist scholars have shown, however, that none of the typical correlates of biological sex conform to the demands of a classification as natural kinds. Within philosophical discourses, a natural kind refers to a category that exists independently of the observer and that can be defined in terms of an essence, a set of properties common to all members of the kind. Feminist scholarship has repudiated the notion of any sexual essence precisely because "there are no behavioral or physical characteristics that always and without exception are true only of one gender" (Kessler and

McKenna 1978: 1). Chromosomes, hormones, sperm production, and egg production all fail to differentiate all men from all women or to provide a common core within each sex. "No matter how detailed an investigation science has thus far made, it is still not possible to draw a clear dividing line even between male and female" (Devor 1989: 1). Both men and women have testosterone and estrogen in their systems, and the human "X" chromosome, wantonly mischaracterized as the "female" chromosome, is not only common to both men and women, but carries a large collection of male sperm genes (Richardson 2012).

Even the insistence that there are two and only two sexes is mistaken. New technologies in DNA sequencing and cell biology conceptualize chromosomal sex as a *process*, not an assignation. More than twenty-five genes affect sex development, contributing to a patchwork of genetically distinct cells within one body, some of which may have a different "sex" than the rest.

> This *mosaicism* can have effects ranging from undetectable to extraordinary, such as "identical" twins of different sexes. An extremely common instance of mosaicism comes from cells passing over the placental barrier during pregnancy. Men often carry female cells from their mothers, and women carry male cells from their sons. Research has shown that these cells remain present for decades. (Ford 2015)

In an early essay, biologist Ann Fausto-Sterling (1993) pointed out that, using strictly biological criteria, there are not two but five sexes "in nature." In addition to males and females, there are multiple modes of intersexuals—"herms" (persons born with both a testis and an ovary), "merms" (persons born with testes and some aspect of female genitalia), and "ferms" (persons who have ovaries combined with some forms of male genitalia). Surveying the evidence presented by endocrinology, genetics, neuroscience, and other scientific disciplines, Fausto-Sterling later concluded: "Our bodies are too complex to provide clear-cut answers about sexual difference. The more we look for a simple physical basis for 'sex,' the more it becomes clear that 'sex' is not a purely physical category. What bodily signals and functions we define as male or female come already entangled in our ideas about gender" (2000: 4).

The social sciences have done no better than the natural sciences in their efforts to identify behavioral differences that conform to the definition of a natural kind. Attitudinal and behavioral "sex differences" reflect social attributions that have nothing to do with natural differences. Within social science research, indicators of "biologically based femininity" typically include interest in weddings and marriage, preference for marriage over career, interest in infants and children, and enjoyment of childhood play with dolls. While indicators of "biologically based masculinity" include high activity levels, self-assurance, and a preference for career over marriage (Devor 1989: 11–15). Psychological inventories of masculinity and femininity manifest the misogynist tendency to define socially valued traits as male (logical, self-confident, ambitious, decisive, knows way around world) and less valued characteristics as female (talkative, gentle, sensitive to others' feelings, interested in appearance, strong need for security) (32). Yet, even with all the cultural bias built into such indicators, empirical studies have not been able to clearly differentiate men and women in the cultures that produced them. "'Normal femininity' of the psychological test variety may actually be a rare commodity. In one study of college-aged females, only 15 percent of the heterosexual sample tested as feminine on a widely accepted sex role inventory. The remaining 85 percent scored as either masculine or as some combination of masculine and feminine" (15). Differences cast in terms of averages, tendencies, and percentages do not meet the criteria of a natural kind.

Rather than being given in nature, sexual dimorphism is imposed by human beings who are trying to make sense of the natural world. As Suzanne Kessler and Wendy McKenna noted, this imposition is as characteristic of scientific inquiry as it is of everyday observation:

> Scientists construct dimorphism where there is continuity. Hormones, behavior, physical characteristics, developmental processes, chromosomes, and psychological qualities have all been fitted into dichotomous

categories. Scientific knowledge does not inform the answer to the question, "What makes a person a man or a woman?" Rather it justi-fies (and appears to give grounds for) the already existing conviction that a person is either a man or a woman and that there is no problem differentiating between the two. Biological, psychological, and social differences do not lead to our seeing two genders. Our seeing two genders leads to the "discovery" of biological, psychological, and social differences. (1978: 163)

Denaturalizing Sexuality

Feminist theorists and queer theorists have also contested the naturalization of sexuality. Whether characterized as an instinctual urge, a species imperative, the means of procreation, a site of pleasure and desire, or a primitive elemental force, sexuality has been enmeshed in intricate systems of social control (Rubin 1993). Whether celebrated as a source of physical delight, denounced as a temptation to sin, or described as the means of generation, traditional depictions of sexuality were often cast as the scene of the first sexual division of labor. In Aristotle's vivid terminology, the male was defined as he who mounts, and the female as she who is mounted, inscribing both a presumption of heterosexuality and an active/passive dichotomy at the core of putatively natural erotic practices (*On the Generation of Animals*, Book I, 2). Noting the power differentials embedded in such a construction of "natural" urges, early feminist scholars suggested that it is a mistake to con-strue sexuality solely in terms of desire, pleasure, and procreation, for it is also a system of domination.

In an early radical feminist analysis, Shulamith Firestone (1970) characterized eroticism as a subspecies of romanticism, a cultural tool of male power that channels women's desire for love into genital sex. Anne Koedt (1970) noted that such channeling quite literally deprived women of the prospects of sexual pleasure. Koedt castigated Freud's psychosexual account of "mature sexuality" because it required women to repudiate the evidence of their own senses—the experience of orgasm through the stimulation of the clitoris—and replace it with the "myth of the vaginal orgasm," defining their sexual satisfaction exclusively in terms of what pleases men. Far from being a space for the free play of desire, radical feminist theorists conceived *heterosexuality* as a political relation of domination and subordination that puts men first and maintains male supremacy (MacKinnon 1987), a social institution of violence that places women in perpetual servitude to men (Wittig 1979), a cosmogony that envisions men and women as complementary because they "fit together" while masking asymmetrical power relations (Delphy 1993), and as a compulsory system that assures men the right of access (physical, emotional, and economic) to women, while requiring that lesbians be invisible in contemporary societies and written out of history (Rich 1980).

By situating heterosexuality in relation to larger structures of male power, early feminist thinkers suggested a strong affinity between lesbianism and feminism. Charlotte Bunch (1972), for example, depicted lesbianism as a "political choice" and as a "revolt against white male power" by women-identified-women who act together to end sexual and political domination. Similarly, Monique Wittig (1979) characterized lesbianism as an escape from the class of women and from servitude to men. Differentiating lesbianism from male homosexuality, Adrienne Rich (1980) envisioned a "lesbian continuum," which encompasses a political stance that entails commitment to the values of feminism and freedom of women as a group, a form of primary emotional intensity among women, bonding against male tyranny, marriage resistance, conscious desire for erotic experience with women, and the strength to break taboos and reject compulsory sexual subordination.

In a pathbreaking book that helped launch the field of queer theory, *Epistemology of the Closet*, Eve Sedgwick questioned the tendency in many feminist works to conflate sex, gender, and sexuality, suggesting the need for greater analytical differentiation of these concepts: "The study of sexuality is not coextensive with the study of gender; correspondingly the study of antihomophobic inquiry is not coextensive with feminist inquiry. But we can't know in advance how they will be different" (1990: 27). In a

related move, Cheshire Calhoun (1994) challenged the conflation of lesbianism and feminism, calling for a clear distinction
between patriarchy (or structures of male domination) and heterosexuality. According to Calhoun, feminist theorists had failed to
recognize that heterosexuality is a political structure of domination
distinct from patriarchy; heterosexuality divides heterosexuals
and non-heterosexuals into different groups with different rights
and opportunities, creating privilege for some, while systematically excluding others. Echoing Audre Lorde's (1985) insight that
heterosexism is the belief in the inherent superiority of one form of
loving, Calhoun defined *heterosexualism* as a political system that
supports male privilege *and* heterosexual privilege. It enshrines the
man–woman dyad as the basic unit of society, privileges reproduction as a heterosexual domain, and produces gender dimorphism,
sexual divisions of labor, and occupational and legal arrangements
that privilege heterosexuals.

Lorde (1985) also pointed out that *homophobia*, which encompasses both a terror of love for the same sex and a hatred of those
who are gay and lesbian, is a powerful mechanism of social control.
Homophobia drives a wedge between gay and straight, while also
deploying the coercive powers of heterosexuality to keep gays and
lesbians closeted. To be "outed" is to risk losing one's biological
children in a custody battle, being denied the possibility of adopting children, losing one's job, being punished for public displays of
affection, facing housing discrimination, being harassed by neigh-
bors, being subjected to "normalizing" therapies, being excluded
from representations of love, being denied the right to marry, and
being subject to physical violence and death at the hands of virulent
homophobes (Calhoun 1994; Pharr 1997). Linking these forms of
coercion to micro-techniques of power that produce "normalized"
and disciplined bodies, Michael Warner (1991, 1993) theorized
heteronormativity as encompassing intricate expectations, demands,
and constraints that sustain hierarchies of difference grounded on
the presumed naturalness of heterosexuality. Heteronormativity is
systemic, pervading cultural production, occupational structures,
legal and political institutions, medical practices, and immigration protocols, as well as religious, philosophical, and scientific

discourses, denigrating and marginalizing those who refuse the strictures of heterosexuality. Indeed, heteronormativity is so pervasive that it has been assimilated within gay and lesbian communities in the form of *homonormativity* (Duggan 2003), a system of values that privileges homosexuals who "mimic" heterosexual norms of monogamy, marriage, and family, while pathologizing dissident forms of queer existence.

Probing the Relations Among Sex, Gender, and Sexuality

With the growth of feminist and queer scholarship over the past five decades, there has been continuing debate about how best to theorize the complex relations among sex, gender, and sexuality. While virtually all scholars working in gender and sexualities studies employ the terms *sex, sexuality, sexual identity, gender identity, gender role*, and *gender role identity*, they do not all use the terms in the same way. Sex, for example, can refer to biological features such as chromosomes, hormones, internal and external sexual and reproductive organs or to erotic practices popularly characterized as love-making. Gender identity typically refers to the individual's own feeling of being a man, a woman, Intersex, or gender variant, but this "feeling" may be defined conventionally as having a conviction that one's sex assignment at birth was "anatomically and psychologically correct" (Stoller 1985: 11), more expansively as a patterned subjectivity that bears some relation to cultural conceptions of masculinity/femininity/nonbinary fluidity, or more critically as a "refiguring of flesh in ways that adhere to normative gender codes . . . making it abide by preexisting gender laws" (Stryker 2006: 247). What is meant by *identity* can also mean markedly different things. It can refer to a psychological sense of "who I am," a sociological notion of a person qua agent prior to assuming specific social roles, a Foucauldian concept that captures an array of regulatory practices that produce the internal coherence of the subject, a philosophical concern with the individuation and unity of a person in the face of change, a narrative construction the individual develops to make sense of one's life, or a political identification with a group or collective, often produced in and through exclusionary political processes and state policies.

Although usage varies from text to text, most scholars grant that there are important conceptual differences between sex construed in biological terms or in relation to the materiality of the body; sexuality understood to encompass sexual practices and erotic behavior; sexual identity referring to designations such as heterosexual, homosexual/gay/lesbian/queer, bisexual, or asexual; gender identity as a psychological sense of oneself as a man, a woman, gender variant or gender queer, a sense that need not be tied to physical embodiment, as transgender and transsexual activism and theory have made clear; gender role as a set of prescriptive, culture-specific expectations about what is appropriate for men and women; and gender role identity—a concept devised to capture the extent to which a person approves of and participates in feelings and behaviors deemed to be appropriate to his/her culturally constituted gender (Kessler and McKenna 1978: 7–11; Barrett 1980: 42–79).

This analytic vocabulary provides distinctions that are integral to efforts to challenge the natural attitude. The distinction between gender identity and gender role identity, for example, opens the possibility that one can have a clear sense of oneself as a woman (or a man) while being thoroughly disaffected from and refusing participation in prevailing conceptions of femininity (or masculinity). This distinction breaks any connection between masculinity/ femininity and sexed bodies, interpreting masculinity and femininity as culture-specific abstractions that mark a chasm between regulative ideal and lived experience, attributed and actual, propaganda and practice.

Once conceptual distinctions that differentiate sex, sexuality, sexual identity, gender identity, gender role, and gender role identity are delineated, then critical questions emerge: What do these phenomena have to do with one another? How are they related? How do their complex interrelations pertain to gender as lived experience or to gender as a power relation? The natural attitude postulates physical sex (male/female) as the determinant of gender identity that flows naturally into a particular mode of (hetero)sexuality and mandates certain gender roles embraced happily by individuals with uniformly positive gender role identities (that is, a person born with a uterus "naturally" develops a nurturing personality, craves association with a member of the "opposite" sex, engages in heterosexual intercourse, gives birth, happily assumes the responsibilities of child rearing, and defines meaningful existence in relation to mothering). Feminist scholars have challenged each of these posited relations. They have advanced varying accounts of the relations that obtain among sex, gender, sexuality, and identity, and investigated how such complex social processes are naturalized, masking the political agendas that inform them.

The final sections of the chapter examine the strengths and limitations of contending accounts of the relations between sex, gender, sexuality, and personal identity, comparing popular biological essentialist views with feminist critiques that foreground performative and structural accounts.

Biological Reductionist Accounts

Operating within the confines of the natural attitude, sociobiologists, evolutionary psychologists, and physical anthropologists have no difficulty explaining putative connections between sex, gender, and sexuality, claiming that they are dictated by the demands of species survival. Defining men as "sperm producers" and women as "egg producers," they suggest sexual dimorphism exists to foster diversity, providing richer opportunities for genetic variation than asexual modes of reproduction, and thereby affording survival advantages for particular gene pools. Sociobiologists, for example, characterize heterosexual intercourse as a form of "cooperation" to produce zygotes; yet they also suggest that species survival "mandates" different sexual practices for men and women. Because, they claim, sperm are "cheap"—males supposedly produce 100 million sperm per ejaculation—sexual promiscuity affords advantages for the promotion of male genes. Eggs, on the other hand, are "costly"—females produce only twenty to thirty viable eggs over the course of a lifetime—therefore, females are more inclined toward fidelity and monogamy as strategies to promote the survival of their gene pool. The putative adaptive advantages afforded by sex-specific sexual practices are claimed to generate distinctive traits associated with masculinity (aggressiveness) and femininity (coyness). Gendered divisions of labor—from fictive accounts of man-the-hunter, women-the-gatherer to contemporary claims about men's overrepresentation and women's underrepresentation in positions of power, wealth, and prestige—are similarly explained in terms of the survival advantages (Wilson 1975, 1978). Rooting their claims in neuroscience, genetics, and evolutionary psychology, best-selling authors such as Simon Baron Cohen (2004) and Steven Pinker (2002) have reinvigorated old debates about innate sexual differences, "hard-wired" in the brain that purportedly affect cognitive abilities, communication skills, and the capacity to perform a host of social and political roles.

Critics have pointed out pervasive and systemic flaws in the sociobiological account of gender. At a methodological level, sociobiology falls prey to circular reasoning that violates the norms of scientific inquiry. Because they assume that existing traits are genetic adaptations, sociobiologists offer no empirical evidence to demonstrate that particular traits or behaviors are "heritable." They advance purportedly universal claims about sex differences drawn primarily from observations of baboons, but offer no justification for their selection bias. Research on some 200 other primate species provides no credible evidence to support sociobiological claims. In particular, claims about "costly eggs" and "cheap sperm" that undergird claims about sex-specific sexual practices have been found to be invalid and unwarranted. In addition, the notion advanced by sociobiologists that the rich and vast domains of culture are "genetically" based mistakenly assigns responsibility to nature for the design of human institutions (Gould 1980; Fausto-Sterling 1985; Fedigan 1992; Tang-Martinez 1997). Unable to provide scientific evidence to support their unwarranted claims, sociobiologists defend a narrow range of male-privileging, heteronormative behaviors by attributing survival advantage to them.

"Scientific" claims about sex differences in the brain are also enormously popular, gaining widespread media attention. Yet, they too are seriously flawed. Rebecca Jordan-Young (2010) has provided systematic evidence that studies that treat the brain as an "accessory reproductive organ" suffer from a host of methodological flaws. Her detailed examination of the "quasi-experiments" and "proxy variables" deployed in "brain organization studies" demonstrate not only that it is impossible to identify any "hard-wired" male-typical or female-typical behavior, but that particular studies are riddled with inconsistencies, ambiguities, and contradictions. To paraphrase the epigraph from Susan Stryker, the Nature that pundits bedevil us with is a lie.

Despite their patent inadequacy as accounts of sex, sexuality, or gendered practices, biological reductionist arguments surface regularly in popular culture and in some feminist discourses. Following the noted anthropologist Claude Lévi-Strauss (1969, 1971), many accept a conception of culture as an elaborate mechanism devised to create interdependence and cooperation in the reproduction of the species. Philosopher Stephen Smith, for example, suggests that species reproduction *requires* sexual differentiation, therefore culture creates that differentiation through processes of gendering in order to ensure the perpetuation of the species, but masks its role by attributing the original difference to sex itself. "Since men and women have significantly different reproductive risks and opportunities in evolutionary terms, their guiding sex-related emotions must be sex-differentiated, that is, there must be different female and male sexual natures" (Smith 1992: 124). Defining gender as a "conventional formation of a plastic humanity" (15), Smith suggests that culture shapes what is perceived as a body. Through "embodiment," "the community stipulates what counts as a male/female body, what life will be like in a male/female body in relation to other bodies, what norms (and latitudes) of character and conduct are associated with these bodies, and who is male and female" (91). When culture takes up the task of molding human nature, then, its aim is to enhance its own *construction* of what is naturally given, marking sex differentiations through language, character, and social roles. According to Smith, "heterosexuality's postulated union of male and female specializations is the basic premise of the gender system" (80). Indeed, he suggests that "Confronting sex differences makes me realize that I need a partner to reproduce ... A gendered being teams with other gendered beings" (71, 55). Echoing sociobiological presumptions, Smith suggests that the cultural creation of gender complementarity serves the larger purpose of species survival.

As Smith's account makes clear, appeal to a biological ground traps accounts of gender within the problematic logic of sexual dimorphism and the heteronormative "ideology of procreation," which construes sexuality and erotic practices only in relation to reproduction (Barrett 1980: 62–77). Despite its nod to culture as the conventional formation of a plastic humanity, these reductionist accounts narrowly define women and accord them an essentialized maternal role "mandated" by culture and nature—a role undifferentiated by race, ethnicity, nationality, age, class, sexual orientation, or any mode of individuality.

Performative Linkages

Judith Butler's influential work, *Gender Trouble*, set out to disrupt the hold of biological determinism by explaining how the "naturalness" of sex, sexuality, and gender are culturally produced. Rather than accepting that sexual dimorphism is given in nature, Butler suggests that the belief in two sexes is discursively produced. Indeed, gender is the "very apparatus of production whereby the sexes themselves are established" (1990: 7). Gender is not a condition, an identity or a set of attributes, but a "doing," a stylized repetition of acts that constitutes the identity that it purports to be (24). By performing subservience, obedience, flirtation repeatedly, for example, some folks come to believe that it is their nature to be subservient, obedient, flirtatious—"feminine." And by taking risks, engaging in dangerous outdoor play, and defying authority repeatedly, others come to understand themselves as daring, adventurous, independent—"masculine."

Keenly aware that there are no biological characteristics that all women and only women share or that all men and only men share, and hence no natural differences that distinguish all men from all women (i.e., no natural kinds), Butler investigates how widespread belief in such differences is created and sustained. "Gender is the discursive/cultural means by which 'sexed nature' or 'a natural sex' is produced and established as 'prediscursive', prior to culture, a politically neutral surface on which culture acts" (7). Gender performs this work of naturalization through the repetition of words, acts, and gestures. The sheer weight of these repetitions leads the actor to believe in and act in the mode of belief. Moreover, the process of repetition constructs the "heterosexual matrix"—the cluster of beliefs that sustain the conviction that dimorphic sex necessarily generates heterosexual desire and heterosexual practice. Gender functions, then, as a regulatory fiction, "a fabrication, a fantasy instituted and inscribed on the surface of bodies" (136).

Becoming gendered is a laborious process, and bringing the self to believe in the natural attitude is arduous; yet the intensity of effort and the power relations that produce this effect are hidden by the very "naturalization" at the core of the gendering process. Butler's account reverses the direction of causality presumed by the natural attitude: the belief in two biological sexes is the effect of gendered performances. But Butler insists that gender itself is the effect of specific formations of power, of institutions, practices, and discourses that establish and regulate its shape and meaning. To explain the forces that produce gender, Butler turns to cultural investment in heterosexuality. "The heterosexualization of desire *requires* and *institutes* the production of discrete and asymmetrical oppositions between 'feminine' and 'masculine' understood as expressive attributes of 'female' and 'male'" (17). Thus Butler, like Smith, appeals to the cultural creation of heterosexuality as the explanation of gender. In Butler's analysis, gender as performativity becomes the cultural force that produces belief in the naturalness of heterosexuality. Gender is both the "effect of compulsory heterosexuality" and a powerful contributor to belief in a "natural" heterosexual world and a heterosexual body experienced as "natural fact."

Gendered performances that naturalize dimorphic sex involve complex psychological processes that eroticize the body. Through an intricate analysis of Freud and Lacan, Butler links eroticization to two cultural taboos—the prohibitions against homosexuality and incest, which differentiate bodily parts and pleasures on the basis of gendered meanings. Although Freud is well-known for his claim that, prior to civilization, human sexual desires were prone to "polymorphous perversity," an inclination curbed only by the institutionalization of the incest taboo, Butler suggests that the incest taboo that fuels the Oedipal conflict makes no sense without a prior prohibition of homosexuality. According to Freud, resolving the Oedipal conflict, that is, repressing the desire to have sexual relations with one's "opposite sex" parent, is the key to normal psychosexual development. Yet, Butler argues, Freud's presumption that Oedipal desire exists only for the "opposite sex" parent proves that same-sex desire has already been forcibly repressed. She notes that Freud's account of polymorphous perversity is structured by sexual dispositions, which he characterizes as "bisexual." But Freud conceptualizes bisexuality in terms of *feminine and masculine dispositions*, "*the coincidence of two heterosexual desires within a single psyche*" (60, emphasis in original). Within Freud's thesis of primary bisexuality, then, there is no homosexuality, sexual desire has already been heterosexualized.

Supplementing Freud's account of a primal incest taboo, Butler argues that culture produces two prohibitions that regulate the shape and meaning of sexuality: the first is the taboo against homosexuality, and the second is the incest taboo. The prohibition against homosexuality both produces sexuality in the form of heterosexual 'dispositions' and "appears disingenuously at a later point in time to transform these ostensibly 'natural' dispositions into culturally acceptable structures of exogamic kinship" (64). Butler emphasizes that the law qua prohibition is also productive: it creates that which it prohibits. Thus, homosexuality and bisexuality cannot be understood as either "before" or "outside" culture, for they too are constructed within the terms of constitutive discourse.

> If the incest taboo regulates the production of discrete gender identities, and if that production requires the prohibition and sanction of heterosexuality, then homosexuality emerges as a desire which must be produced in order to remain repressed. In other words, for heterosexu-

ality to remain intact as a distinct social form, it requires an intelligible conception of homosexuality and also requires the prohibition of that conception in rendering it culturally unintelligible. (77)

The taboo against homosexuality in conjunction with the taboo against incest structure gendering processes that differentiate bodily parts and pleasures, deadening some organs to pleasure and bringing others to life (68–70). Butler's psychoanalytic account accords primacy to the taboo against homosexuality to explain culture's production of compulsory heterosexuality and to explain gender's production of a naturalized body. Where Smith endorsed cultural mechanisms that "harmonize" human relations and foster social integration, Butler denounces the modes of power that produce homosexuality as necessary, yet prohibited; within culture, yet marginalized. Butler is careful to note that the binary relation heterosexual/homosexual is itself a problematic discursive formation, premised upon a false opposition and a fraudulent unity within each term of the binary. Indeed, in criticizing Monique Wittig's radical disjunction between homosexuality and heterosexuality, Butler insists that there are "structures of psychic homosexuality within heterosexual relations, and structures of heterosexuality within gay and lesbian sexuality and relationships" (121). And in criticizing Lacan, Butler cautions against totalizing conceptions of identity that follow from too efficacious and univocal a conception of the Law. She calls instead for a recognition that "multiple and coexisting identifications produce conflicts, convergences, and innovative dissonances within gender configurations which contest the fixity of masculine and feminine placements with respect to the paternal law" (67). The very possibility of such multiple identifications is central to Butler's strategy for confounding gender. Arguing that power can never be escaped, only redeployed, Butler endorses parody as a tactic designed to subvert "the real" or the "sexually factic." Strategies of subversive repetition can dispel belief in the illusions of the "natural" body/desire/sexuality, thereby rendering gender incredible (141, 146).

As a postmodern critique, Butler's genealogy of gender is designed to probe what is left out of discursive formations that construe

sex/gender/desire as natural. She points out that homosexuality as
a legitimate mode of sexuality is omitted from naturalistic accounts.
Given the pervasiveness and persistence of the natural attitude, it
makes sense to attribute its production to powerful cultural forces.
In Butler's analysis, gender as performativity becomes the cultural
force that produces belief in the naturalness of heterosexuality;
gendering is the process that naturalizes and justifies a particular
asymmetry. As the "effect of compulsory heterosexuality," gender
reproduces a "natural" heterosexual world.

Why does gender act as such a helpful handmaiden of compulsory heterosexuality? Butler's response is telling: since "gender is
a project which has cultural survival as its end, the term strategy
better suggests the situation of duress under which gender performance always and variously occurs. Hence, as a strategy of
survival within compulsory systems, gender is a performance with
clearly punitive consequences" (139). Butler's characterization of
gender as a strategy of survival within a compulsory system suggests that gender must perform its function to avoid punishment, a
punishment presumably imposed by culture. But why does culture
insist upon heterosexuality? In a discourse that explicitly eschews
any sociobiological explanation such as species reproduction, the
options seem to be limited to either a simple notion that culture is
a self-replicating system (bracketing the question of the origin of
the cultural preference for heterosexuality), or a Freudian notion
that the renunciation of homosexual desire is the sublimation
that civilization demands. The first option follows from Butler's
characterization of gender as performativity, yet it has conservative implications incompatible with her subversive objectives. She
defines performativity as the repetition of words, acts, gestures.
This definition is virtually indistinguishable from J.G.A. Pocock's
conception of tradition as "an indefinite series of repetitions of an
action," introduced both to vindicate the authority of tradition
and to eliminate unhelpful and potentially destabilizing queries
about origins (1973: 237). Such a conservative project is diametri-
cally opposed to Butler's stated objective of subverting gender. If
Butler's account of gender is not to fall prey to a static conception
of cultural self-replication, then her appeal to "cultural survival"

must be interpreted in a Freudian vein. But in that case, sexuality is offered as the explanation of culture.

Butler's analysis drives a wedge between sex and sexuality, thereby avoiding biological determinism. The belief that sexuality "follows" from sex can be understood only as a relation of political entailment. But what is required to understand culture as "following" from compulsory heterosexuality? Can all of culture's complex domains plausibly be construed as emanating from or mandated by compulsory heterosexuality? Butler tends to conflate culture with phallogocentrism, an androcentric Symbolic system that privileges "the Law of the Father"—a move that accords psychoanalytic discourses greater cultural weight than science, industry, engineering, or other more palpable cultural constructs. Phallogocentrism captures feminist concerns about male domination in history and culture, but it does so at an exacting cost. For by construing culture in terms of a Symbolic system that itself privileges the Phallus, Butler perpetuates women's invisibility, underestimating their role as co-creators of culture. Phallogocentrism fails to provide a sufficiently exhaustive account of culture. Moreover, it indulges a form of anthropomorphism that sustains discussions of what might be called "the cunning of culture," the ingenious means by which culture ensures its own survival through the production of organizational practices and structures independent of the needs or intentions of individuals. Such a reification makes culture appear at once omniscient, seamless, and unassailable, a markedly unhelpful point of departure for those aspiring to feminist transformation. There is also a certain irony in Butler's positing of compulsory heterosexuality as the explanation of culture. Foucault cautioned against the trap of conceiving sex (qua sexuality) as the secret of being, suggesting that such beliefs implicate the subject in ever deeper modes of subjugation. It is unlikely that gesturing toward sexuality as the secret of culture can escape that trap.

By interpreting gender in terms of the cultural production of heterosexual desire and the psychoanalytic production of gender identity, Butler's account makes gender too much a matter of the self—a self that appears peculiarly unmarked by race, class, or ethnicity. Her account privatizes gender, offering little prospect for addressing gender structures beyond the psyche. The operation of gender in social, political, and economic institutions disappears as the psychodrama of the desiring self is played out. This occlusion of gender as an organizational feature of social life that is itself mediated by race and class may explain why Butler's reliance on parody as a transformative mechanism rings so hollow. While parody might help subvert the naturalization of desire, it is unlikely to make inroads against the economic and political forces that circumscribe contemporary lives.

Butler's account of gender succeeds in escaping biological determinism but it advances a functionalist explanation of gender. Moreover, in positing heterosexuality as the explanation of culture, Butler's account of gender comes far too close to Smith's for comfort. For allusions to compulsory heterosexuality do nothing to dispel the ideology of reproduction that sustains the natural attitude. Despite the virtuosity of Butler's account of gender as performativity, it does not provide a conception of gender that breaks definitively from the problematic presuppositions of modernity.

Structural Accounts

In *Gender and Power*, Raewyn Connell advances a "systematic social theory of gender" that strives to account for the historical emergence and variability of gender, the dynamic role of gender in economic, political, sexual, and psychological domains, the relation between personal agency and social structure in gender formation and replication, as well as the turbulence and contradictions pertaining to gender as lived experience. Connell develops a "practice-based" theory attentive to both the constraining power of gender and the myriad struggles people engage in against those constraints. Providing a cogent critique of all modes of biological determinism, Connell notes that the body is never experienced without cultural mediation, and defines gender in terms of the cognitive and interpretive practices that "create, appropriate, and recreate reproductive biology" (1987: 79).

Connell rejects all theories that attempt to derive gender from natural differences, biological reproduction, the functional needs of society, or the imperatives of social reproduction, insisting that they serve only to mask the power underlying these cultural symbolizations in order to justify inequitable distributions of social burdens and benefits. Moreover, she suggests that the social practices constituting gender bear no direct relation to what might be considered "functional" for human reproduction. The patterns of posture, movement, dress, adornment, body shape, body image, sexuality, intonation, speech, skilling, and de-skilling associated with cultural constructions of masculinity and femininity may not be at all conducive to reproduction. Connell also notes that gender as a social practice is more than a mere marking of the human body: "it is the weaving of a structure of symbols which exaggerate and distort human potential" (79).

In developing this account of gender, Connell delineates a conception of human practices in relation to social structures informed by the works of Marx and Sartre. Within this frame, *practices* are the daily actions of human beings who appropriate and transform nature in order to satisfy their needs and in the process transform themselves, producing new needs and new practices. Practices are inherently dynamic transformations of the natural world that open up new possibilities as well as new risks and pressures. Practices can also become solidified, entrenched, institutionalized, creating a degree of intractability in the social world that limits the freedom of future practices. Connell defines social structure in terms of such limits. A *social structure* is a pattern of constraint on practice inherent in social relations. Operating through the complex interplay of power and institutions, "'structure' specifies the way practices (over time) constrain practices" (95). Although structures mark the fixity of the social world—the sedimentation of past practices that limit present action, the dimension of collective life that exists beyond individual intention—they are not impervious to change. "Practice can be turned against what constrains it . . . structure can deliberately be the object of practice. But practice cannot escape structure; it cannot float free of its circumstances" (95). According to Connell, gender can best be understood as an interrelated set of social structures that define men and women in terms of their reproductive role and organize social life around sex and sexuality.

On this view, gender is far more than an attribute of an individual or a characteristic of a social collectivity; it is the active process that reduces people to, and conceives social life in terms of, reproductive function, thereby constraining individual potential (97, 140, 245).

Taking issue with feminist accounts that construe gender structure in terms of a monolithic male domination, Connell argues that gender must be conceived in terms of very specific structures tied to particular social practices of labor, power, and cathexis. As a constraint upon labor, gender structures the allocation of particular types of work, the organization of domestic activity, the division of paid versus unpaid labor, the segregation of labor markets, patterns of production and consumption, wage levels, opportunities for employment and promotion, and even the conditions and terms of labor exchange. Within the domain of power, gender structures authority, control, and coercion, which establish hierarchies in public and private sectors, create a virtual male monopoly on institutional and interpersonal violence, and promote particular domestic and sexual asymmetries. Defining *cathexis* in terms of practices constructing emotionally charged relations with others, Connell notes that gender structures the identities of desiring subjects and the designation of desirable objects, as well as patterns of desire, sexual practices, and the terms and conditions for sexual exchange.

For Connell, gender is the process that relates all the rich and varied levels of human activity to biological reproduction. It is an active force that makes us think constantly in terms of sex. And it is precisely this reductionism that enables gender to constrain so many dimensions of social organization. Yet when Connell so deftly identifies the gender structures operative in the domains of labor and power, it is not at all clear that they gain their force by dragging the mind back to reproductive biology. Do women really earn less because they are capable of bearing children? Does gender make us think so? Is job segregation in clerical work, fast-food industries, secondary education, or nursing really related to women's gestational ability? Are women subjected to domestic violence because of their reproductive role?

Connell notes that "the practices of sexual reproduction are often quite remote aspects of social encounters in which gender is constructed and sustained" (81). But if this is so, how does gender work? Connell introduces Sartre's distinction between a practico-inert series and an intentionally mobilized group to explain gender's operative mechanisms. According to Sartre, a series is a mode of collective unity structured by external social or material circumstances or what might be called the "logic of the situation." Because the commonality that unites the series is imposed by external objects or the actions of others, seriality is passive, implying no conscious awareness on the part of those who make up the series. Sartre used the example of people waiting for a bus to illustrate his conception of the series: they have certain things in common by virtue of their situation even though they may not be consciously aware of any common ties. In contrast, a group is a collection of persons who consciously acknowledge a bond uniting them, whether it is a collective identity, a common project, or shared values.

According to Connell, sex can be understood as a series. The biological differentiation of men and women in reproduction imposes an external logic upon individuals on the basis of a parallel situation. Thus women share a passive commonality by virtue of their reproductive capacity, as do men. In keeping with Sartre's description of seriality as practico-inert (i.e., a product of human action that constrains), Connell notes that construing sex as a series does not imply any awareness of the postulated commonality, any incorporation of the seriality into one's identity, nor any identifica-tion with those others who share the situation. By describing gender in terms of a Sartrean group, Connell suggests that gender's task is *to create* a conscious awareness of reproductive capacity as the basis for solidarity. "To construct the social category 'man' or 'woman', with a common identity and interest, requires a negation of the serial dispersion characteristic of the array of parallel situa-tions constructed by biological categories. This is done in practices that create and assert the solidarity of the sex (or of a group within it)" (81, 137). For gender to accomplish its mission, then, it must negate the passive experience of the body and create a notion of commonality embraced by members of the group, thereby mobilizing women and men as distinctive groups. But how can gender simultaneously negate the biological ground of the series and mobilize reproductive biology as the basis of a shared identity? And if certain social expectations about the sexed body constitute sex as a practico-inert series, structuring the logic of the situation in terms of reproduction, how does gender differ from those initial social expectations? The sex/gender distinction seems to collapse into a vortex of reproduction.

Sartre conceives of the group as a collection of persons whose conscious awareness of shared characteristics serves as the basis for united action, for the initiation of a collective project. But Connell's conception of gender cannot begin to carry men and women that far, for she explicitly acknowledges the deficiencies of any construction of men and women as internally undifferentiated categories. And she is keenly aware of the social cleavages rooted in race, class, ethnicity, age, and homophobia that preclude any collective identification, much less collective action. Thus the group/ series explanation of how gender accomplishes its work founders both in its account of sex as series and its account of gender as group. And despite Connell's numerous caveats, it appears to accord primacy to reproduction in cultural constructions of sex, as well as gender. Without addressing Connell's use of Sartre's conception of seriality, Iris Young (1994) argued that gender should be understood as a series that structures certain commonalities, but that it is activism that mobilizes women as a collective with shared self-understandings and goals—whether that activism is feminist, maternalist, or religious in orientation.

Connell offers several speculations about why belief in gender persists despite all the philosophical arguments and scientific evidence that demonstrate the defects of the natural attitude. "There is a logic to paradoxes such as gross exaggerations of difference by social practices of dress . . . They are part of a continuing effort to sustain the social definition of gender, an effort that is necessary precisely because the biological logic, and the inert practice that responds to it, cannot sustain gender categories" (1987: 81). But if gender is doing its cultural work successfully, what explains the perceived necessity to shore up gender? Connell's account is startling: "The solidarity of the heterosexual couple is formed on the basis of some kind of reciprocity rather than on the basis of common situation or experience . . . Sexual difference is in large part what gives erotic flavor to relationships. It is emphasized as a means of heightening and intensifying pleasure, hence, the systematic exaggeration of gender differences" (113). Despite the enormous complexity of Connell's account, despite her repeated cautions against functionalist explanation, a notion of heterosexual complementarity undergirds her analysis. It provides the fundamental explanation of why gender persists.

Although Connell explicitly tries to avoid heterosexism in discussing gender as a mode of constraint, the notion that "sexual difference" heightens erotic pleasure depends on heterosexist presuppositions. Eve Sedgwick (1990) has pointed out that the heterosexual/homosexual opposition allows for equivocation in the meaning imputed to 'homo'/sexual. As one moves from notions of one sex, to same sex, to self-same, to sameness, an enormous range of differences is elided. And this elision sustains Connell's assumption that there is greater difference, hence greater potential erotic pleasure, across genders than within genders. "The new calculus of homo/hetero . . . owes its sleekly utilitarian feel to the linguistically unappealable classification of anyone who shares one's gender as the 'same' as oneself, and anyone who does not share one's gender as Other" (Sedgwick 1990: 160). But Sedgwick points out that even the most cursory examination of human beings will reveal that being of the same gender cannot guarantee "similarity" any more than being of "opposite" genders can guarantee difference. Moreover, the belief that the gender of one's sexual partner is the crucial difference determining pleasure (rather than differences pertaining to positions, acts, techniques, zones or sensations, physical types, symbolic investments, relations of power, etc.) will not withstand serious scrutiny. Thus, there appears to be a suppressed procreationist premise in Connell's allusion to the best means to heighten erotic pleasure. Once again, the "cunning of culture" seems to insert a procreationist agenda into an explanation of gender.

Complicating Gender

Feminist theorizations of gender have come a very long way since Wollstonecraft's critique of an emerging sexist ideology deployed to exclude women from political life. In addition to drawing attention to the artifice that permeates claims about women's "nature," feminist scholars have advanced sophisticated accounts of gender as "a constitutive element of social relationships based on perceived differences between the sexes, and . . . a primary way of signifying relationships of power" (Scott 1986: 1067). They have shown that gender operates in and through cultural symbols, normative concepts, social institutions and organizations, and subjective identities (1067–8). They have devised compelling accounts of the complex relations that link sex, gender, and sexuality. Yet, as the above analyses of the arguments advanced by Butler, Connell, and Smith suggest, even the most sophisticated accounts of gender tend to be haunted by the "ideology of procreation," a conception of sexuality that reduces the erotic to reproduction (Barrett 1980: 62–77). The assumption that culture functions to enhance species survival is not only heteronormative, but race and class specific. It fails to acknowledge that the cultures associated with "modern civilization" have actively thwarted the reproduction of colonized peoples through policies that ranged from population control to genocide.

Concerned with these limitations, multiple scholars have raised questions about the utility of gender as an analytical category. Susan Bordo identified two currents fueling "gender skepticism" (1993: 216). One current flows from the experiences of women of color and lesbian feminists who suggested that the "multiple jeopardy" characteristic of their lives raises serious questions about the validity of gender generalizations. If gender is always mediated by race, class, ethnicity, and sexual orientation, then an analytical framework that isolates gender or construes it in terms of an "additive model," which presumes gender is a discrete facet of identity that can be variously affected by race, class, ethnicity, and sexual orientation, is seriously flawed and serves only to mask the numerous privileges of white, middle-class, heterosexual feminists who have the luxury of experiencing only one mode of oppression (Spelman 1988; King 1988; Higginbotham 1992). The second current flows from postmodern criticism, which depicts gender narratives as totalizing fictions that create a false unity out of heterogeneous elements. In addition to calling into question the binary opposition that fixes men and women in permanent relations of domination and subordination, postmodern critics also challenged the "ground" of the sex/gender distinction. If gender was devised to illuminate the social construction of masculinity and femininity and naively took the sexed body as given, then it has little to offer in a postmodern world that understands the body, sex, and sexuality as socially constructed.

Theorizing "intersectionality" (Crenshaw 1989; McCall 2005; Hancock 2007a, 2007b, 2016; Cooper 2016), "hybridity" (Anzaldua 1987, Bhabha 1994, Friedman 1998), "articulation" (Hall 1980a, b), and "assemblage" (Deleuze and Guattari 1987; Puar 2007), recent feminist scholars explore embodiment as a matter of the mutual constitution of race, gender, class, ethnicity, sexuality, and nationality. They examine racialization, gendering, and heterosexualization as historically specific and interlocking processes that produce hierarchies of embodied difference and structures of inequality that permeate bodies and minds. These ideas are taken up in Chapter 3.

3

Theorizing Embodiment

Biology is politics by other means. (Fausto-Sterling 2000: 269)

No one yet has determined what the body can do. (Spinoza, *Ethics* IIIP2S)

According to the *Oxford English Dictionary*, to embody is to give concrete form to what is abstract or ideal. The earliest usages of the term were associated with the mystery of incarnation—how the soul or spirit became invested with a body. Some of the musings about embodiment from the ancient world now seem quaint, such as those that attributed basic temperaments to deficiency or excess in bodily fluids. Noted thinkers from Hippocrates (460–370 BCE) and Galen (129–c.200) to Avicenna (980–1037) advanced and refined the doctrine of the "four humors," which explained human moods, emotions, intellectual capabilities, moral inclinations, and behaviors in direct relation to physiological states: sanguine (enthusiastic, active, and social) personalities stemmed from exuberant blood; choleric (independent, decisive, goal oriented) temperaments were caused by yellow bile; black bile contributed to melancholic (analytical, detail oriented, deep thinking and feeling) characters; and strong quantities of phlegm explained those who were phlegmatic (relaxed, peaceful, quiet) (Arikha 2007). The doctrine of the humors shaped the practice of medicine, experiences of the lived body, and philosophical accounts of embodiment well into the eighteenth century. Medical textbooks and philosophical arguments provided graphic images and sophisticated verbal accounts of the intricate relations linking dispositions and afflictions to organs, ducts, and fluids. Astute physicians, jurists, and theorists of human nature grounded their expertise in *physiognomy*—the art of determining character or personal characteristics from the form or features of the body, especially of the face. Signs on the surface of the body were taken as clues to interior states that were neither material nor observable.

Philosophical accounts of embodiment, then, are mired in the politics of representation. They seek to make visible disparate connections: the relation of reality to appearance, essence to actuality, immaterial to material, form to matter, constancy to change, nature to convention, mind to body, cognition to sensation, action to subjectivity, behavior to will and desire. They draw attention to certain kinds of evidence by enabling a particular way of seeing the world. Convinced of the accuracy of their insights, philosophers cast their claims in the language of universals.

This chapter examines some of the claims about embodiment advanced within the Western tradition of political theory to raise questions about the adequacy of their accounts of "human nature." It analyzes a range of abstractions associated with human bodies, and interrogates universal generalizations in order to show how they conflate the experiences of some elite, white, European men with all human experience while simultaneously engaging in gendered racialization that places some modes of embodiment beyond investigation. The chapter begins by examining views of the "rational subject" or the "sovereign self" which have been remarkably resilient in the Western tradition. It then discusses dimensions of embodied existence omitted from or masked by these canonical accounts, demonstrating that "the Eurocentric perspective of knowledge operates as a mirror that distorts what it reflects . . . the image perceived is not just composite, but partial and distorted" (Quijano 2000: 556). The chapter devotes particular attention to racialized and gendered biologization, as the means by which philosophers and scientists associated ideas about different "species of men" with the inhabitants of specific geopolitical regions. It also considers recent theorizations of embodiment that attempt to overcome the raced-gendered distortions that have haunted Western political thought.

Human Nature

Although it is often taught as a tradition that stems from classical antiquity to the present, the Western canon in political philosophy is of fairly recent origin. It is a collection of texts selected in the second half of the nineteenth century as part of a new curriculum offered in secularizing universities in Europe and the United States. Powerfully shaped by Hegel's notion of European history as the unfolding of reason and freedom, the works included in the canon were drawn from cultures and epochs that were believed to have played a key role in Europe's unique civilizational accomplishments (ancient Greece and Rome, the Italian Renaissance, Britain, France, and Prussia during the Enlightenment). Structured around "great debates" concerning human nature, politics, democracy, freedom, and justice, canonical texts suggest that truth is their goal. By exercising their critical intellects, canonical thinkers pierce the mysteries of existence and offer deep insights into the nature of reality. Despite such lofty goals, however, the works included in the Western canon offer accounts that accredit racist, sexist, and heterosexist social relations. Close attention to canonical views of human nature reveals how rationality and political rights come to be the preserve of particular Anglo-European men, who accord themselves not only self-determination but an entitlement to rule over and civilize "lesser" peoples.

In contrast to the theory of the four humors, which explained personality in terms of basic physiological states, canonical political theorists analyzed human nature in relation to gods and beasts. Philosophers sought to identify the *differentia specifica*—that which distinguished humans from the divine and from animals. A.O. Lovejoy (1936) suggested that ancient and medieval theorists shared a theology of the natural world as a well-ordered and divinely ordained hierarchy. Within the "Chain of Being" or *Scala Natura* (scale of nature), all forms of life could be classified on a continuum from the lowest (minerals, vegetables, animals) to the highest (humans, angels, gods). The scale privileged spirit over matter and positioned all living things according to their proximity to an omniscient and immortal deity. Placement within the great chain of being entailed authority: higher beings could legitimately rule over lower forms of existence, but the power they exercised was bounded by moral principles, sometimes described as "laws of nature," also believed to be divinely ordained and accessible to humans through the exercise of right reason.

The conceptions of human nature developed in Western political thought are rich and various. Despite critical differences, however, many theorists ascribe rationality, speech, a capacity for invention, and a capacity for shame to humans. Like the gods, humans can reason, communicate, and create a world of artifice. Unlike gods or animals, humans are not content to move about the world naked. Incessant bodily needs weigh heavily on them and can prove a powerful source of discomfort and shame. Envisioning the psyche, soul, spirit or mind as immaterial, multiple thinkers accorded it immortality, an ability to outlive the body whether through reincarnation or a notion of heavenly reward. Preferring what they had in common with higher beings, some theorists articulated a rift between soul and body, treating bodies as subordinate, inferior in moral status. Some conceive the body as a site of temptation, a distraction from the pursuit of knowledge, a seduction away from God, a capitulation to sexual desire, violence or aggression, a failure of will, a mechanism of death (Bordo 1993: 5). Viewing the body with ambivalence or suspicion, they identify a distance between the "true self" and the body it inhabits. The body is characterized as an appearance, a repository, a temporary vehicle, an entity, a property that one possesses, "as something apart from the true self (which is conceived as soul, mind, spirit, will, creativity, freedom) . . . and as undermining the best efforts of the self" (Bordo 1993: 5). Some philosophers go so far as "to imagine the body as a prison for the soul . . . to conceive flesh as inconvenient matter that limits free expression of our inner and nobler being . . . to be embodied is to be entrapped in a condition of materiality . . . cemented in permanent, hopeless struggle . . . as a condition of existential inadequacy" (Carter 2013: 130).

Captured most famously by Descartes' *cogito*, "I think therefore I am" (1637 [1998]: 19–20), mind/body dualism accords primacy to rationality, while reducing the body to a dubitable shell. Located in the capacity for conscious thought, the self is individual and absolute, freed from the encumbrances of the body. Within modern political thought, the notion of an unencumbered self that pre-exists society and embodied social relations has been enormously influential. It undergirds the social contract tradition, which posits pre-social, rights-bearing individuals who freely contract to create a political system. In Locke's version, developed in *Two Treatises on Government* (1690 [1980]), this "sovereign self" is rational, equal, and free in "the state of nature," and acts always to improve his condition. In fashioning the social contract, this rational subject sets clear limits to state power, and retains a right of revolution against any tyrant who abuses power. Locke suggests that the sovereign self has property in his person and is entitled to acquire additional property by mixing his labor with the abundant resources of the earth. Absent such labor, natural resources have no value; they simply go to waste. For Locke then, embodiment connects reason, rights, labor, and legitimate acquisition in the industrious body.

Locke's language is instructive: "In the state all men are naturally in . . . men are perfectly free to order their actions, and dispose of their possessions and themselves, in any way they like, without asking anyone's permission—subject only to limits set by the law of nature. It is also a state of equality, in which no one has more power and authority than anyone else" (Locke 1690 [1980]: 122). Despite his claims about a universal condition that "all men are naturally in," which make it "simply obvious that creatures of the same species . . . born to all the same advantages of nature . . . should be equal in other ways," Locke subsequently justifies both slavery (132–3) and servitude (135). Slaves are those who have "renounced reason," placing themselves in a "state of war" against others. By engaging in violent aggression, they forfeit all rights to self-determination. Servants are those who voluntarily agree to work for others, signing a contract that accords a "master" entitlement to control the servant's time and talents. By agreeing to transfer control over their labor to another, rather than mixing their labor with the earth's resources and amassing wealth, servants demonstrate that their reasoning powers are suspect. Thus servants benefit from being under the control and direction of their master. Similarly, women manifest weak powers of reasoning when they agree to a marriage contract that perpetually subjects their will to that of their husbands. Consent to marriage implies voluntary subordination, which in turn demonstrates the wisdom of the husband's control over decision making. The universality of the human condition, then, seems to have less to do with generic bodies than with gendered and classed bodies.

Locke scholars have pointed out that his claims about natural freedom and equality exist in tension with views articulated in his other works. While serving as Secretary to Lord Shaftesbury, Locke crafted the *Fundamental Constitutions of Carolina* (1669), the governing document of two British colonies in North America. Article CX of this document makes a provision for slavery, explicitly stating that "freemen will have absolute power and authority, including that of life and death, over their Negro slaves." Locke also owned stock in the Royal Africa Company, which held a monopoly to conduct the British slave trade. There is no evidence to suggest that Locke believed that the African men and women who were kidnapped and transported to "the New World" had aggressed against the slave-traders or in any way conformed to the criteria for justifiable enslavement stipulated in the *Second Treatise* (Ward 2016). Thus his legitimation of slavery in the British colonies stands in stark contrast to his claims about natural liberty and equality. In his *Essay Concerning Human Understanding* (1689 [1997]), Locke's characterizations of "Indians" also fall far short of his claims concerning the rationality and equality of "all men" in the state of nature. In the context of an essay that roots human rationality in knowledge of the laws of nature, Locke positions

Indians along with "children, idiots, and the grossly illiterate" in a category of humans who lack rational capacity (*Essay* I, 2, 27). Indeed, by insisting that Indians lack complex, abstract ideas, Locke suggests that they are closer to non-rational animals than humans (*Essay* II, 11, 10).

Universal accounts of embodiment are often not quite what they appear. As Dipika Nath has noted, "arguments of 'naturalness' inevitably imply universalism because what is 'natural' is seen to be unaffected by what is cultural or learnt . . . the same desires, demands, dissatisfactions are everywhere . . . the result is that people are deracialized, de-nationalized, and degendered." But the inclusiveness suggested by universal claims is deceptive. As theorists read their own cultural experiences into nature, "whatever claims to be universal is only a reflection of the dominant" (Nath 2008: 8). Indeed, theorists frequently allude to a hierarchy of humans "given in nature," thereby masking their own role in envisioning and legitimating inequality.

Racializing and Gendering Bodies

Critical race theorists conceptualize race as "a political division . . . a system of governing people that classifies them into a social hierarchy based on invented biological demarcations" (Roberts 2011: x). Race, then, provides a powerful example of how "biology is politics by other means" (Fausto-Sterling 2000: 269). Dorothy Roberts points out that ethnocentrism (a preference for one's own group) and xenophobia (a fear of outsiders) can be traced to the ancient world, but neither is equivalent to a biological conception of race, which is a product of modernity. Neither ethnocentrism nor xenophobia entails the "partition of all humans into a small number of types . . . or treats visible difference as a marker of immutable distinction that determines each group's permanent social value" (6). Nor does either "read moral and intellectual ability into physical difference" (7).

Biologization as an account of purportedly natural "racial" difference entered the European imagination in the seventeenth century and flowered fully over the course of the eighteenth century (Banton 1998). From the outset, claims about distinctive races included far more than a description of physical characteristics. Scientific taxonomies of race linked observations about pigment, hair texture, and geographical location with racializing stereotypes about intellect and social organization. In the same era that "the individual" was being conceptualized as an autonomous entity, unfettered by membership in a line of descent or kinship ties, science was inventing purportedly natural hierarchies of race that stripped away individuality. In marked contrast to the putative freedom of the abstract individual, science created racial "types"— persons who ostensibly exhibited the characteristic qualities of a class. With the invention of race, European science claimed for itself the prerogative to set the standards by which all humans were to be assessed, positioning Europeans as the pinnacle of human development against which all others must be measured. On the basis of a few observations of particular bodies, Europeans extrapolated "universal" claims about physiognomy, yoking physi- cal attributes to intellect, attitudes, moral inclinations, political abilities, and gendered bodies.

The great Swedish taxonomist Carl Linnaeus (1707–78), for example, set out to categorize all living things into classes, orders, genera, species, and varieties, publishing twelve editions of *Systema Naturae* during his lifetime. Breaking with the divinely ordained order of the great chain of being, Linnaeus identified similarities between primates and humans, while also suggesting that there was a discernible hierarchy among humans. Linnaeus divided the genus *Homo* into two species: *Homo sapiens* (man) and *Homo troglodytes* (ape). He then divided *Homo sapiens* into four natural varieties— evidenced primarily by the males of the "race." Linnaeus's generalizations about these varieties combined observations about geographical region and skin color with opinions about cultural traits, physical appearance, intellectual potential, and aesthetic value.

Dorothy Roberts has adeptly summarized the character traits Linnaeus aligned with particular bodies. At the pinnacle of beauty and intelligence, Linnaeus placed *H. sapiens europaeus*: "Vigorous, muscular. Flowing blond hair. Blue eyes. Very smart. Inventive. Covered by tight clothing. Ruled by law." *H. sapiens americanus*, according to Linnaeus, was "ill-tempered, impassive. Thick straight black hair; wide nostrils; harsh face; beardless. Stubborn, contented, free. Paints himself with red lines. Ruled by custom." Linnaeus described *H. sapiens asiaticus* as "Melancholy, stern. Black hair; dark eyes. Strict, haughty, greedy. Covered by loose garments. Ruled by opinion." And at the bottom, he placed *H. sapiens afer*: "Sluggish, lazy. Black kinky hair; silky skin; flat nose; thick lips; females with genital flap and elongated breasts. Crafty, slow, careless. Covered by grease. Ruled by caprice" (Roberts 2011: 29–30). The "science of race" created a hierarchy of human varieties premised upon the superiority of Europeans, whose association with progress, civilization, and mastery legitimated their rule over descending orders of color, primitiveness, and savagery. This science purported to be based on empirical observation, yet it included claims about moral and intellectual abilities that are not open to visual inspection.

Political theorists played a central role in circulating justifications for such hierarchical ranking of races. David Hume (1711–76), the Scottish Enlightenment thinker, gained international renown for his scathing critiques of his rationalist and empiricist predecessors. As a skeptic, he challenged scholars to interrogate the evidentiary grounds for all their primary impressions. Nonetheless, he advanced remarkably unexamined claims about "Negroes" and "other species of men." In an infamous footnote in his essay, "Of National Character," Hume asserted that there are four or five "species of men" all "naturally inferior to the whites." None of these inferior species have produced a "civilized nation . . . eminent individuals . . . ingenious manufactures . . . arts . . . [or] sciences." Hume attributes these marked distinctions to nature: "Such a uniform and constant difference could not happen, in so many countries and ages, if nature had not made an original distinction betwixt these breeds of men" (Hume 1753: 4, 125n).

The eminent German philosopher Immanuel Kant (1724–1804) developed a complex system of ethics (deontology) around the principle of "universalizability," which stipulates that an action is ethical if it would be the right thing to do for all persons, when confronted with similar circumstances. Kant's categorical imperative, "Act only according to that maxim whereby you can at the same time will that it should become a universal law," sought to establish a foundation for dutiful action binding on all rational beings. Indeed, Kant claimed that universalizability provided an objective, rationally necessary and unconditional principle that humans must always follow despite any natural desires or inclinations to the contrary. Perhaps better known in its second formulation—"So act as to treat humanity, whether in your own person or in another, in every case as an end and never merely as a means"—Kant's categorical imperative celebrates equal human dignity and worth. Thus it is startling to find a discussion of inferior races in Kant's work. In *Of the Different Human Races* (1775), Kant distinguished four human races: "We only need assume four races in order to derive all the enduring distinctions . . . recognizable within the human genus . . . (i) the noble, blond (northern Europe); (ii) the copper-red (America), (iii) the black (Senegambia), and (iv) the olive-yellow (Asia-India)" (1775 [2000]: 11). Replicating the notion that color and geographical origin reveal fundamental character, Kant distinguished the "natural" dispositions of Native Americans from those of Blacks. "The natural disposition of the Americans betrays a half-extinguished life power [so that] one makes use of red slaves in Surinam only in the house because they are too weak for field labor . . . The Negro, who is well suited to his climate [is] strong, fleshy, supple, but who given the abundant provisions of his mother land, is lazy, soft, and trifling" (11). In marked contrast to his categorical imperative that mandates respect for universal human rationality and dignity, Kant consigns the "copper-red" and the "black" to enslaved labor with no moral qualms.

In his *Lectures on the Philosophy of World History* (1837), Georg Wilhelm Friedrich Hegel (1770–1831) commented on this lapse in Kant's thought. Rather than faulting the contradiction in Kant's views, however, Hegel explained the lapse in terms of the limitations of "African civilization." Indeed, he asserted that the "peculiarly African character" lacks the "category of Universality. In Negro life . . . consciousness has not yet attained to the realization of any substantial objective existence—as for example, God, or

Law ... The Negro exhibits the natural man in his completely wild and untamed state" (1837 [1975]: 117). Although Hegel left open the possibility that Africans might one day attain universal consciousness, in the nineteenth century "the SubSaharan African" remained in the grip of "nature." By contrast,

> It is in the Caucasian race that Mind first attains to absolute unity with itself. Here for the first time mind enters into complete opposition to the life of Nature, apprehends itself in its absolute self-dependence, wrests itself free from the fluctuation between one extreme and the other, achieves self-determination, self-development, and, in doing so, creates world-history. (1830 [1971]: §393, Addition)

Writing within the utilitarian tradition, which supplanted deontology's focus on duty with the principle of human happiness as the ground for ethical judgment, British philosopher James Mill (1773–1836) extended racializing logic to the peoples of South Asia. According to Mill, the population of India would benefit from being ruled by a class of "philanthropic men": "the pace of civilization would be quickened beyond all example. The arts, the knowledge, and the manners of Europe would be brought to their doors, and forced by an irresistible moral pressure on their acceptance. The happiness of the human race would thus be prodigiously augmented and the progress, perhaps, of even the most cultivated nations, greatly accelerated" (1813: 30). Incorporating the same racialized assumptions about the inherent superiority of the "noble" white European, Mill depicts colonization as a mechanism to promote the happiness and well-being of the colonized through cultivation of four qualities of mind, namely, intelligence, temperance, justice, and generosity. By bringing manners, education, and administrative and legal systems to those whose civilization was in need of "quickening," colonization would palpably improve the condition of South Asians, alleviating their suffering and providing work to end their impoverishment.

Modern political theorists from diverse intellectual traditions juxtaposed their universal claims about human nature with stark racializing "observations" about non-Europeans. Locke, Hume,

Kant, Hegel, and Mill provide clear demonstrations of how effortlessly racist ideas were naturalized and connected to the bodies of other "species of men." As Saidiya Hartman has noted, "to naturalize race is to make it appear as if it has always existed, thereby denying the coerced and cultivated production of race" (1997: 57). These philosophical accounts of natural difference masked the violent production of race through the slave trade and colonization, and they mired "primitive races" in a fixed temporal relation to Europe. They suggested that "savages" remained fixed in an earlier stage of human evolution or historical development as Europeans ascended to higher levels. The depiction of Europeans as free, self-determining creators of world history implied that the white race had achieved far greater civilizational accomplishments than other peoples. Whether framed in terms of evolution, historical development, or modernization, the "Caucasian race" had attained the height of refinement, manifested in European arts, architecture, culture, philosophy, and science.

The cultivation of two sexes and separate spheres for men and women counted as one of the chief examples of European superiority. In discourses on evolution, "strong sex and gender dimorphism" was proclaimed a world-historical achievement:

> In dominant Western ideology, a strong sex/gender dimorphism often serves as a human ideal against which different races may be measured and all but white Europeans found wanting. This ideal then functions as a measure of racial advancement that admits of degrees determined by the (alleged) character of the relationship between men and women within a particular race. (Markowitz 2001: 390–1)

The association of pronounced sexual differences with higher civilization has a degendering corollary: as distinctions between men and women blur in the "lower races," men of color are feminized and women of color are masculinized. As Sally Markowitz has noted:

> "scientific" classifications of race and sex have long been associated with each other: in temperament, intelligence and physiology,

so-called "lower races" have often provided a metaphor for the female type of humankind and females a metaphor for the "lower race" . . . while "lower races" are often represented as feminine and men of these races as less than masculine, the femininity of non-white women . . . is likely to be denied (the better no doubt to justify their hard physical labor or sexual exploitation). (390)

This association of femininity with lower orders of being also had political consequences. Imagining civilized women to be fragile creatures governed by emotion rather than reason, philosophers and statesmen concurred that they were unfit for public life.

In the 19th century, "woman" consolidated as a being with characteristics and capacities for action that were in direct opposition to those of the constitutional state itself: as the state became one of reason and force, woman became entrenched with emotion and weakness; as the state became one of science, woman became infused with faith and religion; as the state became modern, woman became understood as traditional; as the state turned self-interested, woman was cast as selfless. (Towns 2009: 691)

Theorizing race and gender as inferior modes of embodiment, European thinkers envisioned the full blossoming of rationality as the exclusive achievement of civilized white men. This singular achievement justified certain entitlements—not only self-determination and self-government, but the right to rule over "inferiors," from the women in their families to peoples of all the lands they colonized. The cruel irony is that familial and colonial domination were justified by claims concerning liberty, equality, and rationality.

Gendered Racialization and Colonization

Decolonial theorists have suggested that processes of gendered racialization were central to colonization. Anibal Quijano coined

the term *coloniality of power* to capture a "new politics of population reorganization" that involved both the creation of racial
hierarchies between colonizer and colonized and the obliteration
of cultural distinctions among Indigenous peoples. As the Spanish
and Portuguese colonized the Americas in the fifteenth century,
they imposed "a model of power characterized by the codification of differences between conquerors and conquered under
rubric of 'race'" (Quijano 2000: 533). In contrast to differences
grounded in culture and tradition, race connoted a "different *biological* structure that placed some in a situation of inferiority to
others. Conquistadors made race constitutive of a new form of
domination" (533). As they articulated a purportedly "natural"
hierarchy that positioned "Indians," "Blacks," and "Mestizos" as
lower orders of humanity than the Spanish and Portuguese, the
conquistadors produced the differences they claimed merely to
describe. This production involved the discursive homogenization
of Indigenous populations in conjunction with physical and sexual
violence, exploitation, and dispossession.

Quijano characterizes homogenization as a key technology of
coloniality. The European colonizers

> found a great number of different peoples, each with its own history,
> language, discoveries and cultural products, memory, and identity. The
> most developed and sophisticated of them were the Aztecs, Mayas,
> Chimus, Aymaras, Incas, Chibchas, and so on. Three hundred years
> later, all of them had become merged into a single identity: Indians.
> This new identity was racial, colonial, and negative. The same hap-
> pened with the peoples forcefully brought from Africa as slaves:
> Ashantis, Yorubas, Zulus, Congos, Bacongos, and others. In the span
> of three hundred years, all of them were Negroes or Blacks. (551–2)

The mechanics of homogenization were brutal. As peoples were
dispossessed of their singular historical identities and their modes
of subsistence, they were forced into a stratified labor regime
that became a defining feature of racial difference. Beginning in
1503, the Spanish crown issued *encomiendas* that granted land to
soldiers and colonists, along with a right to demand tribute and

extract forced labor from the Indigenous ("Indian") population who lived on that land. When the *encomienda* system was ended in 1551, the Indigenous were assigned the status of unpaid serfs, but in contrast to the feudal system in Europe, serfs in the new world were afforded neither the protection of a feudal lord nor a piece of land upon which to work. "Africans" who survived the Middle Passage were consigned to forced labor and often worked to death. Resuscitating Aristotelian claims about "natural slaves," the colonizers claimed that "Indians" and "Africans" were unworthy of waged labor, a privilege reserved for "Europeans" and their descendants. The "inferior races" were obliged to work for the profit of their owners. Indeed, the obligation to work was deemed by some colonizers to be fit punishment for Indigenous practices that the Christian conquistadors characterized as "crimes that offend nature." Mestizos, the offspring of European sexual exploitation of Indigenous and African women, were assigned to artisanal and urban clerical positions in colonial society. Only the Spanish and Portuguese, pure in Christian "blood" and ancestry, were granted land ownership by the monarchy, according them control over human and material resources, as well as education and culture in the colonies (538–40).

The racialized gender system developed by European colonizers involved multiple hierarchies of gender difference, altering the lives of European women living in new world as well as Indigenous and enslaved women. The combination of European superiority, male supremacy, and racial degradation that played out in the process of colonization produced complex gradations of raced-gendered hierarchy. The superiority of Europeans over "Indians" and "African" slaves was codified in law, and manifested in all aspects of colonial political, economic, social, and cultural life. But the principle of male supremacy embraced by the colonizers had to be mitigated in the colonial context in order to reinforce European superiority. No Indigenous man or enslaved African male could be acknowledged to be superior to a European woman. Thus, racialized gendering required that European women be subordinated to European men, yet celebrated as more "civilized" than colonized men and women. Toward that end, they were domesticated, ensconced within the private sphere, extolled for their maternal sentiments, yet excluded by their purportedly "natural" inferiority from property ownership and political participation.

By contrast, the Indigenous and the enslaved were dehumanized, which entailed a measure of "degendering." Taking egalitarian relations between colonized and enslaved men and women as evidence of barbarity, Europeans suggested that "savages" manifested biological difference in their relations to reproduction (sex), but they lacked a gender system (Lugones 2010). The European colonizers shored up that "lack" by treating the colonized and the enslaved as beasts of burden, subjecting them to grueling physical labor. Thus Maria Lugones emphasizes the gendered dimensions of the coloniality of power: not only does race demarcate human from sub-human (rather than one kind of human from another), it also distinguishes those who have achieved the civilizational project of gender difference from those ungendered animal-like sub-humans. "Gender hierarchy marks the civilized status of European women and men; its absence defines the non-human, racialized, naturalized non-Europeans, who are sexed but genderless" (Mendoza 2016: 31). Whether cast as hypersexualized animals or beasts of burden, the colonized were fit for breeding, brutal labor, or extermination and the colonizers treated them as such.

Decolonial feminist scholars point out, however, that gender inequality within communities of color was exacerbated under colonization. Focusing on the Yoruba from Nigeria, Benin, and Togo who were imported as slaves to Brazil beginning in 1549, for example, Rita Segato has noted that low-intensity patriarchies became more hierarchical when subjected to the gendered logics imposed under colonization—with devastating consequences for women. As public and private spheres were separated and gendered, Yoruba women were domesticated and privatized, losing the power they once held in the community. Although Yoruba men retained some communal authority, they were humiliated and symbolically emasculated by the depredations of enslavement to such an extent that even their discourses on emancipation adopted a hierarchically gendered logic. Demands for freedom and political rights were cast as claims to restore their "manhood" (Segato 2011).

Examining gender relations in pre-colonized Andean societies, Silvia Rivera Cusicanqui (2004) notes that complementarity within the normative heterosexual couple afforded a measure of equality and reciprocity in private as well as public spheres. Full membership in the community presupposed involvement in a conjugal couple, and power and respect grew with age. Both men and women were entitled to inherit. According to Cusicanqui, this system of complementarity was weakened and eventually destroyed— not at the moment of colonization, however, but later, with the advent of republican systems of governance, modernization, and development. A gradual process of patriarchalization accompanied the encroachment of the modern nation-state upon Andean communities. Over time, the imposition of the European gender system did indeed undermine egalitarian relations between men and women, as the "civilizing" process encouraged the heightened manifestation of gender difference.

In *Black Skin, White Masks* (1952), Frantz Fanon (1925–61) described the process by which colonizers produce the colonized as an inferior racial group as *epidermalization*. Colonizers reduced rich cultures, knowledge systems, and ways of being to a demonized and denigrated "blackness." Fanon suggested that this form of colonial racialization had a profound embodied effect: internalized oppression. The colonized lost their cultural bearings, adopted the language of the colonizer, and accepted the premise that European culture was inherently superior. Immersed in the civilizational discourses of the colonizer, the colonized developed a potent self-hatred as the embodiment of an inferior race. One particularly pernicious aspect of racialization, Fanon argued, is that the colonized are required "not only to be black but to be black in relation to the white man." Judged by the distorting standards of white European civilization, the colonized developed a conviction of their own inferiority, suffering a profound loss of self-respect, cultural pride, and self-confidence.

Within the context of centuries of colonization, racialization involved processes of coerced embodiment. The "nature" of the subordinated was made to conform to the distorted ideas of the colonizers. Extrapolating from Monique Wittig's insight about the oppression of women, one might say that the colonized were "compelled in their bodies and in their minds to correspond, feature by feature, with the *idea* of nature" that the colonizers established for them. They were distorted to such an extent that their deformed bodies became what colonizers called "'natural', what is supposed to exist as such before oppression . . . Distorted to such an extent that in the end, oppression seems to be a consequence of this 'nature' within them (a nature which is only an *idea*)" (Wittig 1992: 9).

Claims concerning racial hierarchies that have permeated moral and political philosophy for centuries are based on a fundamental error—mistaking cause and effect. The inferiority attributed to those outside Europe was not a natural condition but the effect of brutal practices of European colonization. Despite such flawed reasoning, these philosophical notions have circulated as authoritative accounts of human nature, masking the brutality of colonialism and legitimating white supremacy. The rational, sovereign self secured its mastery by legitimating a racialized and gendered version of biological determinism.

From Modern to Postmodern Embodiment

When confronted with claims about putatively natural hierarchies of race and sex, one strategy of rebuttal turns again to science—twentieth and twenty-first century science—as a corrective. Some scholars have relied on the Human Genome Project, for example, to dispel any notion that there are innate biological, intellectual, or emotional racial differences. As Paul Rabinow and Nikolas Rose have noted, "When it became clear that humans shared 98% of their genome with chimpanzees, and the intra-group variations in DNA sequences were greater than inter-group variations, it appeared that genomics itself would mark the terminal point for biological racism" (2003: 18). To rebut claims that there are two and only two sexes, that heterosexuality is mandated by nature, and that gender identity is fixed from birth, some scholars have drawn upon biology and primatology to document how nature is far more diverse than sociobiologists, evolutionary psychologists, and modern political theorists acknowledge. Joan Roughgarden, for example, explores categories of sexual difference beyond male and female, gender diversity, and transgender in thousands of species in *Evolution's Rainbow: Diversity, Gender, and Sexuality in Nature and People* (2004). Bruce Bagemihl compiles a "Wondrous Bestiary" in *Biological Exuberance: Animal Homosexuality and Natural Diversity* (1999) that documents same-sex behaviors, including "courtship, affectionate, sexual, pair-bonding, and parenting" in countless different species of mammals and birds. Myra Hird and Noreen Giffney catalog an extraordinary range of diversity in *Queering the Nonhuman* (2008).

> The diversity of sex and sexual behavior among known species is much greater than human cultural notions typically allow . . . Homosexual behavior occurs in more than 450 species of animals, is found in every geographic region of the world, in every major animal group, in all age groups, and with equal frequency among females and males . . . Sex is not restricted to reproduction (many species continue to have sex when females are pregnant) . . . Pleasure is an organizing force in relations between nonhuman animals . . . Nonhuman animals display a wide variety of sexual behavior . . . and also display a wide diversity of sex. Nonhumans eschew the assumption that sex involves two (and only two) distinct (and opposite) entities (male and female) and further that these two sexes behaviorally complement each other. Virtually all plant and many animal species are intersex, i.e., are both sexes simultaneously— which means that there are not really two sexes after all. Most fungi have thousands of sexes—Schizophyllum, for example, has more than 28,000 sexes . . . Nor are living organisms sex dimorphic. People may have XXY, XXXY, XXXXY, XXYY, and XXXYY chromosomes . . . Many species are also transsex . . . functioning as one sex during one breeding season and the "other" sex during another breeding season . . . in some families of fish, transsex is the norm. (Hird 2013: 159)

Given this proliferating diversity in nature, Hird (2004) notes that heteronormative researchers have engaged in all manner of contortion to impose a stable form—sexual dimorphism—on what remains unpredictable, mutable, and always emergent. The evidence suggests that "the majority of living organisms on this planet could make little sense of the human classification of two sexes" (Hird 2013: 159).

Placing humans on a continuum with nonhuman animals provides one approach to a postmodern account of human existence that offers a powerful alternative to "mastery," the presumption that the sovereign self has a right to use the world "for his own edification, as he casts the 'other' as a passive, silent object or resource" (Colebrook 2012: 193). This version of posthumanism explicitly breaks with human "exceptionalism"—the tendency to emphasize characteristics that humans purportedly have in common with gods, which permeated ancient and modern political theory. Stacy Alaimo has noted the ethical implications of the abandonment of exceptionalism.

> Once the human is conceptualized as a material creature that has happened to appear as a being in the same way that other beings have happened and who continues to exist as the very stuff of intra-acting agencies—not a creature made exceptional by his reason, independence, and transcendence—then the grounds for ignoring or dismissing the lives, the suffering and the concerns of other creatures make little sense. (Alaimo 2016: 545)

Although focusing on the lessons afforded by genomics and nonhuman animals is a tempting means to debunk flawed accounts of embodiment, the strategy also has its drawbacks. Myra Hird has cautioned that many analysts invoke evidence from nonhuman animals to reinscribe a problematic nature/culture dichotomy. "Nonhuman animals have for some time been overburdened with the task of making sense of human social relations . . . Nonhuman animals supposedly exemplify human animal qualities like the family, fidelity, selfless care for the young, and perhaps, above all, sex complementarity" (i.e., the view that masculinity and femininity are categorically different and complementary) (2013: 157). In these instances, nature carries a suppressed moral premise: the "natural" is deemed to be morally superior to the "unnatural" and to the "artificial." But these judgments have far less to do with how nonhuman animals behave than with how humans interpret the meaning of that behavior. Arguments from animal existence seldom escape anthropocentrism. "When animals do something that we like, we call it natural. When they do something that we don't like, we call it animalistic" (Weinrich 1982: 203). Appeals to the natural diversity of sexes, genders, and sexualities replicate the notion that biology has lessons that humans can ignore only at their peril, shoring up rather than displacing the nature/culture binary.

In calling attention to interpretations that mediate every conception of the natural, Hird underscores the point that embodiment is never exclusively a matter of bodies. Embodied "nature" is a cultural conception of a material entity. Poststructuralist theorists view the body "not as a ready surface awaiting signification, but as a set of boundaries, individual and social, politically signified and maintained" (Butler 1990: 44). Feminist and queer poststructuralists understand the body as simultaneously material and beyond the individual, constituted through discourse and power-knowledge relations, including scientific accounts and the technologies they create to measure and maintain health (Rupp and Thomsen 2016: 897). In the words of Donna Haraway, "nature" does not exist as some essential, eternal, or exploitable material or form but instead is "artifactual," something made, but "not entirely by humans; it is a co-construction among humans and nonhumans" (1991a: 297).

To illuminate nonhuman contributions to the "co-construction" of embodiment in the twenty-first century, some theorists draw attention to the role of technology. Beatriz Preciado, for example, traces the way that "soft technologies—injectable, inhalable, and incorporable technologies—permeate contemporary bodies" (2013: 271). "At the beginning of the millennium, four million children were being treated with Ritalin for hyperactivity and so-called attention-deficit disorder, and more than two million consume psycho-tropics to control depression" (268). The contraceptive pill regulates the fertility of millions of women, just as Viagra structures the sexual performances of millions of men. Synthetic androgens and estrogens, along with manifold other pharmaceutical molecules, "enter the body to form part of it; they dissolve in the body; they become the body . . . power acts through molecules that become part of the immune system . . . neurotransmitters modify ways of perceiving and acting, hormones systematically affect hunger, sleep, sexual excitation, aggression, and the social codification of femininity and masculinity" (271). These new technologies of the body are deployed

> to modify the "deviant" body to bring it into accordance with pre-existing prescriptive ideals for feminine and masculine bodies. If in the nineteenth century disciplinary system, sex was natural, definitive, untransferable, and transcendental, then gender now appears to be synthetic, malleable, variable, and susceptible of being transferred, imitated, produced, and technically reproduced. (272)

Pulsing through cells, these chemical molecules produce an interior knowledge about the self, a sense of authenticity, a conviction about normality; they "produce mobile ideas, living organs, symbols, desires, chemical reactions, and conditions of the soul" (269). In this context,

> science gains "material authority" by inventing and producing techno-living artifacts . . . by transforming the concepts of the psyche, libido, consciousness, femininity, masculinity, heterosexuality, homosexuality, intersexuality, and transsexuality into tangible realities . . . There is nothing to discover in nature, there is no hidden secret . . . it is no longer about discovering the hidden truth in nature; it is about the necessity of specifying the cultural, political, and technological processes through which the bodily as artifact acquires natural status. (269)

In contrast to the modern mythos of human mastery, which imagined the sovereign subject as capable of autonomous self-making and control of nature, *posthumanists* and *new materialists* repudiate "faith in the unique, self-regulating and intrinsically moral powers of human reason," along with the assumptions about universalism, exceptionalism, and dualism that inform that faith (Braidotti 2016: 677). Although there are many versions of new materialism, science studies scholars and humanities scholars influenced by Gilles Deleuze and Félix Guattari's "philosophy of immanence" draw insights from Baruch Spinoza (1632–77) to rework the notion of embodiment. Spinoza explicitly rejected the mind/body dualism that had dominated the Western philosophical tradition, insisting that nothing stands outside of nature, not even the human mind. Indeed, Spinoza's materialist metaphysics suggests there is only one unique self-creating substance in the universe, although it is variously called God or Nature. "Nature is an indivisible, uncaused, substantial whole—in fact, it is the *only* substantial whole. Outside of Nature, there is nothing, and everything that exists is a part of Nature and is brought into being by Nature with a deterministic necessity. This unified, unique, productive, necessary being just *is* what is meant by 'God'" (Nadler 2016).

Physical bodies are modes or expressions of the extension of matter. According to Spinoza, "a mode of extension and the idea of that mode are one and the same thing, but expressed in two ways" (*Ethics* IIP7S). Because of the fundamental and underlying unity of Nature, the only existing Substance, "Thought and Extension are just two different ways of 'comprehending' one and the same Nature . . . The human mind and the human body are two different expressions—under Thought and under Extension—of one and the same thing: the person" (Nadler 2016).

Spinoza's materialism rejects human exceptionalism as well as dualism. The human being is a part of Nature, and as such, is governed by the same causal nexuses as other beings. "Nature is always the same . . . the laws and rules of nature, according to which all things happen, and change from one form to another, are always and everywhere the same. So the way of understanding the nature of anything, of whatever kind, must also be the same, viz. through the universal laws and rules of nature" (Nadler 2016). Within this determinist frame, the notion of free will loses all meaning. According to Spinoza, "Men believe themselves to be free because they are conscious of their own actions and are ignorant of the causes by which they are determined" (*Ethics* IIIP2S). Subject to the same causal forces as all other existents, human "affects"—love, anger, hate, envy, pride, jealousy—"follow from the same necessity and force of nature as the other singular things."

New materialism within a feminist frame selectively appropriates aspects of Spinoza's metaphysics. Deleuzian feminists accept the premises of monistic philosophy and explore their implications for embodiment. Rejecting the devaluation, denigration, or indeed, "somatophobia" (hatred of the body) that permeated the canon, feminist new materialists theorize "'vital politics,' premised on the idea that matter, including the specific slice of matter that is human embodiment, is intelligent and self-organizing and not dialectically opposed to culture, nor to technological mediation, but rather continuous with them" (Braidotti 2016: 681). Taking the body as "not simply a sign to be read, or a symptom to be deciphered, but also a force to be reckoned with" (Grosz 1994: 120), Elizabeth Grosz analyzes "agency and contingency within living and nonliving worlds . . . [a]s neither free nor determined but both constrained and undecidable" (1999: 19). She conceptualizes the possibilities and limits of bodily action in the context of the "brute world of materiality . . . the precarious, accidental, contingent, expedient, striving, complicated, resistant . . . world regulated by the exigencies, the forces of space and time" (Grosz 2004: 2).

Although explaining embodiment as a mode of "vital matter," feminist new materialists are markedly less deterministic than Spinoza. Attuned to the magnitude of indeterminacy associated with quantum physics as well as mutation in evolutionary theories, they envision corporeality as a site of political possibility tied to the agential capacity of bodily matter. Following Deleuze and Guattari (1987), feminist new materialists construe living matter as a "process ontology," a constantly changing and variable constellation of self-organizing forces that interact in complex ways with social, psychic and natural environments, producing multiple ecologies of belonging (Guattari 2000). Feminist versions of vital bodily materialism reject dichotomous systems of valuation that treat the first term in a binary as positive (e.g., male as strong, rational and free) while defining the second term negatively (e.g., female as "male minus," weak, irrational, enslaved by desire). Materialist process ontology involves a "more complex vision of the subject . . . that foregrounds an open, relational self-other entity framed by embodiment, sexuality, affectivity, empathy and desire as core qualities" (Braidotti 2016: 681). Understood in terms of a thoroughly entwined nature-culture, matter—the stuff that comprises humans, nonhumans, and nature—is not given or passive, but dynamic and agentic, contributing both content and form to processes of world-formation (Wingrove 2016: 455).

Matter is a co-constituting force, an "actant" whose power is both restrictive and productive, constricting and enhancing individual capacities and skills. As Preciado notes in her discussion of soft technologies:

> Contemporary society is inhabited by subjectivities defined by the substance (or substances) that supply their metabolism, by the cybernetic prostheses and various types of pharmaco-pornographic desires that feed action and through which they turn into agents . . . Prozac subjects, cannabis subjects, cocaine subjects, alcohol subjects, Ritalin subjects, cortisone subjects, silicone subjects, hetero-vaginal subjects, double-penetration subjects, Viagra subjects, $ subjects. (2013: 269)

Co-constitution, then, refuses "additive" models that presuppose discrete entities, which separately contribute to an embodied outcome, insisting instead on dynamic, interactive, and historically contingent processes of mutual constitution. "Culture and politics are not inscriptions on the surfaces of bodies but rather dynamic presences" (Wingrove 2016: 462). Abandoning base/superstructure models of embodiment, feminist new materialists conceive the corporeal body as a material, signifying, agentic matrix sutured by the interaction of multiple forms of organic and inorganic matter (Tuana 1997: 57).

Queer and trans* theorists have been impressively creative in disrupting the linear logics that enforce dualist thinking, shattering the illusion that the social body is layered on the biological body and that the biological body is fixed by nature (Sedgwick 2003: 8). Indeed, as Pat Triarch has humorously put it, "Gender queers and trans-folks are 'deconstruction workers', who by quite literally putting misfitting bodies on the (disassembly) line, begin to resist and rebuild the man-made gender imperatives that pass as those of nature" (cited in Noble 2013: 257). Advancing a theory of embodiment that does not seek fixity, totality or coherence of self, Jeanne Vaccaro analyzes how "body, memory, and time fold into each other to produce the subject . . . whose myriad forms of bodily capacity . . . integrate bodily experience with material, social, and political modes of being and becoming" (2013: 93). Rather than privileging constancy and stability, trans* theorists celebrate the "yet-to-be-determined" aspect of bodies—their transience, instability, and openness to encounter. Reminiscent of Spinoza, trans* theorists insist that "no one yet has determined what the body can do" (*Ethics* IIIP2S). In the words of Julian Carter, "enfleshed is not necessarily a trap but rather the condition of possibility for movement toward one another . . . to comport one's body in a particular way . . . to embody one's intention . . . to assume open-ended responsibility for what one becomes" (2013: 130).

Mary Weismantel draws upon her expertise in archaeology to provide an example of an alternative understanding of enfleshment. She explores Pre-Columbian traditions in the ancient Americas to excavate a conception of embodiment at great remove from the unencumbered, self-contained, pre-social rational subject. "Bodies and persons are not conceptualized as discrete, bounded, individuals, but as constellations of qualities and potencies that come alive through constant interaction with others" (Weismantel 2013: 331). In contrast to Western political thought, "bodies and selves were understood to be multiple and composite in their very essence" (330). Within this context, the body was

> permeable and protean, growing throughout life through physical and metaphysical intercourse with others . . . Actual bodies were assembled over life rather than given at birth—and this process of accumulating bits and pieces of others was a beneficial process, even though it necessarily involved giving away part of oneself . . . they conceived of life as a process of constant exchange between bodies, and wished such exchange to continue after death. (328–30)

Indeed, attainment of human excellence required that men "rise above the limitations of the birthed body by incorporating the bodily aspects of others. To show femininity in this context made a man more powerful, not less . . . Living beings gained power and beauty through appropriating the body parts of others" (328). Within this belief system, "physical properties of the flesh are not inescapable markers of absolute difference and limitation, but desirable and detachable gifts that can be exchanged in real and imagined interactions between mutable social agents" (331).

Surveying evidence from multiple ancient cultures, Weismantel challenges the "damaging modernist fiction of the natural that denies the existence of bodies assembled rather than birthed" (321). Instead of conceiving matter as inert, stable, concrete, and unchangeable, the ancient world envisioned inspirited matter subject to contingency, transformation, regeneration, a view compatible with gender fluidity and gender atypicality as forms of human flourishing. Evidence from these ancient civilizations, then, provides one means to move beyond rigid mind/body dualisms as well as sexual dimorphism. Thus, Weismantel notes:

> The dominant vision of human history is an oppressive one: an unbroken legacy of manly men and womanly women compelled by biology to create nuclear families devoted to reproduction . . . The accumulated weight of the archaeological data does not support this vision of human history . . . [but] reveals this normativizing narrative as the distorting, selective, constructed artifice that it is. (321)

Conclusion

Demonstrating that embodiment is profoundly political is one of the most distinctive contributions of feminist scholarship. Although Western political theorists portray embodiment as a matter of discovering the naturally given, their accounts are better characterized as the culturally freighted inventions of a particular class of elite European men. Under the guise of nature or divine ordination, canonical thinkers have entrenched notions of dichotomous sex, procreational heterosexuality, and hierarchies of race that have sustained multiple modes of coerced embodiment. They have allowed white androcentrism to masquerade as human nature and masked racialized biologism with assertions about equality, rationality, and freedom. For centuries, these deceptive universals have legitimated divisions of the world into public and private in ways that narrowly constrain liberties and rights, as well as understandings of state action and the scope of injustice. These issues are explored in the following chapters.

4

Refiguring the Public and the Private

At bottom, the separation of home and workplace, the rise of the new domestic woman, the separation of the spheres, and the construction of public and private all describe the same phenomenon in different words.
(Vickery 1998: 166)

Bodily privacy is a privilege regulated by systems of power and control.
(Clare 2013: 264)

Disputes over the boundary between public and private remain a central feature of political life in the twenty-first century. Policy debates over cigarette smoke, domestic violence, dress codes in schools and workplaces, driving while Black, erotic practices, gun ownership, hate speech, marijuana use, pornography, racial exclusion, sexual harassment, sex work, travelling while Muslim, transgender access to toilets, and transwomen's participation in training sessions for sexual assault counseling raise contentious claims about the scope of individual liberty versus the appropriate sphere of governmental regulation. These complex debates tend to focus on where to draw the line between public and private, not on the validity of the public/private distinction itself.

Within common parlance, "the public pertains to the people as a whole, to community or nationwide concerns, to the common good, to things open in sight, and to those things that may be used or shared by all members of the community" (Landes 1988: 3). Despite such universal and inclusive connotations, the etymology of the *public* suggests a far narrower reach. The *Oxford English Dictionary* traces the origin of the word to the Latin, *publicus*, referring to that which is "under the influence of the *pubes*—adult men or male population." Joan Landes has noted that the original meaning continues to resonate in certain contexts:

> A public man is one who acts in and for the universal good . . . on the other hand, a public woman is a prostitute, a commoner, a common woman. A public action then is one authored from or authorized by the masculine position. Only the latter is truly general, community-spirited, and universal in its consequences. Surreptitiously, language works to effect a closure, one that dictates women's absence from political life. (3)

This chapter examines how designations of public and private have raced and gendered "material and experiential consequences in terms of formal institutions, organizational forms, financial systems, familial and kinship patterns, as well as in language," which raise important questions about the validity of this liberal construct (Davidoff 1998: 165). The first part of the chapter traces how political theorists' analyses of public and private have contributed to the consolidation of racialized and gendered understandings of citizenship, liberty, and social order. The second part considers how contemporary feminist, critical race, queer, and trans* theorists have probed the public/private distinction to illuminate and challenge forms of power and domination in the domains of family, sexuality, embodiment, and subjectivity.

Canonical Accounts

In her pathbreaking work, *The Sexual Contract*, Carole Pateman noted that "a fundamental assumption in political theory is that the patriarchal separation of the private or natural sphere from the public or civil realm is irrelevant to political life" (1988: 13). Feminist theorists have challenged that assumption, seeking to demonstrate how the public/private distinction operates to establish and preserve male power. In one of the first major feminist critiques of Western political philosophy, *Public Man, Private Woman* (1981), Jean Bethke Elshtain used the public/private distinction as a "prism" though which to examine women's relationship to the political. Elshtain noted that political theorists have disagreed about whether the demarcation of public from private is natural or conventional, whether "notions of the public and private are prerequisites for and constitutive features of social life itself" or "arbitrary, culturally relative artifacts that exist at the level of convention alone and which can be dispensed with if we are but rational and bold enough" (1981: 11). Nonetheless, they have been unrelenting in structuring their analyses of political order around that distinction. Whether or not social life is universally organized around privacy and publicity, Elshtain argued, political theory is.

Elshtain analyzed the "dense web of associational meanings and intimations" of public and private, arguing that they operate as "twin force fields to create a moral environment for individuals, singly and in groups; to dictate norms of appropriate or worthy action; to establish barriers to action, particularly in areas such as the taking of human life, regulation of sexual relations, promulgation of familial duties and obligations, and the arena of political responsibility" (5).

Exploring changing conceptions of public and private from Plato and Aristotle to twentieth-century feminist theory, Elshtain suggested that these concepts reveal "a society's intersubjectively shared realm . . . the ideas, symbols, and concepts that are not only shared but whose sharing reverberates within and helps to constitute a way of life on both its manifest and latent levels" (5). Noting that the public was routinely defined in terms of the political world, and the private in terms of the family or household (4), Elshtain observes that a perennial "problem for women is not just their exclusion from political participation but the terms under which this exclusion has occurred" (xiv). Throughout the Western tradition, the public qua political has been "part of an elaborate defense against the tug of the private, against the lure of the familial, against evocations of female power" (15–16). Thus, Elshtain advanced a psychoanalytic interpretation that positioned women's exclusion from the public as constitutive:

> Men fear the sexual and reproductive power of women. This is reflected in the lengths to which they have gone to protect themselves by projecting that fear toward outward social forms, by embedding the need to defend themselves against women in institutions and activities, including those called "political," historically inseparable from war-making . . . In this complex inner-outer dialectic, rejected or hostile feelings are expelled. Their embodiment in an external form is one way the male mind works unconsciously to denude images of women of much of their force—especially the image of the Mother. On the other hand, operating on a level that is both conscious and uncon-scious, is the conviction that women are weak and soft. Men define themselves by that which is "not-woman," therefore not vulnerable. To fend off both the unconsciously embedded image of female power and the recognition of the "weakness of woman" as that which one cannot accept in oneself, men have, over the years, created hard, exter-nal institutions of enormous power both as a match for the vision of the powerful Mother within and as a protection, a hedge against their own "weak, female" self. (142–3)

By analyzing the inherent relation between the public and the private in psychoanalytic terms, Elshtain casts women's exclusion from public life in universal terms. Construing the public world as a defensive reaction against powerful fears and attractions of the intimate and familial, she envisions an inherent antagonism driven by psychological forces that are unlikely to change. While such an explanation draws attention to the persistence and pervasiveness of exclusionary practices, it also has a number of drawbacks. In addition to the anachronism of reading more than two thousand years of political thought through a twentieth-century Freudian lens, Elshtain's confident assumption that works of political theory provide a reliable guide to the life worlds of specific cultures fails to take into account the fact that the Western canon is itself a product of nineteenth-century European efforts to systematize knowledge and reform the educational curriculum. What appears as universal explanation, then, may itself be the effect of a particular modernist analytic lens.

In a lucid critique of Elshtain's argument, Mary Dietz (1985) raised important questions about the tacit liberal presuppositions informing *Public Man, Private Woman*. Situating Elshtain's work in the context of long-standing liberal efforts to defend the private against the state and against theorists who fail to prize the familial and the maternal, Dietz suggested that Elshtain's argument turned on a reductive reading of Aristotelian concepts. Dietz acknowledged that it is not difficult to isolate certain Aristotelian claims that pit the private realm as a domain of "mere life" against the *polis* as the mechanism for pursuit of the "good life," structuring a dichotomy between the "realm of necessity" and the "realm of freedom." Within this oppositional frame, preserving mere life—the task of women and slaves—is undertaken in silence and obedience in a hierarchically structured order where propertied, male citizens engage in deliberative speech and action. Yet, Dietz suggests, this reductive reading misses important Aristotelian insights into the relation between public and private, insights valuable to the feminist transformative project.

Dietz offered a "generous reading" of Aristotle emphasizing that human existence involves multiple complex practices and associations pertaining to the production of necessities for survival, human reproduction, the creation of aesthetic objects and cultural rituals, provision of common defense, and structures of decision making about collective concerns. Amidst these integrally connected domains, the public sphere takes precedence because it holds the potential to effect and reshape the other relations.

Politics is primary because all other human acts and occupations are examined in its light and made its subject matter . . . family life and privacy, social practices and economic issues are matters of political decision-making. Family practices, control over property, the rights of children, the nature of schooling and child labor laws, benefits for single mothers, the regulation of birth control . . . are potentially open to political control and may be politically determined. Even the decision to allow them to remain private . . . is ultimately political . . . The questions of who we are allowed to be and what rights we are allowed to exercise, even in the supposed sanctity of the family, have always been and will continue to be determined by political determinations. (Dietz 1985: 28–9)

Rather than setting up a stark and unwavering opposition between public and private tethered to universal claims about male and female psyches, Dietz suggests that the specific contours of public and private are politically constituted. Moreover, politics affords the means to restructure dimensions of social life in the future. Aristotle's conception of citizenship turned on a distinction between politics (a deliberative relation among equals) and rulership (a command relation among unequals). Although Aristotle placed women and "natural slaves" under the dominion of male citizens, democratic states extended citizenship to women, creating opportunities for them to participate on equal terms with men. Public engagement, then, is a means of transformative practice. Rather than resign the public sphere to the perpetual grasp of defensive male egos, Dietz holds out the possibility that women can not only claim the public sphere but use it to restructure private relations. Through "public speeches and debates, organized movements with expressly political goals, and democratic activities . . . feminist citizens challenge the 'givens' and seek to revitalize democratic values with a view toward the generations of citizens to come" (34).

Seeking to free conceptions of the public and private from the spell of the universal, feminist historians have traced the blurred boundaries between the two in particular eras. Some point out that the family has often been a "public unit" in the sense that it is created and regulated by civil law as well as by religious codes and courts (Poole 1995; Vickery 1998). Others note that the public/ private binary distorts the complexity of classed households in various epochs: the households of the elite have been domiciles, worksites, places of production and conspicuous consumption, sites of political intrigue and active state politics (Tillyard 1995; Smith 1998), while the domiciles of the poor have often afforded no privacy whatsoever. Moreover, within monarchical systems, the political was far less public than contemporary readers might imagine. Within feudal structures of authority, "lordship was some- thing publicly represented . . . but it was not constituted as a social realm or public sphere; rather it was something like a status attribute" (Landes 1998: 138; Habermas 1962 [1989]). Feudal lords staged performances of authority, displaying themselves as embodiments of "higher power" before audiences of loyal subjects, but these performances coexisted with arbitrary and capricious exercises of sovereign will beyond any mundane mechanisms of accountability. For reasons such as these, Diane Willen has argued that "The very existence of two spheres, private and public at least in the modern sense, remains problematic for Tudor and early Stuart England" (1989: 155–6). Similarly, Kristen Poole (1995) and Amanda Vickery (1998) have suggested that the "spheres" for early modern women and men were so multiple and overlapping that the theory of "separate spheres" actively distorts this era.

Jürgen Habermas' *The Structural Transformation of the Public Sphere* (1962 [1989]) sought to theorize and historicize the public sphere, advancing a conception of the public quite distinct from ancient and feudal notions of governance and politics. Indeed, Habermas argued that the public sphere is unique to bourgeois society, emerging in the context of the innovations in social organization and communication networks of early modern territorial states. Urbanization, capitalist commerce, stock markets, the develop- ment of print and epistolary cultures, growing literacy, as well as new modes of state apparatus for taxation and policing of subject populations played central roles in the production of "the public." Habermas characterized the public sphere as a dimension of social existence quite separate from the intimacy and familiarity of the private domain and from the increasingly impersonal authority of the state. Emerging in the bourgeois cultural institutions of certain European cities, the public sphere involves a way of coming together in coffee houses, clubs, reading and language societies, libraries, concert halls, opera houses, theaters, lecture halls, and salons to discuss, debate, and deliberate. Fueled by the proliferation of novels, journals, commercial presses, and publishing companies, a literate public develops practices of critical reflection upon and engagement with contemporary issues. For Habermas, the bourgeois public sphere signifies the hitherto "private people" coming together as "a public" through the historically unprecedented use of their "public reason." Changing practices in policing, taxation, and the administration of justice aid the cultivation of the public sphere, as interaction with the state stimulates the critical judgment of a public making use of its reason. Print culture fosters forms of interiority, self-reflection, and self-assertion characteristic of individualism at a moment when the commodification of culture enables the middle classes to enjoy a degree of adornment and self-fashioning once possible only for the nobility. As economic power shifts from land to manufacture and trade, the new bourgeois public begins to challenge monarchy in order to advance the interests of the commercial economy.

Habermas argued that the bourgeois public sphere is governed by norms of rationality, equality, and publicity, although they are only imperfectly realized. Embracing norms of rational discourse, the bourgeois public asserts equality as a regulative ideal—in the sense that the merits of arguments rather than the status of speakers are supposed to determine outcomes. Envisioning itself as a universal class, the bourgeoisie appeals to general, abstract, objective, and permanent norms in constructing "constitutional law," which is "public" and "universal" in application, admitting no status distinctions among citizens. Even as it advances claims to publicity, however, the bourgeois public exists largely as private individuals discoursing within private spaces. And despite its claims to rationality and equality, class, gender, and race relations within bourgeois culture remain at great remove from egalitarian ideals.

Although Habermas acknowledged the failure of bourgeois

culture to fully instantiate the norms of the public sphere, Joan Landes (1988, 1998) has suggested that he did not take seriously enough the implications of this failure. Embracing the myth of imperfect realization, Habermas holds out the hope that rationality and equality, the ideals of the public sphere, could in principle escape the limitations of bourgeois culture and attain full realization. Landes, on the contrary, argues that closer examination of the gendered dimensions of the public sphere leave little reason to be sanguine about such a possibility.

Through sustained investigation of women's experiences in liberal and republican politics in the late eighteenth and nineteenth centuries, Landes debunks the view that women's exclusion from the public sphere was simply the residual effect of traditional practices. Exclusion of women from the public was *not*

> the accidental consequence of the lesser status of women in pre-liberal society, to be amended in a more democratic order. Rather, the resistance of enlightened liberal and democratic discourse to femininity was rooted in a symbolization of nature that promised to reverse the spoiled civilization of *le monde* where stylish women held sway, and to return to men the sovereign rights usurped by an absolutist monarch. Furthermore, when women during the French revolution and the nineteenth century attempted to organize in public on the basis of their interests, they risked violating the constitutive principles of the bourgeois public sphere: in place of one, they substituted the many; in place of disinterestedness, they revealed themselves to have an interest. Worse yet, women risked disrupting the gendered organization of nature, truth, and opinion that assigned them to a place in the private, domestic, but not public realm. Thus an idealization of the universal public conceals the way in which women's (legal and constitutional) exclusion from the public sphere was a constitutive, not a marginal or accidental feature of the bourgeois public from the start. (1998: 143)

Contrary to the facile assumption that women experienced unwavering subordination prior to the nineteenth century, Landes demonstrates that the "eighteenth century marked a turning point for women in the construction of modern gender identity: public-private oppositions were being reinforced in ways that foreclosed women's earlier independence in the street, in the marketplace, and, for elite women, in the public spaces of the court and aristocratic household" (1988: 22). She suggests that anti-monarchist sentiment blended a virulent animosity against the aristocracy with an equally potent distaste for "public women"—both the elite women in salon society ("*le monde*") and the militant women who founded the Society of Revolutionary Republican Women and harnessed republican rhetoric to demands for "free womanhood" and the rights of *citoyennes*. Within male republican circles, this combination of animosities gave rise to trenchant critiques of the *ancien régime* and of women's political activism. The male republican political agenda encompassed not only the revolutionary overthrow of the monarchy but the domestication of women, and both projects played a central role in their theorizing.

Landes points out that Montesquieu, in his *Spirit of Laws*, was the first to advance a proposal for the domestication of women. His rationale was simply put: in order to avoid the effeminacy of men imposed by absolute monarchy and the corruptions of "unnatural women" in the salons, the republic *must* domesticate women:

> The forward march of civilization, he cautions, requires the domestication of women; in a more advanced society women will be sure to occupy their proper place. The domestic woman is accommodated to her new surroundings, her narcissistic vanity and licentious use of freedom are curbed, and her nature, like that of a domesticated animal, is made to fit a depoliticized domestic environment . . . Private virtue within the male-defined, restricted family, Montesquieu hopes, will provide the foundation for a patriotic and virile political constitution. (Landes 1988: 38)

In contrast to Habermas' optimism about its egalitarian potential, feminist scholars suggest that the bourgeois public sphere made gender socially relevant in a way that it was not hitherto. Under feudal monarchy, masculinity carried some privileges, but they were not vast. Under ordinary circumstances class status trumped sex in determining a person's life prospects. Within emerging republics, however, "sexual difference" was written into law. At just the moment that bourgeois claims to universality raised hopes for the elimination of all social distinctions before the law, gender discrimination was encoded into the founding constitutions of "free nations." Thus Landes has argued that the republic's most important legacy was the cultural inscription of gender in social life. As an emerging national form, "the Republic was constructed against women, not just without them" (171). Similarly, Claire Moses has pointed out that women were "reduced to the status of a legal caste at the same time that the ancient regime legal class system was abolished for men" (1984: 18).

Constitutive Contradictions:
Liberal Patriarchy

Examining the social contract tradition from the seventeenth-century works of John Locke to the twentieth-century arguments of John Rawls, Carole Pateman has suggested that far from grounding the rights of the individual, the liberal social "contract is the means through which modern patriarchy is constituted" (1988: 2). Pateman acknowledges that "patriarchy refers to a form of political power . . . rule by fathers . . . that political theorists insist has not existed for the past three-hundred years" (19). Yet, her close readings of social contract theorists demonstrate that the social contract tradition couples a story of freedom for property-owning men with a story of women's "natural" subjection. "The contract establishes men's political right over women, establishes men's orderly access to women's bodies . . . the original contract establishes 'the law of male sex right'" (2). In marked contrast to their claim to have repudiated ascription standards that fix a person's life prospects from birth, "contract theorists justified modern civil subjection" (40). The public/private distinction provides ideological cover for the patriarchal and class hierarchies perpetuated through liberalism. Insinuating that "women's natures are such that they are properly subject to men and their proper place is in the private, domestic sphere, and that men properly inhabit and rule within both spheres," liberal theorists obscure and mystify the social reality they help create (Pateman 1989: 119).

Liberal bourgeois domesticity was inherently political, then, even as the private sphere was proclaimed pre-political and "protected" from the intrusions of state power. By situating women in a domain beyond the reach of the state and barring them from public speech and political participation, the public sphere naturalized women's subordination, allowing the rhetoric of motherhood and separate spheres to mask the explicit acts of men that produced women's subordination.

Asymmetrical power relations established by the liberal patriarchal contract permeated the "multiple publics" theorized by Habermas. Leonore Davidoff (1998) has pointed out that, in the nineteenth century, women were effectively excluded not only from coffee houses, political clubs and associations, and legislative assemblies, but also from educational institutions, the professions, the practice of science, and the worlds of art and cultural production. By 1850, women were excluded from the leadership of unions. And although poor women always worked outside the home, repeated efforts were launched in the nineteenth century to bar women from factories, mines, and other skilled crafts. As feminist labor historians have demonstrated, the invention of the "male breadwinner" and the quest for a "family wage" were well-orchestrated attempts to mask the pronounced presence of women in the industrial labor force and to remove them from desperately needed waged labor (Anderson 2000; Landes 1988; Offen 2000). Defining women by their familial relationships, placing them under the legal guardianship of men, and denying them the right to enter into contracts, effectively precluded women from selling their labor freely in the marketplace. Liberal bourgeois law produced *homo economicus* as an exclusively white male identity. Thus Amanda Vickery notes that the "separation of home and workplace, the rise of the new domestic woman, the separation of spheres, and the construction of public and private all describe the same phenomenon" (1998: 166).

Critical race theorists have demonstrated that the myth of imperfect realization also renders invisible the systemic racial subjugation of Indigenous and enslaved peoples. As Saidiya Hartman has noted, recognition of liberal bourgeois humanity, "licensed by the innovation of rights, and justified on the grounds of liberty and freedom, unleashed unheralded forms of racialized violence and domination" (1997: 6). Core liberal concepts such as privacy, consent, will, intentionality, and action were utterly meaningless for the enslaved, who were subjected to the master in all things. Deprived of mobility, the freedom to use their labor power, the right to marry and to form families, the enslaved had no privacy or private sphere. In the words of the infamous *Dred Scott* decision, the enslaved had "no rights that white men had to respect" (*Dred Scott* v. *Sandford* 60 U.S. 393, 1857). Even the rape of slave women was not illegal under common law or statutory provision. Slave codes prohibited harms that impaired labor power of slaves; because rape did not interfere with laboring, it was not prohibited (Hartman 1997: 95–9). On the contrary, the generation of children as result of rape increased the master's property; hence the organized rape of enslaved women was endemic to the institution of slavery (Morgan 2004). When an enslaved woman sought redress in the Mississippi courts for rape by another slave in 1859, the Mississippi Supreme Court ruled: "our laws recognize no marital rights as between slaves; their sexual intercourse is left to be regulated by their owners," thereby placing slaves outside the protection of the law, excluding them not only from legal personhood but from humanity (Rosen 2009: 10).

Reserved for the "unencumbered self, the citizen, the self-possessed individual, the volitional and autonomous subject," the public as "proper political" completely denied the agency of the dominated (Hartman 1997: 61). "The slave [wa]s the object or the ground that makes possible the existence of the bourgeois subject and, by negation, or contradistinction, defines liberty, citizenship, and the enclosures of the social body" (62). In the words of Jean Comaroff, the "enslaved were neither envisioned nor afforded the privilege of envisioning themselves as part of the imaginary sovereignty of the state . . . their relation to the state [was] mediated by another's rights—the property owner's . . . the spatial organization of domination confined the slaves to the policed precincts of the quarters unless given a pass" (1985: 261).

Even free African Americans were denied birthright citizenship—the rights "of every other person in the community under like circumstances"—and had no redress when they were expelled from democratic states such as Missouri and Arkansas under laws stipulating that those who refused to leave would be enslaved for one year, after which the earnings from their labor would be used to relocate them (Rosen 2009: 96–7). Excluded from privacy and publicity, Blacks were consigned to "the social . . . an asylum of inequality . . . allegedly beyond the reach of the state . . . less an autonomous zone than an arena of collusive, contradictory, and clandestine practices between the state and its purported other, the private" (Hartman 1997: 201). Within this frame, the historical construction of public and private spheres—with all the attendant rights and liberties—seems nothing more than a discursive mechanism of domination.

When feminist critical race theorists identify the division between the private and public spheres as a *political problem*, then, they are suggesting more than that the artificial entrenchment of that binary within liberal theory is problematic. They are seeking to politicize the creation of a private domain as part of a white, masculinist political agenda that places racial and gender oppression beyond redress. Moreover, they want to insist that the allegedly private sphere performs multiple political functions, most important of which is the perpetuation of race, gender and sexual subordination. By incorporating an unequal conception of raced-gendered citizenship at the heart of the polity, the public world of men relegates women, people of color, sexual minorities and gender variant people to a shadow world, which continues to restrict their fate despite constitutional guarantees of equality before the law.

Contemporary Engagements with the Public/Private Binary

Liberals defend the public/private distinction as a means to protect "negative liberty," a private sphere over which the individual alone is sovereign, free from intrusion by the state. Negative liberty in realms of association, employment, education, commerce, living arrangements, religion, sexuality, reproduction, and interpersonal relationships appears to be a gender- and race-neutral category. A right to privacy would seem to be of equal benefit to all persons. Hobbes pointed out, however, that the sphere of negative liberty exists only if the state chooses to recognize and defend it. Privacy rights presuppose state action. And critics note that the apparent neutrality of privacy rights masks a history of racial, gender, and sexual oppression and the role of the state in producing and sustaining that oppression. When property is deemed a private matter, for example, and women are designated by law to be the property of their husbands and slaves are accorded the legal status of personal property of particular masters, protecting the privacy of husbands and masters entails state complicity in the subordination of wives and slaves. A focus on protecting privacy, including "private property," renders invisible state action to define certain people as property. Similarly, when the family is considered to be beyond the reach of the state, laws governing marriage and adoption are made invisible, as is domestic violence. When sexuality is assumed to be a private matter, the role of the state in criminalizing particular sexual acts is made invisible. When privacy is taken to be a constitutional right, brutal "genital verification" as a recurrent mode of transphobic violence that is committed with impunity is inconceivable. The concept of negative liberty, then, is more complicated than it first appears. At one level, the concept captures an ideal of limited state power, yet at another level it masks the operation of state power. At one level, it suggests that the private realm is the domain of untrammeled individual freedom, yet at another level it obscures manifold structures of power that circumscribe private relations. Contemporary critics of the public/private binary illuminate these constitutive contradictions.

Marriage

Marriage is an institution that illustrates inherent contradictions in the liberal construction of public and private. A matter of public record, licensed by the state, marriage is nonetheless perceived as the most private of relations—a site of intimacy organized through voluntary agreement and insulated from unwarranted intrusions by the state. Yet even in the most egalitarian households, conjugal relations and sexual divisions of labor are profoundly unequal and these pervasive inequalities affect women's prospects in employment and public life (Okin 1989: 134–69). In the *Sexual Contract*, Carole Pateman argues that marriage irrevocably weds "juridical equality to social inequality . . . to form a coherent social structure" (1988: 229). Pateman notes that liberal political theorists justified women's subordination to men not only because women possessed inferior rational capacities, but also because women were unable to sublimate their passions and thus posed a "perpetual source of disorder" (98). Absent male control, women presented a danger to a well-ordered society. "Women, their bodies and bodily passions, represent what must be controlled and transcended if social order is to be created and sustained" (99).

Although common law recognized the legitimacy of male control, the locus of patriarchal power resided in the private sphere—in the family, the home, and in conjugal relations. Under the doctrine of coverture, a woman experienced "civil death" upon entering marriage. She ceased to exist in the eyes of the state. "A wife was required to live where her husband demanded . . . her earnings belonged to her husband and her children were the property of her husband, just as children of the female slave belonged to her master" (121). A wife who worked full time in the conjugal home was not entitled to pay; she was entitled only to subsistence in return for her labors. Until 1884 in Britain, "a wife could be jailed for refusing conjugal rights, and until 1891, husbands were allowed forcibly to imprison their wives in the matrimonial home to obtain their rights" (123). Rape within marriage was politicized only in the 1970s through feminist activism around the globe, but it is not yet prohibited in all nations.

The marriage contract, then, is a contract of specific performance covering sexual services, reproductive labor, child care, and house work as well as love, affection, and companionship. The conjugal power accorded to men through the marriage contract creates a structural asymmetry in the private sphere: "men dictate the terms and women comply" (146). Unlike other valid contracts, the marriage contract "requires that one party gives up the right to self-protection and bodily integrity" (163). The marriage contract is also sexually ascriptive: "man is always the husband, woman, the wife" (167). Because conjugal power is structural, the asymmetrical "terms of protection and obedience cannot be altered . . . no husband can divest himself of the power he obtains through marriage" (166, 157).

Liberal and conservative political theorists naturalize marriage and the family, viewing them as ontologically prior to and distinct from the sphere of politics. Yet the conjugal power accorded to husbands in their private capacity has also been shored up by state laws and court decisions. Court decisions in the nineteenth century upholding statutes barring inter-racial marriage unambiguously articulated the role of the state in upholding white hetero-male power. In 1871, in a decision upholding an anti-miscegenation statute, the Indiana Supreme Court held that

> marriage is a public institution established by God himself . . . and is essential to the peace, happiness and well-being of society . . . The right of all states to regulate and control, to guard, protect and preserve this God-given, civilizing, and Christianizing institution is of inestimable importance, and cannot be surrendered, nor can the States suffer or permit any interference therewith. (*State* v. *Gibson*, 36 Indiana 403)

In 1877, the Alabama Supreme Court reaffirmed this view: "marriage is not a mere contract, but a social and domestic institution upon which are founded all society and order, to be regulated and controlled by the sovereign power for the good of the State" (*Green* v. *State* 58 Alabama 190). A century later, the Minnesota Supreme Court articulated the same claim in upholding the law prohibiting same-sex marriage: "The institution of marriage as a union of man and woman, uniquely involving the procreation and rearing of children within a family, is as old as the book of Genesis" (cited in Daum 2017: 355). Although anti-miscegenation statutes were struck down in many nations in the second half of the twentieth century, heteronormative and procreationist assumptions remain widespread.

As of August 2017, twenty-six of 200 nations in the world permitted same-sex marriage (Pew Research Center on Religion and Public Life 2017). Thus, Ellen Anderson points out, only "individuals in positions of systemic power have the privilege of ignoring the 'public' aspect of marriage, instead conceptualizing marriage as a 'private' relationship, taking the very real legal and political implications of the institution for granted. As individuals are increasingly marginalized, the public aspect of marriage becomes increasingly important" (2017: 391). Despite the prevalent Western tendency to "speak of marriage in the language of love, romance, and commitment, it is also a legal contract creating a web of rights and obligations . . . the nexus for the allocation of a host of public and private benefits" (390). Proponents of same-sex marriage note that marriage is a "primary means of distributing symbolic and economic capital"; thus, "those denied the right to marry are excluded from the promise of respectability, belonging, and material benefits accrued through marriage . . . [and] stigmatized as second class citizens" (Daum 2017: 360). These benefits include rights to inherit property, adopt and retain custody of children, receive tax benefits and health insurance coverage, and the power to make critical legal and medical decisions on behalf of an impaired partner.

Intimately connected to conceptions of citizenship, and a precondition for the enjoyment of civil and social rights that afford social as well as legal status, "marriage is a private institution, but it is emphatically a public one as well" (Anderson 2017: 376). Contemporary debates about marriage reform raise fundamental questions: Can a sexist and heterosexist institution, long associated with white hetero-male entitlement, be transformed? Can its patriarchal, heteronormative, and white supremacist roots be extirpated? There is no consensus on these issues among theorists or activists. Some argue that marriage is so ensnared in hetero-patriarchy that the institution should be abolished (Spade and Willse 2016). Some suggest that as long as marriage continues to be a pillar of adult citizenship replete with state-sanctioned rights and privileges, it should be available to all citizens—and indeed, that same-sex marriage might model a more egalitarian mode of marital relations (Gullette 2004). Some suggest that the power of the state could be used to reshape spousal relations in accordance with principles of equality (Nuti 2016). Others argue that marriage should be privatized, reduced to the status of a private contract accompanied by no state recognition and no state benefits (Metz 2010; Chambers 2013). As Clare Chambers notes:

> Abolishing state-recognized marriage means that the state no longer provides a bundle of rights and duties to people because they are married. It does not mean making it illegal for people to participate in the symbolic institution of marriage or to call themselves married. Without state-recognized marriage people could still engage in private religious or secular ceremonies of marriage but these would have no legal status. (2013: 133)

Queer theorists such as Lisa Duggan (2003), Dean Spade and Craig Willse (2016) caution that returning marriage to the private sphere would shore up homonormativity, further marginalizing those who refuse the heteropatriarchal terms that discipline love, romance, and sexuality. Privatizing marriage will not alter pervasive assumptions that naturalize gendered divisions of labor with respect to child care and house work. It will not diminish the power of religious traditions that continue to posit marriage as the only permissible site for sexual expression or lessen their focus on the ideology of procreation. Indeed, Carole Pateman argued that privatizing marriage simply replicates the strategy of the social contract tradition in claiming that "conjugal power is not political" (1988: 53). It does nothing to subvert heteropatriarchal power, "the power of every husband to order things of private concernment in the family . . . and to have his will take precedence" (53).

Sexuality

Pateman's discussion of "male sex right" extends well beyond marriage. In the realm of sexuality, "liberalism's romance with privacy" also obscures manifold operations of power (Heberle 2016: 598).

Feminist scholars and activists have sought to dispel those obfuscations and make that power visible and actionable. In *Sexual Politics*, Kate Millett argued that heterosexual erotics are shaped by power dynamics:

> Coitus can scarcely be said to take place in a vacuum; although of itself it appears a biological and physical activity, it is set so deeply within the larger context of human affairs that it serves as a charged microcosm of the variety of attitudes and values to which culture subscribes. Among other things, it may serve as a model of . . . power-structured relationships, arrangements whereby one group of persons is controlled by another. (1969 [2000]: 43)

Placing heterosexual intercourse on a continuum with rape as "political relations that structure male superiority and female inferiority," Barbara Mehrof and Pamela Kearon suggested that "The sexual act renews the feeling of power and prestige for the male, of impotence and submission for the female. Rape adds the quality of terror. Terror is an integral part of the oppression of women. Its purpose is to ensure, as a final measure, the acceptance by women of the inevitability of male domination" (1971 [1973]: 230). In "Rape: An Act of Terror," Mehrof and Kearon asserted that rape plays a particular role in normalizing relations of domination. Rape not only positions "woman qua woman outside the protection of the law," but also produces a form of demoralization and powerlessness that perpetuates male domination (230). Carole Sheffield elaborated this theme in "Sexual Terrorism":

> Violence and its corollary, fear, serve to terrorize females and to maintain the patriarchal definition of woman's place. The word terrorism invokes images of furtive organizations of the far right or left, whose members blow up buildings and cars, hijack airplanes, and murder innocent people . . . But there is a different kind of terrorism, one that so pervades our culture that we have learned to live with it as though it were the natural order of things. Its targets are females—of all ages, races, and classes. It is the common characteristic of rape, wife battery, incest, pornography, harassment, and all forms of sexual violence. I call

it sexual terrorism because it is a system by which men frighten and, by frightening, control and dominate females. (1984: 3)

Terror is a form of extra-judicial violence that targets innocent parties. When radical feminists identified rape and various practices of violence against women as acts of terror, they sought a vocabulary that could articulate a form of coercive control masked by formal guarantees of equal protection of the law. They sought to make visible structures of power that allowed and condoned the use of violence and intimidation against women who had committed no crime. They sought to situate these acts of violence in a political framework in which the perpetrators of violence (men) quite literally had control of the state, using its lawmaking powers to create laws reflecting their own interests, and using formal police powers to ensure that they could engage in extra-judicial violence with impunity. To borrow a term from Giorgio Agamben (2005), they sought to demonstrate the existence of a "state of exception." Anticipating Michel Foucault's conception of "discipline" and Achille's Mbembe "necropolitics," radical feminists analyzed sexual violence as a microphysics of power that produces docile bodies and damaged psyches. They theorized sexual terror as a mode of subjection that produces the feminine body as a specific repertoire of gestures, postures, modes of adornment and movement trained to deference. In the words of Susan Brownmiller, "women are trained to be rape victims" (1975: 343). Through feminine socialization, "they learn not only how to survive as prey, but how to eroticize and aestheticize the experience of their own victimization" (Grant 2016: 235).

Theorizing rape as an act of power and aggression that was sexually enacted most often by men, most often upon women, Brownmiller suggested that rape was always about domination. "Even male-on-male rape reinforced the patriarchal link between male violence and gendered hierarchy insofar as it was a crime in which one man treated another man as though he were a sexually subservient woman" (Grant 2016: 234). Examining gang rapes of black women by white men in the late nineteenth- and early twentieth-century United States, Hannah Rosen illuminated the racial dynamics of white "patriarchal rationales for rape—in particular, the notion that men rape women to get at other men" (2009: 217).

> This patriarchal framing—that men can be punished and dominated through the rape and thereby the dishonor of their women—seems to be part of the assailants' fantasy enacted through rape. It also posits black men's patriarchal possession of the women in their families only to defy it. The fantasy performed through rape, then, became one of white male domination of both black women and men through the articulation of this patriarchal framework. Interactions among assailants suggest that they needed one another's participation to create the desired illusions about their violence. In this way, night-rider violence contributed to solidarity among white men . . . [the] collective dynamics of night riders helped to produce an anticipation that violence would be pleasurable. It also suggests the need of some assailants to see themselves reflected in the actions of others in order to normalize their brutality and to reinforce their construction of it as a reflection of black women's dishonor rather than their own. (Rosen 2009: 218)

In recent years, LGBTQ activists have documented increasing numbers of "curative" or "corrective" rapes against lesbians, transmen, and transwomen. In the course of these brutal attacks, the perpetrators make it clear that they seek to punish those who violate the norms of compulsory heterosexuality and the conventions of sex assignment at birth (Thomas 2013). As a mode of raced-gendered domination, rape involves far more than unrestrained sexual impulses or the conscious pursuit of power. It is performance of social and political inequality whose very possibility is conditioned upon interlocking investments in conventional gendered identities and heterosexuality (Rosen 2009: 8). Rape, then, is political in ways that defy liberal constructions of the public/private dichotomy. Rape is a private but political act that occurs in public and private spaces, which violates the privacy and physical integrity of the victim, but is enacted with impunity. In putatively democratic states, where negative liberty is enshrined, rape is widespread—experienced by 20 to 25 percent of women in the course of their lives. Yet, it is the least reported of violent crimes. Less than 3 percent of rapists are prosecuted, convicted, and punished.

Although the rights to bodily integrity and decisional privacy concerning intimate matters are central to negative liberty, they remain elusive for nonnormative citizens. Talia Mae Bettcher (2007, 2016) has theorized "sex verification" as a brutal form of forced genital exposure imposed upon trans people. Clothing is typically conceived as a matter of personal taste and a means of preserving modesty according to individual choice; yet it is also a mode of gender presentation. In everyday interactions, a person's sex (construed in terms of genitalia) and gender identity (sense of self as a man, a woman, gender variant or gender queer) are routinely *inferred* from style of dress and deportment. "Gender presentation is generally taken as a *sign* of sexed body, taken to mean sexed body, taken to communicate sexed body" (Bettcher 2007: 52). For cisgender people (those whose gender identity coincides with their assigned gender at birth), clothing confers a privacy right—the right to privatized genitalia, to have one's sexed embodiment taken on trust. Trans people are not afforded that right. They are construed as "deceivers" or "pretenders." A transwoman's gender identity is invalidated when she is characterized as "a man living as a woman," a man because she has not been a girl or a woman since birth. Thus she is subjected to a double violation: identity invalidation (her own sense of self is repudiated); and in far too many cases, violent sex verification as assailants forcibly expose her genitalia to prove her "true" sex. As in the case of rapists and night riders, the transphobic marauders who engage in these brutal assaults remain fairly confident that they can act with impunity. The state seldom comes to the aid of victims of trans violence, and even when it does, the police often exacerbate rather than mitigate the violence.

Commodification of Bodies

Liberal political theorists typically ensconce the market in the private sphere. Providing an alternative to mercantilism (an economic system controlled by the feudal state), the market is the means by which equal, rational individuals order relations of production, exchange, and consumption. Motivated by self-interest, individuals freely enter into contracts that specify the goods and services to be produced and exchanged, the conditions of labor, and the monetary costs of the transaction. Because these exchanges are negotiated among equals, the state is assigned a minimalist role, ensuring that all parties keep the terms of the contract, and settling disputes that arise from violations of the contract. From Adam Smith to John Stuart Mill, some liberal theorists suggested that the state should also monitor market relations to ensure that they were free from fraud and did not cause harm to third parties (e.g., consumers, the environment). But the freedom to buy and sell, bargain and exchange, are hallmarks of negative liberty. When the commodity to be purchased is flesh, however, in the form of sexual services, some feminist activists and theorists have suggested that presumptions about equal parties to the contract require interrogation.

Prostitution
The sale of sexual services is markedly gendered. Although heterosexual men and women, gays, lesbians, trans persons, and children are all active in sex markets, the majority of sex workers are women, and the vast preponderance of clients are men. In contrast to the market ideal of equal individuals negotiating free from governmental interference, state action to regulate prostitution has long skewed the sex work contract to the advantage of the male client. In the nineteenth century, feminists drew attention to increasing state regulation of "vice" as a means to assign sexual authority over women's bodies to men. Laws regulating prostitution acknowledged that men had sexual appetites that required access to "public women" on a cash basis. Bourgeois women's putative "asexual" nature made it necessary that men pursue sexual satisfaction through private contracts with sex workers. Yet the state's concern for public health mandated that they control prostitutes to limit the transmission of infectious diseases. In 1875, Josephine Butler founded the International Federation for the

Abolition of Governmental Regulation of Vice to contest the way that state institutions (the Parliament, the army, the police, and the judiciary) in collusion with the medical profession regulated women's bodies for the use of men (Harrington 2010: 47). Mandatory vaginal examination of prostitutes denied women's bodily integrity while leaving men with sexually transmitted diseases free to spread infection without state interference. Butler pointed out that the law played a crucial role in creating sexual inequalities that fueled sex work. As laws barred women from gainful employment, higher education, and professional training, they narrowed women's economic options to an unhappy choice between marriage or prostitution. The law structured asymmetric power relations by granting men a monopoly on property ownership, paid work, education, and public policy, while insulating them from prosecution by criminalizing prostitution but not the purchase of sex.

As nations mobilized for war across the twentieth century, and peacekeeping forces have been deployed for "humanitarian" purposes in the twenty-first, militaries routinely organized access to brothels populated by disease-free sex workers to keep combatants happy and preserve order within the ranks. National, international and military police collude in organizing prostitution at nightclubs in close proximity to military bases and popular spots for rest and relaxation. Although prostitution remains illegal in many nations where troops are deployed, the local police typically assist in the recruitment of women to work in these clubs, ignore the sexual and economic exploitation of sex workers, and tip-off club owners prior to raids (Harrington 2010: 154).

As Carol Harrington has noted, soldiers who buy sex "share much in common with sex tourists" (170). They have a measure of economic privilege compared to the sex workers. They enjoy short leaves where "normal" moral rules are suspended. They believe that tolerance for rule-breaking is deserved due to their stressful assignments. They perceive a visit to a brothel as a pleasurable experience of male bonding and a chance to win status and influence among male peers. One study of Swedish and Finnish men deployed on peacekeeping assignments explored how the purchase of sex detached the men from national norms of gender equality and enabled them to "form powerful homosocial bonds that elude them at home" (176). They explained their recourse to the purchase of sex both in terms of a putative uncontrollable male sex drive and sexually assertive local women and girls who prefer white men. "Even when they pay for sex, they do not see it as prostitution—but rather as generous or altruistic behavior given the impoverishment of local women and girls" (175). Rather than grappling with the structural inequities associated with the commodification of sex, "military men assume that the women they pay for sex freely choose and enjoy sex with them . . . that prostitution is good for the women and for their local economy" (176).

Some feminists have argued that the commodification of sex is no different than the commodification of any other service. As autonomous individuals, women have a right to do with their bodies as they choose. Yet others point out that the presumption of autonomy on the part of sex workers overlooks the structural inequities that haunt transactional sex. The law structures relations of domination by criminalizing the sex worker, but not the "'john', the 'punter', the man who contracts to use the services of the prostitute" (Pateman 1988: 203). Purchasing sex can foster male bonds precisely because access to women's bodies is part of the construction of masculinity. Sex workers are required to perform servility and submission as sexually satisfying in order to preserve their client's illusion that he is generous, altruistic, and humane—even as he sets the terms of the encounter and she complies with his commands. Physical and psychological violence are rampant in sex work—perpetrated by clients, police, and prison officials. Moreover, although some sex workers are independent entrepreneurs who determine the conditions of their own labor, the multi-billion-dollar global sex industry mercilessly exploits sex workers to maximize the profits of the pimps and club owners who facilitate the sale of sex.

Feminists disagree about how to address the systemic inequities in sex work. "Abolitionists" argue that sex work should be prohibited because the sale of sexual services is incompatible with human dignity and equality. Others argue for an end to the criminalization of sex work because these laws make the conditions of sex workers more dangerous, driving them off the streets and into the hands of criminal syndicates, while also subjecting them to arbitrary arrest and abuse by police. Some Nordic nations have decriminalized the sale of sex, but criminalized the purchase of sex, in an effort to shift the power relations that inform commercial sexual exchanges (Global Network of Sex Work Projects 2017). Despite such disparate prescriptions, feminist analyses suggest that the pervasive power imbalances in transactional sex reveal gendered-racialized relations that canonical conceptions of negative liberty render invisible or deem irrelevant.

Pornography

As a global industry that includes the mass production and circulation of texts and images in print and online, pornography is very much part of the public sphere. Yet, consumed as a form of personal entertainment, it is often discussed as a private matter. Prohibited by obscenity laws in many nations in the nineteenth and twentieth centuries, pornography has been characterized by its defenders as a victimless crime, a mode of artistic expression, and a key component of sexual freedom.

In the early 1980s, Andrea Dworkin and Catharine MacKinnon challenged this characterization of pornography as harmless and victimless by defining it narrowly as the graphically depicted and sexually explicit subordination of women. Distinguishing pornography from erotica (sexually explicit depictions of consensual, mutual sexual satisfaction) and sex education materials, Dworkin and MacKinnon argued that pornography coerces, entraps and exploits women who are involved in its production, while also disseminating the fallacious message that women enjoy sexual subordination. Pornography teaches that women take pleasure in being raped, humiliated, mutilated, and tortured. Indeed, pornography eroticizes sexual domination, conquest, violation, exploitation, possession, and use. By circulating such noxious representations, pornography reinforces women's second-class status. As such, it should be understood as a discriminatory practice based on sex that denies women equal opportunities in society.

In the fall of 1983, at the request of the City Council of Minneapolis, Dworkin and MacKinnon drafted a civil rights ordinance to give individuals who had been harmed by pornography a right to sue for damages. The ordinance proposed to amend Minneapolis' existing civil rights code to enable anyone who had experienced physical or economic harm through "trafficking in pornography, coercion into pornographic performances, forcing pornography on a person, or assault or physical attack due to pornography" to sue the manufacturers of the pornography for monetary compensation (Dworkin and MacKinnon 1988: 101). The logic underlying the ordinance was economic: if porn producers had to pay large settlements to those harmed by their products, they might be driven out of business. Nothing in the proposed ordinance authorized censorship prior to publication of pornographic materials. It simply gave those harmed a right to seek redress for their injuries.

The Minneapolis City Council passed the "Dworkin-MacKinnon ordinance" twice between December 1983 and July 1984, but it was vetoed by Mayor Don Fraser both times. The Indianapolis City Council passed a similar ordinance in spring 1984, but it was struck down by the federal courts as an infringement of the First Amendment guarantee of free expression. Although the court case was initiated by the American Booksellers Association and supported by the American Civil Liberties Union, there was also significant opposition to the Dworkin-MacKinnon ordinance within the feminist community. "Sex radical feminists" argued that the ordinance's definition of pornography was "unconstitutionally vague" and would amount to a license to censor a virtually limitless number of materials, including experimentations in feminist art (Hunter and Law 1987: 108, 89, 101). Moreover, the ordinance shored up sexual stereotypes by suggesting that sex is harmful and degrading. Insisting that the ordinance constituted censorship, some opponents argued that it would hinder women's efforts to develop their own sexuality, exacerbate the oppression of lesbians and other sexual minorities, harm women who voluntarily work in the sex industry, and undermine essential aspects of human freedom, including sexual freedom (Strossen 1995; 1993).

As the "sex wars" roiled in the United States, the Supreme Court of Canada upheld a MacKinnon-inspired interpretation of pornography in 1992, categorizing it as "hate speech" against women that violates the equality clauses of the Canadian Constitution. The German Federal Constitutional Court upheld an interpretation of pornography as an offense against human dignity incompatible with the Basic Law's pledge to treat all human beings with dignity and respect.

In the realm of the market, the boundaries of public and private, the equality of contracting parties, and the appropriate role of the state remain matters of intense contestation. Anita Allen (1988) defined privacy as a condition of inaccessibility of the person, his or her mental states, or information about the person to the surveillance of others. In cases of marriage, rape, gender verification, and commercial sexual transactions, "bodily privacy is a privilege regulated by systems of power and control" (Clare 2013: 264). Marriage, heterosexuality, and commodified sex continue to be structured by systemic gender inequalities, despite formal equality. The displacement of lesbians, gays, and trans people from the safety and protection of the private sphere is central to their subordination (Calhoun 1994). Gays and lesbians are afforded no privacy in the bedroom because specific erotic acts are criminalized in seventy-five nations (Keating 2017: 437; Duncan 2017). Trans folks have no privacy guarantees in public or private spaces.

Racialized gender hierarchies and systems of compulsory heterosexuality operate freely within the private sphere. They are reproduced through gendered assumptions that naturalize relations of domination and subordination—a naturalization that masks white heteropatriarchal power (Rupp and Thomsen 2016: 897). Within these naturalized circuits, female, queer and trans citizens, like citizens of color, enter the public sphere on markedly different terms than their white, cis, hetero-male counterparts. They are public, in the sense that they are subjects of collective concern and subject to regulation in the collective interest, but they are sorely lacking in the beneficial aspects of privacy. Analyses of the constitutive contradictions of the liberal construction of public and private spheres, then, lay the groundwork for a systematic reconsideration of the nature of the state. That topic is taken up in the next chapter.

5

Analyzing the State and the Nation

The chief principle of a well-regulated police state is this: that each Citizen shall at all times and places . . . be recognized as this or that particular person. No one must remain unknown to the police.
(Fichte 1796 [1889]: 378)

The sex/gender binary, which is in perpetual crisis, is actually preserved—not by physiological requirements guaranteeing permanence and irreversibility, because they can't—but by the legal machinations the state requires of its people. (Currah and Moore 2013: 619)

In Iran in the 1970s, the emergence of visible non-heteronormative maleness was widely perceived as a moral corruption of Iranian culture through Westernization. Any public spectacle of non-masculine maleness, non-heteronormative sexuality, or gender ambiguity was taken as a sign of "Westoxification" (Najmabadi 2013: 387–8). Manifestations of "gender confusion" in clothing, lifestyles, or work of men and women that was "too similar" was denounced as a "threat to today's civilization" (389). Associated with the corruption of the Pahlavi regime, violations of the gender binary became the target of state action after the establishment of the Islamic Republic in 1979. Mandatory veiling policies dramatically altered the dress of Iranian women in public spaces. Criminalization of "passive" homosexuality, accompanied by threats of arrest, imprisonment or the death penalty profoundly altered nonnormative behavior in public space. Ayatollah Khomeini's approval of "sex change" operations at public expense placed increasing pressure on transgender people to alter their bodies to conform to heteronormativity, and catapulted Iran into the limelight as the nation that provides the highest number of sex-confirming surgeries in the world (395).

In the United States in 2006, the Ninth Circuit Court of Appeals issued a ruling upholding the right of employers to enforce grooming policies designed to ensure that men look and act like men, conforming to conventional standards of masculinity, and women look and act like women, complying with cultural norms of femininity. At issue was the "Personal Best" policy of Harrah's Casino, which required that women wear makeup ("face powder, blush, mascara and lip color must be worn at all times") and prohibited men from doing so. Women could wear colored nail polish, but men could not. Women were required to tease, curl, or style their hair. Men were not permitted to have ponytails; indeed, men's hair "must not extend below top of shirt collar" (*Jespersen v. Harrah's Operating Co.*, 444 F.3d 1104 [9th. Cir. 2006]; Carbado 2013). Mandated gender conformity in workplaces resonated with concerns articulated in a 2003 Advisory issued by the Department of Homeland Security (DHS) that linked gender ambiguity to national security threats (Beauchamp 2009 [2013]: 51). Warning that "terrorism is everywhere in disguise . . . male bombers may dress as females in order to discourage scrutiny," the DHS advisory "fused terrorist-in-disguise with gender transgression, marking particular bodies as deceptive and treacherous" (46, 49).

In these examples, two states with radically different political regimes, belief systems, and public images enforce regulatory practices and state surveillance policies "deeply rooted in the maintenance and enforcement of normatively gendered bodies, behaviors, and identities" (47). These practices stand in marked contrast to accounts of the state advanced by modern political theorists from Locke to Weber, who conceptualize the state as a collection of impartial institutions, governed by neutral and rational procedures, designed to foster formal equality before the law, equal rights of participation, and practicable mechanisms of account-ability. Within canonical accounts, sex, gender, and sexuality are construed as individual attributes or demographic characteristics that exist outside of politics and have no direct relevance to the nature or operations of the state. The previous chapter showed how demarcations of public and private mask power relations that permeate the private, "pre-political" sphere, reinforcing gender, race, and sexual subordination with powerful ramifications for public life. The present chapter will show how the state itself is far from an impartial institution; on the contrary, it plays a crucial role in producing raced, classed, gendered and sexualized subjects and citizens. Leading conceptions of the state mystify these power relations, fostering sanctioned ignorance of the role of the state in racing, gendering, and heterosexualizing citizens.

This chapter explores competing theorizations of the state, the nation, and citizenship. It begins with a comparison of accounts of the state advanced by canonical thinkers including Hobbes, Locke, Weber, Marx, Madison, and Foucault, and considers some of the limitations of these views identified by critical race, femi-nist, queer, and trans* scholars. It then shows how understandings of "the nation" complicate standard theories of the state, while also creating possibilities for making sense of race, ethnicity, sex, gender, sexuality, and able-bodiedness as political categories that carry legal status and ground citizenship rights. The final section of the chapter examines a range of policy areas that illuminate how nation-states create and maintain status hierarchies among citizens through the production and regulation of bodies and identities. Through birth certificates and registries, passports, driver's licenses, draft cards, credit applications, marriage licenses, death certificates, dress codes, and regulations of behavior, nation-states affix raced-sexed legal status to citizenship, sculpting the contours of individual freedom and belonging in ways that ensure that domination and subordination are thoroughly corporeal.

Conceptions of the State in Western Political Theory

"State" is a remarkably versatile concept. Long before it was associated with political systems, a state referred to "a particular way or manner of existing—a condition." In its earliest usage, a state involved a "condition of mind or feeling," or indeed "the mode of existence of a spiritual being." With the emergence of modernity, the meaning expanded to encompass "a physical condition as regards make or constitution." Later, the term connoted "a person or class of persons regarded as part of the body politic and participating in government," and referred particularly to feudal lords. As feudal relations succumbed in the age of revolutions, state began to refer to "a particular form of polity or government, the body politic as organized for supreme civil rule and government, a body of people occupying a defined territory and organized under a sovereign government" (*Oxford English Dictionary*).

Within political theory, the nature of the state is a subject of continuing controversy. Despite disagreement on multiple questions, however, theorists do concur on a few points. They agree that the state has a geographically identifiable territory with a body of citizens; that it claims authority over all citizens and groups within its boundaries; and that it embodies more comprehensive aims than other associations (Vincent 2004). As Thomas Hobbes so famously put it in *Leviathan* (1651), the state is defined by a monopoly of force within a particular territory, which is the basis of sovereignty. Sovereignty is the power to make and enforce the civil and criminal law with the penalty of death and all lesser penalties. Hobbes was thoroughly cynical about the content of law. As the "word of the sovereign," the law was quite simply whatever the sovereign declared it to be. People complied with the law solely from fear of punishment. Thus Hobbes articulated an *absolutist theory of the state*, which subjects all equally to the will of the sovereign.

Subsequent theorists within the liberal tradition insisted that the rule of law set limits on sovereign state power. Locke, for example, argued that because it proceeded from the consent of the governed, sovereign power could be neither absolute nor arbitrary, for rational subjects would never consent to laws that made them worse off. To ensure limited state power, Locke argued for the separation of legislative, executive, and judicial functions, and accorded citizens a perpetual "right of revolution"—a right to overthrow tyrannical government whether enacted by legislative or executive branches. Laying a foundation for a *constitutional theory of the state*, Locke envisioned electoral mechanisms to hold legislators accountable to the citizens and separation of powers to prevent state institutions from abusing power. The constitution, whether written or unwritten, was understood to identify the official institutions of governance and the scope of their activities, establish specific procedures for office holding and removal from office, specify criteria for citizenship and the rights of citizens. By establishing the ground rules for the political system, the constitution differentiated between the authority of the state and the actions of any particular regime or set of officials. Embodying the principle that no one is above the law, the constitutional theory of the state suggests more than the existence of the "rule of law." As subsequently developed, the constitutional theory suggests that political institutions are impartial, governed by neutral and rational procedures, and that office holders are ultimately accountable to the people.

   Theorizing the development of political systems in the twentieth century, Max Weber (1864–1920) identified rationalization and bureaucratization as two central forces shaping the *modern administrative state* (1919 [1946]). The rule of law would necessitate the growth of large administrative bureaucracies in which official conduct was governed by hierarchies designed to impose strict discipline and accountability. Recruitment for specialized roles within these administrative agencies would be based on merit, demonstrated through competitive examination. With the institutionalization of impersonal merit-based authority, policy making would be based on technical expertise in accordance with the norm of political neutrality. As governance became fully rationalized, public policy would be driven by scientific investigation of the most efficient means to achieve social objectives. Rational comprehensive decision making by technical experts would foster the common good.

In a series of essays published in the 1840s, Karl Marx pointed out that the state was far less impartial than the constitutional theory made it out to be. Far from being accountable to all the people, Marx suggested, the *state was an instrument of class oppression*—representing the interests of the ruling class and accountable only to the ruling class. For Marx, however, class relations were inherently dynamic. He contended that, in the mid-nineteenth century, European states were still in the hands of feudal aristocracies, although the bourgeoisie (the emerging capitalist class) was fighting for political representation as a means of wresting control of the state from the *ancien régime*. Yet precisely because it was lobbying for universal male suffrage, the bourgeoisie was laying the foundation for its own overthrow. Indeed, in the *Communist Manifesto*, Marx and Engels suggested that one strategy for revolution was to "win the battle for the ballot box." Because the working class was so much larger than the bourgeoisie, once the vote was secured, workers could use their votes to elect parties that would represent the interests of labor. Thus Marx advanced a *social democratic theory of the state*, which posits the state as a class-based instrument but envisions a time when democratically elected socialist parties govern in the interests of the workers who comprise the vast majority of the population.

In the United States, where socialist parties never succeeded in gaining popular support at the polls and where workers regardless of income tend to identify as "middle class," *a pluralist conception of the state* took root, starting from arguments about human nature advanced by James Madison in the *Federalist Papers* (Hamilton, Madison, and Jay 1787 [1980]). Madison suggested that because human beings are self-interested, short-sighted, and contentious, prone to form factions (interest groups) at the least provocation to press for private advantage, politics should be understood as a process of interest accommodation. As subsequently articulated by Charles Lindblom in *The Intelligence of Democracy* (1965), politics is here conceived as a process of partisan mutual adjustment, a process of bargaining, negotiating, conciliation and compromise through which self-interested individuals seeking markedly different objectives arrive at decisions with which all are willing to live. Within the pluralist frame, the state is sometimes characterized as the "arena" of politics, the space in which interest accommodation takes place. Alternatively, some pluralists depict the state as an "umpire" ensuring that the rules of the game are enforced. Both versions suggest that the state 1) recognizes the heterogeneity of citizens and protects the rights of all to participate in the political process; 2) acknowledges the validity of multiple power bases in society (for example, wealth, numbers, monopoly of scarce goods or skills); and 3) accords each a legitimate role in policy making. Although some versions of pluralism cast the state as disinterested—officially refraining from taking sides in these contests over values and interests—other versions suggest that competing interests exist within the official institutions of state itself. On this view, state institutions must also be understood to act as factions, whose behavior is governed by organizational interests, partisanship, and private ambitions rather than impartiality (Allison 1971). Whether or not the state itself is seen as an interested party in these policy negotiations, pluralists treat all power bases as equal, suggesting that no particular advantage is afforded by wealth or political office. Insisting that "formal equality" guarantees equal rights of participation and influence, the pluralist conception of the state denies that disproportionate advantage accrues from insider status within political institutions or economic power in determining political outcomes.

The *new institutionalist conception of the state* grew out of a critique of pluralism and suggested that the notion of the state as a political arena or as an umpire failed to take account of the distinctive power and interests of state institutions. Rather than being construed as impartial or as merely reflecting particular social interests, the state plays a formative role inculcating values and molding individual interests and choices. Emerging in specific national contexts, each state embodies norms, formal rules, and standard operating procedures that reflect particular historical legacies and shape and constrain the behavior and decisions of those acting within them. Indeed, the new institutionalist theory of the state suggests that institutional norms and rules establish the criteria of intelligibility for political action; they frame the most basic understandings about what is rational, permissible, and possible within political life. Precisely because particular histories shape the norms of political behavior of rulers and ruled, patterns of action of individual states may be distinctive, but they are also predictable. Legacies of authoritarian practice, for example, will structure state behavior differently than norms of individual rights. The historical development of political institutions within particular states fixes repertoires of actions, institutional agendas, sets of expectations and loyalties, patterns of conflict and cooperation, and a modus operandi with powerful effects on future state action.

As neoliberalism has gained global ascendency since the 1970s, Michel Foucault's conception of *governmentality* has gained purchase as an explanation of contemporary state action. Foucault theorizes governmentality as "an explosion of numerous and diverse techniques for achieving the subjugation of bodies and the control of populations" (1978: 140). Situating these technologies of governance in relation to concerns about the "protection of life" that have preoccupied states since the early nineteenth century, Foucault suggests that governmentality obliterates the classical boundaries between public and private. Moving beyond the spectacles of monarchical rule designed to ensure obedience by manipulating fear of death, the state undertakes the regulation of health, sexuality, bodies, dispositions, and desires as part of its legitimate terrain. Political technologies that facilitate the "conduct of conduct" produce individual identities—resisting identities according to Foucault, but identities also invested in particular orders of desire (Foucault 1994: 237).

Rather than concentrating power in the official institutions of state, governmentality as a modern technology of power is diffused through manifold "capillaries"—power-knowledge constellations that permeate professions (law, medicine, education, psychology, social work), institutions (courts, families, hospitals, prisons, schools, the market, the military), and processes (discipline, normalization, socialization) (Foucault 1977). In the neoliberal era, states diffuse power by devolution, allocating responsibilities to supranational, regional, and subnational organizations; by "contracting out" responsibilities to private firms and corporations; and by fostering the exercise of autonomy as a duty to manage oneself according to neoliberal principles, such as rational and responsible "choice" (Novas and Rose 2000; Rose 2000). Foucault called attention to the central contradictions of neoliberal governmentality: power proliferates under the guise of privatization; heightened surveillance accompanies self-regulation; the responsible management of risk confronts individuals with impossible choices; and manifold technologies of governance foster profit-generating consumption far more than meaningful freedom.

The State as a Gendered Institution

As diverse as these classic accounts of the state may be, they converge in suggesting that the state is disembodied—unmarked by race, sex, gender, or sexuality. In her analysis of the state, Catharine MacKinnon (1983, 1987, 1989) suggested that, far from being disembodied, the state was inherently male. Whether claiming objectivity and disinterestedness, or to represent universal interests, the state simply conflates male interests with the common interest. "The male perspective is systemic and hegemonic . . . In this context, objectivity—the non-situated, universal standpoint, whether claimed or aspired to—is a denial of the existence or potency of sex inequality that tacitly participates in constructing reality from the dominant point of view" (MacKinnon 1983: 636). According to MacKinnon, the state's norms of accountability are cast only in terms of men; its sources of power are drawn exclusively from men; and the state's primary constituency is men. "The law sees and treats women the way men see and treat women. The liberal state coercively and authoritatively constitutes the social order in the interest of men as a gender, through its legitimizing norms, relation to society, and substantive policies" (634).

In theorizing the state as a gendered institution, subsequent scholars have drawn attention to its composition (women and

racialized minorities remain markedly underrepresented in elective
and appointed offices), its practices (standard operating procedures
in legislative halls and committee rooms, courts and bureaucratic
agencies, are neither gender inclusive nor gender neutral), and its
products (laws and policies create and entrench gender hierarchies,
gendered symbols, and gendered identities). In marked contrast
to notions of impartiality, the state actively produces difference,
political asymmetries, and social hierarchies that simultaneously
create the dominant and the subordinate.

Carole Pateman traced the means by which nascent welfare
states produced white male advantage by constructing "independence" as a gendered criterion for public citizenship. Claiming
merely to consolidate the capacity for self-protection, states created
"three elements of 'independence' . . . related to the masculine:
the capacity to bear arms, the capacity to own property and the
capacity for self-government" (Pateman 1998: 248). States used
mandatory male military service, conscription, and militia duty as
means to construct white men as "bearers of arms." Women, on
the other hand, were "unilaterally disarmed," barred from military
service and from combat duty, as men were assigned responsibility
for the "protection of women and children." Through laws governing freedom of contract, states created the most fundamental
property owned by "free men," the property in their own person
and in their labor power. By constructing women as the property
of their fathers or husbands, states denied women the right to freely
contract their labor. By structuring marriage laws to guarantee
men perpetual sexual access to their wives, states denied married
women autonomous ownership of their bodies. Moreover, by creating the category "head-of-household" and restricting it to men,
states created men's capacity for governance not only of themselves
but of their "dependents."

Pateman points out that census classifications in Britain and
Australia officially recognized the male worker as "breadwinner"
and his wife as his "dependent," regardless of her contributions
to household subsistence and income. Between 1851 and 1911 in
Britain (1891 in Australia), women's domestic labor was reclassified
from being a form of productive activity to a mode of dependency.

This reclassification was coupled with efforts to remove married women from the paid labor market in the belief that women workers depressed men's wages. The campaign for a "family wage" paid to the male "breadwinner"—actively promoted by the trade union movement—enshrined the principle of unequal pay for women in law, as it simultaneously masked women's presence in the industrial and agricultural labor force, and rendered their role as family providers invisible. In 1912, 45 percent of male workers in Australia were single, yet they were paid the family wage; while women workers, one-third of whom were supporting dependents, were paid 46–50 percent less than male wages on the basis of the legal fiction that they were not breadwinners. Thus the state created and reinforced women's identity as "dependent" both directly and indirectly, even as it used that dependency to legitimate women's exclusion from political life: regardless of their actual earnings or wealth, women were declared "trespassers into the public edifice of civil society and the state" (248).

The state also used pronatalist legislation to encourage white women to bear children, and prohibited abortion and contraception in order to circumscribe their reproductive autonomy. Ruth Miller has pointed out that when reproduction is defined as women's political duty and motherhood is conflated with women's citizenship, wombs are politicized in order to assert "the biological rights of the collective"—the nation. When abortion and contraception are criminalized, "crimes against the biological collective" are located within women's wombs (Miller 2007: 362). Indeed, because the *only* crimes that a citizen could commit against the biological collective involve contraception and abortion, women alone can pose this threat to the nation; hence the state's rationale for policing women's reproductive practices. Pronatalist policies are always racialized. Some citizens are encouraged or required to reproduce, while others are restricted or prohibited from reproducing through "eugenics" initiatives, sterilization campaigns, or, in the case of genocide, annihilation. To foreground this connection between state action, nationalism, ethnic privilege and racialized disadvantage, Jackie Stevens (1999) coined the term "race-nation."

Nations and States

Feminist scholars have made a compelling case in arguing that the full scope of state action to consolidate gender, racial, and sexual hierarchies cannot be understood unless the nation is theorized (Stoler 1995; McClintock 1997; Yuval Davis 1997, 2006). As a political concept, the "nation" suggests the existence of a "people" with intricate ties to the land quite independently of the state. Andreas Wimmer and Nina Glick Schiller (2003) have pointed out that contemporary conceptions of the nation presuppose a mode of belonging associated with an ethnic group tied by "blood," origins, ancestry, language, culture, and history. As a domain of identity, the nation suggests membership in an ethnicity that pre-exists the power politics of state formation. As the metaphors of blood and lines of descent suggest, national belonging implies organic ties, something akin to an extended family that requires solidarity, shared sacrifice, and mutual support. The emphasis on common language, culture, and history also suggests a linked fate, a common destiny as well as a shared geography. In certain formulations, the nation is taken to manifest certain inherent characteristics, a "national character" which forges ties across generations. In the words of Edmund Burke, the nation involves a "partnership not only between those who are living, but between those who are living, those who are dead, and those who are to be born" (1790 [1993]: §165).

Johann Gottlieb Fichte (1807 [2013]) theorized "interior frontiers" as the essence of the nation. Coexisting with formal equality before the law, the notion of interior frontiers subtly shifts the meaning of citizenship from legal equality to possession of a certain sensibility—a set of shared moral values, cultural orientations, and refined perceptions, which some may be said to lack. Traditional criteria of citizenship, such as place of birth (*jus soli*) or lines of descent (*jus sanguinis*), are augmented by a notion of a national community united by an ineffable set of invisible bonds. Equating the "essence of community" with an intangible moral attitude, particular righteous sentiments, and an enhanced patriotic sensibility, the state—aided and abetted by dominant racial, religious, ethnic, and gender-based organizations—primes the citizenry to recognize and act upon a panoply of internal distinctions within the nation. Those who embrace this heightened patriotic sensibility often feel compelled to act in defense of the nation, carrying out policies to preserve and protect what they hold dear. Thus, in Benedict Anderson's famous formulation, the nation is an "imagined community," and like all communities, nations are constituted by exclusion (1991: 101).

Fichte's conception of interior frontiers provides a way of understanding exclusionary practices by states that make little sense when citizenship is conceived only in terms of formal equality and legal status. Conceptions of national belonging characterized in terms of "blood ties" suggest notions of purity or authenticity that can be corrupted by mixture with outside elements. Those concerned with a mythos of national purity may act to protect the "body politic" from outside contaminants by controlling marriage (prohibiting miscegenation, marriage across racial, ethnic, or religious lines), by policing the population (ostracizing, imprisoning, institutionalizing, sterilizing, or eradicating those perceived to have physical, cognitive, or moral disabilities), and by restricting immigration. Laws limiting educational and professional opportunities and voting rights, laws imposing racial and intellectual classifications, and laws enforcing "eugenic" policies—whether on the basis of disability, poverty, or race— have been justified as means "to protect the integrity, superiority, and purity of the nation" (Stoler 1995: 150).

Although the mythos of nationalism emphasizes popular unity, nation-states have institutionalized gender difference, both to restrict access to the resources of the nation-state to a cohort of privileged men (McClintock 1997: 89) and to ensure that certain women reproduce the nation (Yuval Davis 1997; Farris 2017: 67). To increase birthrates, for example, Mussolini heavily taxed unmarried individuals and discriminated against them in the labor market, while granting tax exemptions to families with seven or more children (Farris 2017: 72). Although privileged citizens may be rewarded handsomely for reproducing the nation, eugenic policies target those considered "unfit" to reproduce (people of color, the poor, immigrants, the disabled, the "criminal"). Entire communities have been socially controlled through the creation and implementation of coercive laws, policies, and medical practices designed to preclude their reproduction (K. Price 2017: 82). Drawing attention to state practices that deliberately stunt, maim, experiment upon, and physically disable subgroups within a population, Jasbir Puar (2017) has theorized "debility" as a sovereign power claimed by the state that is linked to, but not the same as, the right to kill.

State action that links familial arrangements to public order makes sense in terms of assumptions about national identity structured in accordance with the "interior frontiers" of a particular race-nation. Heterosexual marriage is privileged as the basis of the nation—the mechanism by which the nation is reproduced. Other forms of sexuality are perceived as threats that subvert not only the "natural" order, but the nation. Privileged racial and ethnic groups are afforded the right to marriage to preserve imagined blood ties; others are excluded from that privilege. At this most elementary level, the state creates and sustains hierarchies of gender, sexuality, race and ethnicity within "the nation." In contrast to the liberal presumption that the state does not recognize differences among citizens, cultural and political discourses about national identity frame citizenship, loyalties, and allegiances in relation to social distinctions among citizens and often mobilize one part of the population against another. By enacting measures to regulate sexuality, marriage, family forms, and immigration, the nation-state not only controls citizenship as a legal status but produces citizens with particular racialized, gendered, and sexualized identities.

The nation-state involves far more than territorial boundaries, populations, forms of governance, and types of political authority. The concept of the nation's interior frontiers illuminates the state's role in subjectivation, the production of historically specific forms of personhood, knowledge, and experience. Foucault (1977, 1978) theorized power as a productive force that permeates life, shaping new forms of desires, relations, discourses, and modes of subjectivity. The subject does not precede power relations but is

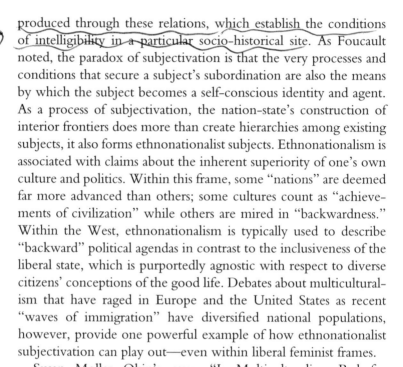

produced through these relations, which establish the conditions of intelligibility in a particular socio-historical site. As Foucault noted, the paradox of subjectivation is that the very processes and conditions that secure a subject's subordination are also the means by which the subject becomes a self-conscious identity and agent. As a process of subjectivation, the nation-state's construction of interior frontiers does more than create hierarchies among existing subjects, it also forms ethnonationalist subjects. Ethnonationalism is associated with claims about the inherent superiority of one's own culture and politics. Within this frame, some "nations" are deemed far more advanced than others; some cultures count as "achievements of civilization" while others are mired in "backwardness." Within the West, ethnonationalism is typically used to describe "backward" political agendas in contrast to the inclusiveness of the liberal state, which is purportedly agnostic with respect to diverse citizens' conceptions of the good life. Debates about multiculturalism that have raged in Europe and the United States as recent "waves of immigration" have diversified national populations, however, provide one powerful example of how ethnonationalist subjectivation can play out—even within liberal feminist frames.

Susan Moller Okin's essay, "Is Multiculturalism Bad for Women?," suggested that there is an inherent tension between feminism and multiculturalist commitments to group rights for ethnic minority populations. This tension is fueled by "claims of minority religions or cultures that conflict with gender equality that is at least formally endorsed by liberal states (no matter how extensively they violate those norms)" (1999: 9). Okin defined "feminism" as the belief that women should not be disadvantaged by their sex, should have human dignity just as men do, and have opportunities to live a fulfilling and freely chosen life (10). She defines multiculturalism as the protection of the group rights or privileges of "indigenous peoples, formerly colonized, ethnic, racial, and religious minorities" living within liberal nation-states (11). Although Okin's conception of feminism invokes a group (women), whose rights she seeks to protect, she subsumes this demand under the "liberal value of individual freedom," which should not be trumped by the rights of any group (particularly illiberal groups). Okin argues that subnational multicultural issues predominantly involve "oppressive gender practices, that is, male control over women," ranging from child marriages, forced marriages, and divorce systems biased against women to polygamy, clitoridectomy, and purdah (17–18). According to Okin, these practices repudiate any notion of women's human rights and endorse a cultural message that women are ancillary to men. Arguing that these practices deny women and children in minority cultures equal protection of the law and expose them to greater levels of male violence, she rejects the notion of group rights. "The fundamentals of liberalism require that the well-being of all members of a group be advanced; there can be no justification for assuming that the groups' self-proclaimed leaders—invariably composed mainly of their older and their male members—represent the interests of all the groups' members" (24).

Okin's critics have questioned her interpretation of minority cultures as mired in backwardness, unrelentingly misogynist, and unchanging; her assumption that the heinous acts of particular individuals are representative of whole cultures; and her depiction of women within minority cultures as either devoid of agency or, worse, as instruments of their own oppression. They have pointed out that Okin presumes the validity of a liberal conception of individual agency, driven by a universal urge to be free and unencumbered by the weight of tradition and custom. That presumption, the critics argue, naturalizes a particular conception of freedom that orientalizes African, Arab, Muslim, East Asian and South Asian women and lays the foundation for a version of feminist politics that seeks to save "Third World Women" from "death by culture." Critics have also pointed out that the chauvinism of this Western liberal perspective seriously distorts the agency and subjectivity of women in minority communities, and sustains policies that can worsen their condition (Narayan 1997; Abu Lughod 2002; Mohanty 2003; Mahmood 2005).

When a liberal version of ethnonationalism anchors the way of seeing political life, a great deal about the origins and operations of contemporary nation-states is obscured. A romanticized notion of a people bound by blood masks the historical origins of nations in war, conquest, and colonization. In the case of colonial settler societies, it masks the brutal construction of the racialized and gendered boundaries of belonging that reserved property ownership and citizenship to an elite white cohort. It hides the diversity within the population and the political force expended to suture the nation together, from quelling riots, subduing dissent, and breaking strikes to civil war. The myth of a stable, homogeneous population also masks the extensive immigration and migration that have shaped current populations. In contrast to the myth of a stable, homogeneous people, "the national population is . . . an assemblage of different legal categories that are not on the same pathway to citizenship . . . the citizenry is just one population among many that reside in the national territory alongside populations of noncitizens," including tourists, immigrants, refugees, "guest workers," and the undocumented (Kretsedemas 2008: 560). This plurality is not only masked by but constructed as a political problem within ethnonationalist frames.

National territory has never been a uniform political space. While the state has afforded some privileged persons rights, free land, and the possibility of self-determination, it shackled, enslaved, and exploited others, and annihilated still more. In *Seeing Like a State*, James Scott (1998) pointed out that states have devoted great efforts to producing a national population—efforts that have involved massive transformations of the physical landscape, the built environment, economic policies, educational practices, systems of regulation, as well as the appearance and demeanor of the people themselves.

To make a society legible, states develop social simplifications that make a society seem to be administratively manageable. In this process, they marginalize local knowledges that challenge managerial orderings. Social statistics, models, physical representations of space and place involve sweeping projects of social change informed by the ideology of high modernism: a vision of rational engineering all aspects of social life to improve the human condition. The goal is transformation. Toward that end, the state creates a population with characteristics easier to monitor and manage. Those who do not fit the model are left out of the frame, characterized as anomalies or pathologies which need to be transformed. (Bergeron 2006: 30)

States have devised complex technologies to cultivate a sense of national identity that is sufficiently strong to overcome some differences associated with class, ethnicity, religion and gender—while designating certain "others" unassimilable. States have funded programs to build connections between the aspirations of authorities and the activities and self-understandings of individuals and groups.

[Through the state's] inculcation of habits, standardization of systems of training, professional specialisms and vocabularies, invention of devices, surveys, health regimens . . . actors come to understand their situation according to similar language and logic, to construe their goals and their fate as in some way inextricable, they are assembled into mobile and loosely affiliated networks. Shared interests are constructed in and through political discourses, persuasions, negotiations, and bargains. Common modes of perception are formed, in which certain events and entities come to be visualized according to particular rhetorics of image or speech. Relations are established between the nature, character, and causes of problems facing various individuals and groups . . . intrinsic links form the basis for solutions. Regulatory techniques installed within citizens align their personal choices with the ends of government. (Rose and Miller 1992: 19–20)

In contrast to liberal notions of the state as a neutral vehicle, racialization, gendering, and heterosexualization are part of the daily operations of state power, deployed as means for particular states to realize their visions of national identity and national order (Stevens 1999). Raced-gendered-sexualized patterns of skilling and deskilling, differences in political rights and economic opportunities, and modes of political visibility and invisibility structure the identities, self-understandings, and life-prospects of citizens. Rather than succumb to mythic constructions of the nation-state that emphasize ties of blood and ancestry, feminist, critical race, queer, postcolonial and trans* scholars have traced how state actions have produced physical characteristics, modes of subjectivity, and behaviors associated with particular populations.

Racialization, Gendering, and Heterosexualization within Nation-States

Leading accounts of nation-states have been remarkably successful in masking the use of power to produce hierarchies within the population. To show how privilege and disadvantage related to race, class, gender, sexuality, and disability are created and maintained through law, institutional processes, practices, images, ideologies, and distributional mechanisms, the remaining sections of this chapter explore the micropolitics of racialization, gendering, and heterosexualization.

From Sumptuary Laws to Dress Codes

According to Fichte, "the chief principle of a well-regulated police state is this: that each Citizen shall at all times and places . . . be recognized as this or that particular person. No one must remain unknown to the police" (1796 [1889]: 378). Little attention is paid in democratic nations to the complex ways that states have mandated that individuals become known. Sumptuary laws were one means to "construct an order of appearance that allowed relevant social facts, in particular about social and economic status, gender, and occupation to be read from the visible signs disclosed by the clothes of the wearer" (Capers 2008: 7). Restrictions were intended to mark and police boundaries of gender, class and race, designating some as illustrious and others as subordinates.

Many assume that stringent dress regulations are a feature of authoritarian rule and ascription systems that fix an individual's life prospects from birth. It comes as something of a surprise, then, to find such laws in liberal democratic nations such as the United States, which enshrine individual liberty, self-making, and upward mobility as defining characteristics. Yet between 1850 and 1870, "at a time when the racial order was being overthrown by civil war and Reconstruction, the women's suffrage campaign was challenging the gender order . . . and lesbian and gay subcultures were emerging in large cities, municipal laws were passed prohibiting 'dress not belonging to [one's] sex'" (Capers 2008: 8). These ordinances made it a crime to appear in clothing belonging to the "opposite" sex, specifically prohibiting individuals from "masquerading in another person's attire for unlawful purposes" (9). Between 1848 and 1914, forty-five cities in twenty-one US states passed laws against cross-dressing (Sears 2013: 555). These laws were designed to prevent "gender fraud," particularly by women posing as men to gain economic, social or political advantage. Included in new municipal codebooks, these "offenses against good morals and decency" carried heavy penalties—fines from $500 to $1,000 or six months in jail. Deployed to stamp out gender "deviance," the laws also inscribed dimorphic gender divisions and enforced the disciplinary production of gender.

> Being an adult male meant that one must dress like a man, be a man; being an adult female meant that one must dress like a woman, be a woman . . . these divisions had to be readily visible and maintained . . . these prohibitions signaled to everyone what dress, and what behavior, was appropriate. It was not enough that in every government form, in every government census, an answer was demanded: male or female. One had to act and appear it too. (Capers 2008: 9)

As Clare Sears has noted:

> these laws did much more than police the types of clothing that belonged to each sex; they used the visible marker of clothing to police the types of people who "belonged" in public space . . . Between 1863 and 1900 more than 100 arrests for cross-dressing snared feminist dress reformers, female impersonators, 'fast' women who dressed as men for a night on the town and people whose gender identifications did not match their anatomical sex. Those arrested faced police harassment, public exposure and severe financial penalty along with loss of freedom. (2013: 555)

In the twentieth century, these laws became a key tool for policing transgender and queer communities. If arrested, sexual and gender variant people risked institutionalization in prisons and psychiatric facilities or deportation if they were not US citizens (555). Thus, exclusion from public space became a powerful means to regulate gender transgression. Fear of arrest led some people to modify their public appearance and confine their cross-dressing to private spaces.

> Legal segregation excluded cross-dressers from everyday activities (walking in parks or neighborhoods, shopping, political rallies, civic participation, democratic participation), thereby making cross-dressing a secretive practice . . . and producing an artificially narrow range of gender identities in public life . . . removing different gender appearances and identities from public view. By policing gender hierarchies through public exclusion, cross-dressing law reinforced the very notion of difference as anomalous by exaggerating the prevalence of the "norm." (556)

After more than a century of enforcement, prohibitions against cross-dressing were struck down by the courts in the final quarter of the twentieth century in the United States. Ordinances prohibiting "'dress not belonging to [one's] sex' were deemed unconstitutionally vague given current dress habits . . . yet dress codes persist in schools, the military, workplaces, in courtrooms, in legislative halls" (Capers 2008: 10–11). As the opening vignette in this chapter demonstrates, the courts have ruled it permissible for employers to require highly conventional gender presentation as a condition for employment. Gendered dress practices also surface in judicial decisions in criminal cases in particularly pernicious ways: judges give light sentences to rapists, or refuse even to convict them, because the woman's dress "invited" the attack; jurors have acquitted a rapist who repeatedly assaulted a woman over a five-hour period, claiming her mini skirt indicated that she was "asking for it" (Capers 2008). In addition to exculpating men accused of sexual assault, women's dresses have been used as a "shaming" means of punishment. In 2001, for example, a judge in Columbus,

Ohio sentenced two men to wear dresses while walking down Main Street, deeming this form of shaming appropriate to punish them for having thrown beer bottles at a car and been rude to the woman driver (Doulin 2001: C13).

The Western press pays a good deal of attention to mandatory dress policies in some nations. "Veiling" practices imposed by Islamic states garner instant and sustained international attention as evidence of the authoritarian inclinations of particular regimes or the "backwardness" of particular civilizations. But state investment in gendered dress practices in the West gets far less attention. Indeed, state involvement in the hierarchical marking of bodies often goes unnoticed.

Normalizing the Body Politic

In 1879, two years after the US federal government abandoned efforts to secure the equal rights of African Americans, Senator William Windom of Minnesota noted, "The black man does not excite antagonism because he is black but because he is a citizen" (Singh 2004: 24). In the aftermath of Reconstruction, following the withdrawal of Union troops from the states of the former Confederacy, southern states demonstrated the impressive inventiveness of law as they crafted statutes that criminalized a host of behaviors when enacted by Blacks. Absence of a formal labor contract, for example, became evidence of the crime of vagrancy. For Blacks, standing on public sidewalks was criminalized as loitering. Failure to step into the gutter when a white person passed on a sidewalk was deemed a disruption of public order. Criminalization of these acts was part of a cruel subterfuge to undermine the 14th Amendment guarantee of equal protection of the laws by expanding the range of crimes for which Blacks could be arrested and sentenced to "involuntary servitude."

> To meet its economic needs, the South built a criminal justice system around imprisoning Blacks. Fines for minor infractions morphed into jail time. Selective prosecution of Blacks surged. New crimes made their way onto the books . . . then jails leased convicts out as laborers

... At one point, Alabama earned nearly 12 percent of its total annual revenue from leasing convicts to private enterprise (plantations, corporations, mines, steel manufacturing) ... Those men and women swallowed alive by the prison-leasing system were almost always ... arrested by self-serving sheriffs and tried before venal judges for trivial offenses ... The system's ubiquity and caprice assured that virtually no Black was safe unless under the protection and control of a white landowner or employer ... Blacks went into sharecropping, a relationship itself akin to slavery, partly because they needed white bosses to protect them. (Haney Lopez 2014: 39–41)

In addition to criminalizing black behavior in public space, Black Codes mandated segregation in public accommodations, created fees for movement across state lines (applicable only to African Americans), and imposed literacy tests and poll taxes to prevent black men from exercising their franchise. When these racist state statutes were challenged in the courts, justices declared these systemic violations of liberty to be reasonable and legitimate (Hartman 1997: 199). The US Supreme Court ruled in *Plessy* v. *Ferguson* (163 U.S. 537, 1896) that "separate but equal" treatment was compatible with the demands of formal equality, ensuring that "the safety, health, morals, and comfort of the public were predicated upon the banishment and exclusion of blacks from the public domain" (Hartman 1997: 199).

Black Codes and the convict-leasing system are particularly egregious examples of the means by which nation-states make citizens intelligible through disparate treatment. In the words of James Scott, "states have historically been very bad at designing or legislating for complexity; they tend to impose order by categorizing and rationalizing their subjects and territories, by imposing constraints on 'natural' bodies" (1998: 136). By ordering citizens according to categories of race, sex, gender, and sexuality, nation-states identify certain attributes as foundational, immutable, and not subject to dispute. They also make it appear that these characteristics are visible, readily discernible, and unproblematically knowable. Encoded on birth certificates, national identification cards, passports, driver's licenses, death certificates, certain demographic features are solidified, given state recognition, and integrated into a sense of national belonging. Specified as criteria for inclusion, these racialized, gendered, and sexualized markers of citizenship also exclude.

Consider, for example, the 2004 French law on "secularity and conspicuous religious symbols in schools," which prohibited wearing religious symbols such as headscarves in primary and secondary schools, but did not prohibit jewelry featuring a cross, a crucifix, or a Star of David. Under the rubric of "secularism," Christianity and Judaism were accredited as French as Islam was declared to be alien. In September 2010 the French Senate ratified by an overwhelming majority (246 in favor, 1 opposed) a bill approved by the National Assembly in July 2010, which makes it illegal to wear garments such as the *niqab* or *burqa* anywhere in public. Under this new law, which took effect in 2011, women appearing in public in a full-face veil would be subjected to a fine of 150 euros. Although French legislators framed secularism as a means to defend individual liberty and national identity, Muslim citizens in France who want to wear the veil for religious reasons are deprived of liberty and autonomy. The regulation of women's dress both creates hierarchy among French women citizens and positions women as bearers of national identity in ways that legitimate state regulation of their presence in public or, indeed, their exclusion from public space.

In her study of "integration" policies in the European Union, Sara Farris investigated processes of gendered racialization as nation-states determined which migrants would be allowed to take up permanent residence:

Integration narratives situate nonwestern migrant women in a double relation to the state: as victims of oppressive cultures in need of rescue; and as mothers who can take on and advance the western project of eradicating oppressive practices by reproducing national culture . . . They are not addressed as individuals, but as vectors of integration, bearers of the collective, and bridges between hosted and hosting communities, that is, they embody the mediating role assigned to women as reproducers of the nation. (2017: 102–3)

Through detailed examination of integration programs in Italy, the Netherlands, and the United Kingdom, Farris concluded that "nationalism and racism are the animating forces of civic integration" (113).

> Civic integration policies make long-term residence of migrants dependent on tested results, language acquisition, cultural competence, and allegiance to values such as gender equality and LGBT rights . . . Mandatory integration requirements emphasize equality in the private sphere (monogamy, prohibition of family violence; mother's involvement in schools and neighborhoods). Messages concerning women's equality in the public sphere are far more ambiguous . . . Gender equality is promoted not predominantly in the labor market, or in the realm of political participation . . . but above all in the family as the main social unit within which women, on the one hand, allegedly need protection qua victims of backward cultures, and on the other hand are pushed to assimilate in order to promote their agency as "proper" mothers. (101, 110)

Contemporary European nation-states craft integration policies that share assumptions embedded in Okin's discussion of multiculturalism. Ignoring the fact that the majority of women migrants (64 percent) had been employed outside the home prior to migration, state integration programs presume that migrating women remain locked within the domestic sphere. Work assignments are portrayed as a means to "undo gender" via paid employment. Yet, government programs designed to facilitate employment channel women migrants toward work in the care sector, hospitality, cleaning, and restaurant work. Rather than liberating women, these placements perpetuate racial stereotypes and conventional job segregation by sex. Forty-two percent of women migrant workers in the EU are concentrated in care work either in private households or in hospitals; many working at jobs for which they are greatly overqualified (Farris 2017: 157). Nonetheless, European governments insist that integration is an inherently progressive experience. Requiring that migrants "denationalize—neutralize their nation of origin—and renationalize" by adopting a western European mothering style,

EU member states replicate assumptions about the superiority of European civilization (103). While positioning European culture as more advanced, more tolerant, and more inclusive, integration policies trade on racist stereotypes, reinforcing "migrant women's employment segregation, traditional gender roles, and the gender injustice they claim to be combating" (118). They also make it appear that all Europeans are far more committed to gender equality, anti-racism, and LGBTQ rights than polling data warrants.

New arrivals are not the only citizens subjected to the normalizing logics of contemporary nation-states. In "Bodies of the State: On the Legal Entrenchment of (Dis)Ability," Katie Ledingham argues that the "disabled body is constituted in the British legal system through a politics of othering, which contributes to the rise of hate crimes against the disabled" (2013: 133). Within the field of disability studies, Ledingham suggests, "disability is defined as either a medical condition intrinsic to an individual body or a negative societal infliction imposed by psychological beliefs in inherent superiority and inferiority," but both frames neglect the role of the state in constituting disability (135). Subjecting the 1995 UK Disability Discrimination Act to a thorough discursive analysis, Ledingham shows how it entrenches the notion that a person with a disability is dependent and ineffective. "By legally defining the disabled person as 'impaired' and with a 'diminished capacity' to perform normal day-to-day tasks, the law places the disabled person at odds with capitalist notions of efficiency, performance, and productivity that dominate employment" (137). By constructing an abled/disabled binary, the state masks the variance in strength and ability characteristic of the human population, whether considered in terms of physical, cognitive, or social competences, and contributes to the underemployment and unemployment of the disabled (only half the disabled population in the UK is employed compared to 80 percent of abled) (137). Identifying the disabled body as problematic and dysfunctional, the state construes disabled individuals as "different, as a form of other" (138). Thus the legal construction of the disabled body is itself a mechanism of discrimination, a means of securing a social order that privileges the "normal" (white, male, unmarked) body while

entrenching prejudiced expectations about "abnormal," pathologized bodies.

Heterosexualization

Disability rights activists have drawn attention to the pervasive
and pernicious role of expectations in pathologizing bodies. Their
insights raise a host of questions about state expectations concerning "normal" bodies. In the twenty-first century, it is taken as
given that "sex designation along with date and location of birth,
and parentage (when known) make the person intelligible to the
state" (Currah and Moore 2013: 608). But what exactly is the state
recording under the category of "sex"? If, as demonstrated in earlier
chapters, sex is not a dichotomous variable, how does the state deal
with people of "doubtful sex" (Beck and Beck 1863: 179)? Zine
Magubane has suggested that gender variant people "did not excite
antagonism simply because their genitals were strange and their
bodies unclassifiable but because they were *citizens* with strange
and unclassifiable bodies; to exercise the rights of citizenship, one
had to be either a man or a woman" (Magubane 2014: 771). In
her study of the surgical alteration of "ambiguous bodies" in the
United States between 1850 and 1904, Christine Matta found
that "legal and medical authorities alike struggled to identify what
hermaphrodites really were and what rights they might possess"
(2005: 75). When the designations male and female carry markedly
different rights, political judgment must be exercised to preserve
the power of the privileged from encroachment by those whom
the state defines as inferior.

In recording sex as a legal identity, the state is determining the
category of belonging that will dictate the individual's future rights
and responsibilities. Indeed, it is determining whether a person will
be allowed to belong, and if so, under what conditions. Historians
suggest that states have developed very different policies about
criteria for membership and the appropriate treatment for those
deemed not to belong.

Bodies perceived to be "abnormal" have been subject
to restraint, correction, or elimination. In ancient Greece, for

example, "women whose bodies were determined by authorities to be partly male were put to death by public drowning or burning" (Weismantel 2013: 320). The language used to describe those condemned to death is instructive. What does it mean to be a woman whose body is partly male? What did authorities perceive that justified execution? Medical discourses in ancient Greece adhered to the "one sex model." Men and women were believed to have the same genitalia and sexual organs; the notable difference was that men's organs of generation were external and women's were internal to the body. What then did authorities see that warranted the death penalty? Did the aberration involve bodily parts, sexual acts, violations of gender roles or gender identities? With only fragments of evidence surviving, these questions may not be answerable, but they do call attention to the slipperiness of the category "sex."

The treatment of those who did not fit easily into a male/female binary seems to have been far more humane in Medieval and Renaissance Europe. According to Emma Heaney, at the moment of baptism, the father or godfather decided the initial gender of rearing for hermaphrodites. When the individual reached adulthood, s/he could choose how s/he wished to live for the remainder of life, a choice that would determine social role, sexual partners, and manner of dress. Although the choice itself was constricted by a sex binary—the only options available were male or female—the individual was afforded far greater freedom in eras prior to the emergence of biological determinism (Heaney 2017: 222).

European colonization offers a range of examples of state intervention to sustain binary sex. Some Indigenous peoples in the Americas had far more fluid conceptions of gendered bodies than their European conquerors (see Chapter 3). Some recognized and accorded a special social role to "Two-Spirit" people—"boys" who were raised as "girls," assigned women's roles in adulthood, including marriage to men, and who were given special training to perform critical roles in funeral rites that required a capacity to transcend gender. On September 23, 1513, Vasco Nuñez de Balboa ordered forty Indigenous men dressed as women (*joyas*, according to the language of the conquerors) to be torn apart by dogs—mastiffs and greyhounds brought by the Spanish to use as weapons against the Indigenous in the New World (Miranda 2013: 353). Deborah Miranda coined the term "gendercide" to refer to the brutal extermination of the "Two-Spirit tradition" within the Native American populations by the Spanish colonizers. "Gendercide is an act of violence committed against a victim's primary gender identity" (350).

Afsaneh Najmabadi (2005) has demonstrated that heterosexualization was an important facet in the European colonization of West Asia. As Europeans imposed a centralized state upon colonized territories in Persia, they criminalized erotic relationships between men and organized campaigns to eradicate long-established sexual and romantic relationships between men. Najmabadi's history of gender and sexuality in the Qajar period of Iran (1794–1925) traces the heterosexualization of love bonds that entailed the erasure of "beardless men" (*amrad* or *ghilman*) as socially accepted objects of male desire. Prior to the late nineteenth century, it was public practice for an older man to keep a younger man as a companion or "beardless beloved." These relationships were considered completely compatible with heterosexual marriage, understood as a reproductive contract. Characterizing *amrads* as "backward," Europeans demanded heteronormalization of eros and affect as a condition of achieving "modernity." The colonizers called for a reconfiguration of emotional bonds within family life, as well as the heterosocialization of public space. Modernization required the mixing of men and women at all levels. But, as Emma Heaney has pointed out, "the very notion of mixing assumes a binary of two kinds . . . heterosocialization became, paradoxically, productive of gender as a binary" (2017: 250).

The binarization of all people into either male or female was the mechanism through which love and desire were heterosexualized in Qajar-era Iran (Heaney 2017: 251). In earlier eras, sexual difference was associated with sexual role (i.e., an active or passive role in copulation). Informed by modernist convictions about biological determinism, Europeans insisted that sexual difference be defined morphologically. Construing *amrads* as usurpers of a woman's right to her husband's body and attention, norms of reciprocal monogamy required that men give up their beardless beloveds. Criminalization of sodomy was a means both to alter sexual practices and to change the cultural assumptions about appropriate romantic and sexual relationships. Modern companionate marriage in Iran was coercively constructed by European colonizers who deployed arrest and imprisonment to banish "gender-deviant depravity" from their colonies (Heaney 2017: 206). The eradication of the *joyas* and the *amrads* provide powerful examples of how "the sex/gender binary, which is in perpetual crisis, is actually preserved—not by physiological requirements guaranteeing permanence and irreversibility, because they can't—but by the legal machinations the state requires of its people" (Currah and Moore 2013: 619).

Emma Heaney has noted that the anti-sodomy laws imposed by the British in South and West Asia did more than persecute those with same-sex desires. This coercive gendering established "that only female-assigned bodies will be penetrated" (2017: 251). Colonial heteronormalization, then, had an important ideological dimension. It excised the "trans feminine" from history and from the public imaginary. Heaney defines the trans feminine as people who were assigned male sex at birth, and "who avow a female or feminine gender identity by using female pronouns, identifying with one or more vernacular trans feminine terms (around the turn of the twentieth century in the United States, Britain, and France, these terms included fairy, Mary, molly, queen, *tante*, and *molle*) and/ or identifying as women" (xiii). In the early twentieth century, in the metropole and the colonies, "people whose social expressions of gender and sexuality were incompatible with the modern dictate that genitals determine social role were disappeared" (251). Excised from history, the fairy was made anachronistic, enabling the transwoman to emerge within the orbit of sex change, a modern medical possibility (251). "In the conflation of trans women with sex change, sex became cis" (252). Heaney defines cis as "an adjective that indicates a rough alignment between sex assigned at birth and the sex with which one identifies. *Cissexism* is the presumption that assigned sex and identified sex always align and the rejection of any evidence that this is not a universal condition . . . In order for sex to become cis, the penetrability of all bodies must be denied" (xiii, 252).

Heaney points out that Foucault and Butler link the biological determinist conception of sex to the naturalization of sexual orientation, engendering distinctions between normal (normative) and deviant bodies and sexualities (226). State regulations regularize bodies as male or female, thereby providing the conceptual foundation for the naturalization of heterosexuality. Once entrenched, the male/female binary places the trans feminine who identifies herself as a woman and who prefers the company of women, and the trans masculine who identifies as a man and prefers the company of men, outside linguistic, cultural, and legal conventions. Thus the state plays a crucial role by forcing all bodies to be registered as male or female, grounding that registration on genitalia, and using its coercive power to force trans communities underground. Removed from public space and historical memory, the vibrant experiences of trans communities are reduced to tools to facilitate theoretical insight. In Butler's account, according to Heaney, "Trans expose the link between binary categories of gender and the heterosexualization and normalization of heterosexuality . . . Trans feminine and trans masculine gender experiences and representations work to denaturalize . . . sex and show that gender is the discursive/cultural means by which sexed nature or natural sex is produced" (228). Heaney warns, however, that reducing trans vibrancy to theoretical insights also masks specific state action to render trans communities invisible and make trans life impossible.

Vek Lewis has emphasized that trans oppression is not a relic of the distant past but continues to operate through state action. Focusing on Latin America, Lewis shows how gender variance is constructed as a "threat to the 'patria'—the virile, masculine entity . . . Publicly visible same-sex erotic practices and cross-dressing are taken as apocalyptic signs of the end of an order, the end of an era, the destruction of the civilized nation" as gender variant people are depicted as "criminals, low-lifes, bad seeds who threaten order and represent forces of anarchy" (2013: 460). Similar to discourses that denounce race-mixing, heteronormative cultures figure nonnormative genders and sexualities as "obstacles to progress and

modernity . . . backward, uncivilized . . . Weak in their dispositions and unnatural in their passions, both racial and sexual subjects
are perceived as a threat to the harmony of the imagined social
corpus and theorized as a contamination of the national body"
(462).

Taking twenty-first-century Japan as the focus of her analysis,
Laura Norton has shown how Law 111 passed in 2003 trans-
forms state recognition of trans citizens into a cruel mechanism
of exclusion. The proposed law was initially introduced by Aya
Kamikawa, Japan's first openly transgender elected official, with
progressive intent—to allow transgender people to petition the
courts to change their legal sex designation in Japan's national
registry of citizens (the *koseki*). During the legislative process,
however, the content of the "Law Concerning Special Cases in
Handling Gender for People with Gender Identity Disorder"
was dramatically altered. Indeed, the language of the bill, which
passed unanimously, restricted opportunities to alter one's recorded
sex on the family registry to "those who have no children and
have no capacity to ever have children" (Norton 2013: 596). Law
111 reduced the category of transgender to a small minority of
post-operative transsexuals who have completed sex confirmation
surgery and been *sterilized* in the process.

The Japanese case illuminates both the cost of state recognition and the powerful negative consequences of medicalizing
trans experience. The law reduces the rich trans spectrum—which
"encompasses transsexuals, drag queens, butch lesbians, cross dressers, feminine men, masculine women, FTM, MTF, gender queer,
trans woman, trans man, butch queen, fem queen, transy, drag king,
bi-gender, pan-gender, femme, butch, stud, two spirit, people with
intersex conditions, androgynous, gender fluid, gender euphoric,
third gender, and man and woman" (Enke 2012: 4)—to a tiny
minority of post-operative transsexuals. It creates a mechanism for
state recognition of transsexuals only to exclude the much larger
category of transgender people. Moreover, the legal recognition of
trans was both medicalized (contingent on a diagnosis of gender
identity disorder) and linked to the amendment of Japan's "Eugenic
Protection Law," which defines "sex reassignment surgery" as a

form of sterilization that removes or incapacitates the reproductive organs (Norton 2013: 595). Recognition by the state, then, involves both pathologization and sterilization. The conservative majority in Japan's National Diet (legislature) "insisted that reproduction had to be restricted on the basis that a parent who had changed his/her sex would 'shock a child'" (597). Norton notes the irony that "Fears of unduly shocking Japan's children . . . are moot because Law 111 mandates childlessness as a condition for realigning gender on the birth registry" (596). The unanimous passage of this law shows how state recognition can institutionalize transphobia. Although sterilization as a precondition for "being allowed to exist according to the dictates of their consciences violates international conventions that guarantee rights of reproductive self-determination and bodily integrity," in the sovereign nation-state of Japan this is the law of the land (597).

Drawing attention to the punitive dimensions of trans recognition in many states, Susan Stryker analyzes narrow constructions of transsexuality as "somatechnology," a technique for the administration of embodied subjects who contest the double binary of man/woman and hetero/homo that governs identity.

> Transsexuality is an administrative solution, with biopolitical consequences, particular to certain kinds of problem bodies within Eurocentric modernity—for bodies whose natal sex registration does not match their bodily habituses, whose gendered comportment does not accord with their societal gender status, whose subjective gender identification with gender categories are not congruent with those typically associated with their reproductive roles or capacities . . . It is the juridico-medical apparatus of an institutional, state-sanctioned power that enmeshes itself with the bare life of individuals whose embodiment problematizes the regulatory function of the gender system. (Stryker 2013: 551)

Rather than being unproblematic aspects of the natural condition, race, sex, gender, and sexuality are constructed within regulatory regimes. Legal classifications of race, sex, gender, and sexuality are imposed by nation-states even though they do not and cannot adequately address the diversity that exists within the human species. Heterosexualization of the citizenry can take many forms. Recent efforts "to make sex cis" or to restrict the meaning of trans to those who have undergone surgical procedures may ease social anxiety over gender ambiguity, but they do so at an exorbitant cost—shoring up and perpetuating racialized heteronormativity and masking state violence. In a world in which sex, gender, and sexuality are fluid and open to expression in manifold ways, state imposition of binary legal classifications involves a form of injustice that escapes notice in traditional political theory. Mapping the scope of that injustice is the subject of the final chapter of the book.

6

Reconceptualizing Injustice

As our (modern Western) world is now, failure to conform to the norms of gender is socially stigmatizing to an unbearable extent: To be human just is to be male or female, a girl or a boy, or a man or a woman. Those who cannot be readily classified by everyone they encounter are not only subject to physically violent assaults, but perhaps even more wounding, are taken to be impossible to relate to humanly. (Scheman 1997: 132–3)

Legal equality arguments require those making them to articulate existing legal structures as generally fair and neutral but for the exclusion focused on and to portray the excluded group as a population that deserves inclusion.
(Bassichis and Spade 2014: 199)

When science is accorded the authority to make definitive claims about bodies, it is easy to believe that characteristics attributed to bodies are pre-political or apolitical. Within this frame, state classifications of race and sex appear unproblematic: they simply record the given. Consider, however, the power deployed by medical science to make certain bodies conform to state requirements for classification as male or female. Dan Irving (2013) has pointed out that state recognition of trans citizens requires both medicalization and pathologization. States routinely delegate sex identification to doctors, who have been trained to define sex exclusively in terms of genitalia. Although they may have learned in medical school that manifold chromosomal and genital configurations occur in nature, obstetricians fit physical variation into statistical categories of "normal" (i.e., average, modal or typical) and "abnormal" (i.e., rare). Within this mathematical frame, doctors assign sex at birth, filtering diversity into the binary classification, male or female. The state records this statistical judgment in birth registries.

To contest this judgment, trans people cannot simply point out a misjudgment on the part of the physician, nor are they allowed to protest the medical conflation of rarity with statistical "abnormality." Less than 5 percent of the nations in the world recognize a "third gender" or allow individuals to alter their gender identity on official documents. Those states that are willing to consider making administrative changes to birth certificates insist that trans people seek medical treatment for a "set of mental maladies" diagnosed as gender dysphoria or gender identity disorder (Irving 2013: 18). In the twentieth century, doctors who worked in gender identity clinics "accepted only one transsexual narrative—which subscribed to heteronormative and hegemonic categories of sex/gender." They insisted that their patients must seek surgical assistance to rectify a "wrong body problem" and demonstrate a vision for their future life that conformed to culturally approved gendered expectations (24). "Prior to surgery, candidates had to prove they could live successfully as the 'opposite sex' without being provided any of the hormones that would have facilitated their transition. Those who succeeded in withstanding daily harassment and discrimination were determined eligible for surgery" (20). Irving notes that the gendered conventions to which trans people had to conform to qualify for surgery were race and class specific and markedly sexist. Female-to-male trans people (FTM) were "expected to be economically industrious . . . demonstrate their authentic masculinity by participating in the labor market . . . and become reliable providers" for their families (20). They were required not only to seek certain kinds of gendered employment, but to be unreservedly heterosexual. Doctors refused to approve surgery for transsexuals who were gay, bisexual, or lesbian (20). Medical expectations for male-to-female transsexuals (MTF) manifested prevalent cultural denigrations of women and tolerance for institutionalized sex discrimination. MTF candidates were "quizzed on their willingness to accept lower status jobs and lower wages as women . . . the success of their sexual reassignment was measured partly through their complacency (an ideal mark of femininity) and their ability to assimilate into gendered and exploitive relations" (21).

Medical transition is designed to eliminate any vestiges of nonnormative gender and sexuality. Rather than recognize trans as a category of existence, "medical science relies on standardized, normative gender presentation, monitoring trans ability to pass seamlessly as non-trans . . . as if they had never been transgender to begin with" (Beauchamp 2009 [2013]: 47). Rather than affirming diversity and fluidity, "medicine and law work together primarily to 'correct' individuals whose bodies or gender presentations fall outside the expressed norm, promoting concealment of trans status in order to reestablish that norm" (48). By normalizing "unruly transgender bodies through surgery and hormones," medical interventions reinscribe notions of "deviant gendering" in relation to mental, physical, and behavioral states. They "create a non-threatening body that is undetectable as trans in any way. Transgender bodies that conform to a dominant standard of dress and behavior may be legible to the state not as transgender at all, but instead as properly gendered and 'safe'" (49).

State recognition does not simply record what is given; it produces accredited categories and requires bodies to conform to them. It imposes certain identities, converting pigmentation into race and bodily fluidity into dichotomous sex. It suppresses certain modes of embodiment (intersex and trans) and erases that suppression by premising state recognition on individual identification with state-sanctioned categories. It imposes the restriction that "to be human just is to be male or female, a girl or a boy, or a man or a woman" (Scheman 1997: 132), and requires surgical and psychiatric interventions to produce conformity with that gender order.

Bodies, then, do not exist outside politics and beyond the reach of the state. Sex and race are products of state action that accords legal status and determines citizenship rights. State classification affects educational and employment opportunities, levels of income and wealth, and access to prestige and power. The institutions that require sex/gender legibility and consistency are multiple and pervasive, including social services such as rape crisis centers, homeless shelters, medical clinics, job training services, housing and public accommodations such as restrooms, marriage and family formation, inheritance, health insurance, incarceration in "gender-appropriate" facilities, and identity records such as passports, social security cards, and driver's licenses (Enke 2013: 245). Sex/gender legibility is always mediated by norms pertaining to race, class, sexuality, and nationality.

Canonical political theory seldom acknowledges the state's role in the creation of subordinated and stigmatized subjects. As discussed in Chapters 3, 4, and 5, the state's innocence is enabled by the naturalization of racial and gender hierarchies, the treatment of "difference" as a private matter that has no bearing on state action, and by conceptualizing racism, sexism, and heteronormativity as matters of individual sentiment rather than state policy. The innocence of the law has been preserved by claims that the state does not create human nature and cannot change it; moreover, any attempt to do so would involve a massive violation of individual liberty. Conceived as innocent and bounded by the limits of human nature, the state has been positioned as the key institution for the administration of justice.

To understand the sovereign state as the maker of law and the dispenser of justice requires sanctioned ignorance of a great deal of state action as well as a very narrow conception of injustice. This chapter challenges that ignorance and probes the adequacy of that conceptualization of injustice. It begins with an examination of a range of canonical conceptions of justice and their relationship to the state. It then presents multiple examples of state injustice in order to question the scope of popular theories of justice and expand the conceptualization of injustice in ways that make pernicious state action and omission visible and actionable. In the final section, the chapter considers a range of remedies for injustice that have been advanced by critical race, feminist, Indigenous, postcolonial, queer, and trans* theorists.

Justice and the State

Within the Western tradition, justice has been conceived as a virtue of individuals and institutions, but the specific character of that virtue has been the topic of intensive debate. In the *Republic*, Plato (c. 428–347 BCE) conceived justice as a well-ordered soul in which reason governs interests, inclinations, and passions. The virtue of just souls could be mirrored in a just political order if those governed by reason (philosopher kings) ruled over those inclined toward martial arts and warfare and those driven by appetites and desire for creature comforts. A just polity was hierarchically organized, but within this system each individual was content because the system of rewards gave each person what s/he most prized. The state distributed social roles and material benefits appropriate to those roles on the basis of individual aptitude and interest. Those who were interested in creating things to meet human needs were assigned jobs as artisans and farmers, devoted their energies to producing goods, and were allowed to accumulate material possessions. Those who loved physical exertion, competition, and manifestation of their military prowess were assigned the task of defense of the polity and provided with free food and accommodations, allowing them to devote their time to cultivating their strength and demonstrating their valor. Those who loved learning and wished only to develop their rational faculties were encouraged to spend their lives thinking, discovering truth, and contemplating the good. They too were provided free accommodations and food, but they were asked to use their knowledge for the well-being of all by taking a turn in political leadership. Having great minds rotate in office would ensure wise public policy and prevent both the accretion and the corruption of power. In prescribing a division of labor that met pressing social needs for subsistence, the production of goods and services, a common defense, and shrewd leadership, and assigning these roles to individuals best suited to them by inclination and ability, Plato envisioned a core principle of justice—to give each person his or her due. He also framed this notion of desert to accommodate human differences, recognizing that people wanted different kinds of lives and different forms of reward. In Plato's ideal *Republic*, individual happiness coincided with social justice.

The key to individual happiness and collective justice in Plato's ideal *polis* turned on state action. The philosopher kings had to devise an educational system that correctly identified the interests and aptitudes of each individual in order to assign them the appropriate role in the division of labor. If these aptitudes and interests are "given in nature," then the task of the educational system is straightforward—to cultivate each person's natural talents to their fullest ability. If, however, individual potential is open-ended and its realization depends on a host of social factors rather than natural givens, then the role of the state in determining individual life-prospects becomes much more controversial. If the state shapes individual desires and aspirations, then assigns social roles and hierarchical status according to its own judgments about individuals, the possibilities for injustice proliferate. Plato was aware that the state would play a role in shaping desires, aspirations, temperaments, and the population itself. Anticipating the modern "science of eugenics," he envisioned politically organized mating rituals, designed to ensure that each category of citizen reproduce only with their "own kind."

Aristotle built upon Plato's insights in developing a conception of justice that distinguished between distributive justice and corrective or compensatory justice. Although equality featured in Aristotle's account of a just social distribution of benefits and burdens, it operated in accordance with his conviction that human beings were inherently unequal. In keeping with his belief that those who devote their lives to earning a living are incapable of living a human existence, Aristotle argued that justice required that "equals be treated equally and unequals unequally" (*Nichomachean Ethics* V.§6). According to Aristotle it is as unjust to treat unequals (e.g., propertied men v. women and natural slaves) in the same manner as it is to treat equals differently. And it is the task of politics as the master science to make these critical determinations about equality and difference in order to ensure that all members of the *polis* live "well."

Some political theorists have amended Aristotle's distributive principle to fit modern presumptions concerning natural equality. On this view, justice requires that individuals be treated the same, unless they differ in some way that is *morally* relevant. Theorists have disagreed about what might count as morally relevant for the purposes of differential treatment. In Marx's famous dictum, "From each according to ability to each according to need," justice requires that the fundamental human needs should govern distributive decisions. Within this frame, the needs of starving people should be given priority over additional treats for the well-fed; the requirements of the worst-off should carry greater moral weight than the comforts of the affluent. Other philosophers have argued that individual "desert" is far more morally relevant than need, that is, people should be rewarded on the basis of individual effort and contribution to society.

In addition to his account of distributive justice, Aristotle's conception of retributive justice has been profoundly influential. Justice as a remedial principle is designed to rectify wrongs in ways that both punish the wrongdoer and compensate the wronged for their injury. As a reparatory transaction between one person and another, Aristotle suggested that punishment should be proportionate to the harm done. Its primary objective is to compensate the injured party—to nullify the injury by restoring the status quo ante, the condition prior to the injury. In an instance of theft, for example, the thief would be required to return the stolen property. Although the principle of rectification makes a good deal of sense for certain crimes such as those pertaining to property, other kinds of crimes allow no restoration of the status quo ante. There is no way to restore what is taken from a rape victim; there is no way to undo the harm of murder or mutilation.

Corrective justice is often associated with the creation of judicial procedures designed to establish culpability in relation to the seriousness of harm inflicted and the intent of the wrongdoer, and to determine appropriate punishment. Procedures concerning the selection of judges and jurors, introduction of evidence, the presence of attorneys for the prosecution and the defense, and the manner of deliberation concerning the verdict and the punishment to be imposed accord a critical role to the state in ensuring fair trials and protecting the rights of those accused in the process of adjudicating allegations of wrongdoing. Acknowledging that procedures alone cannot guarantee a just result, many states create appeal processes in an effort to ensure outcomes that punish the guilty and acquit the innocent.

In modern political thought, justice has been associated with the rule of law. Hobbes provided pragmatic grounds for this association. If people are to obey the law, the law must be made known and enforced. By definition, the sovereign holds the monopoly of power, and, as such, is the only possible enforcer of the law. Moreover, as the sovereign's word is law, only the sovereign can make the law known. Thus it is in the sovereign's interest to publish the law widely and enforce the law equally on all subjects. Conceptualizing law as a constraint on individual behavior, Hobbes suggested that a subject is free where the law is silent.

Locke reframed law as a codification of the moral requirements of natural law rather than a coercive instrument of an all-powerful sovereign. According to Locke, the task of legislators was finite—to use their right reason to discern the precepts of natural law and to codify them in the state's constitution. Because natural law is accessible to all rational beings, there is no inherent opposition between law and freedom. In his *Second Treatise on Government*, Locke insisted:

> Law, in its true notion, is not so much the limitation but the direction of a free and intelligent agent to his proper interest and prescribes no farther than the general good . . . So that, however it may be mistaken, the End of *Law* is not to abolish or restrain but to preserve and enlarge Freedom . . . where there is no law, there can be no freedom . . . That ill deserves the Name of Confinement which hedges *us* in only from *Bogs and Precipices*. (1690 [1980]: 148)

Because the law is knowable and guides intelligent agents to do what is right, Locke suggested that all rational beings have an obligation to enforce the law in the state of nature. But he acknowledged that allowing men to be judges in their own cases could lead to conflict and violence. Thus rational beings agreed to create the state to dispense impartial justice, thereby remedying one of the "inconveniences" of the state of nature—the absence of a known and impartial judge.

In contrast to Locke's association of justice with rationality and the rule of law, some political theorists associated with the utilitarian tradition offered more cynical interpretations of justice. In *A Treatise on Human Nature*, Hume suggested that justice was nothing more than a set of property rules that allowed constant possession of goods acquired by inheritance, industry, or effort. Although there was nothing inherently fair about perpetuating the permanent possession of readily transferable objects, property relations benefitted society by providing stability. Thus Hume insisted that justice had nothing to do with benevolence: "It is only from the selfishness and confined generosity of men, along with the scanty provision nature has made for his wants, that justice derives its origins." Nonetheless, the rules pertaining to the "stability of possession, of its transference by consent, and of the performance of promises" were beneficial to society and hence considered moral. Indeed, "Tis on the strict observance of those three laws, that the peace and security of human society entirely depend; nor is there any possibility of establishing a good correspondence among men, where these are neglected" (Hume 1738 [1987]: 526). Concurring in Hume's assessment of the social utility of justice, Bentham sought to subsume justice under utility altogether: "justice, in the only sense in which it has a meaning, is an imaginary personage, feigned for the convenience of discourse, whose dictates are the dictates of utility, applied to certain particular cases" (1789 [1948]: 125–6).

In the *Philosophy of Right* (1820), Hegel argued that theorists such as Hume and Bentham confused justice and self-interest and failed to differentiate civil society from the state. Within civil society, individuals understand themselves as "rights-bearers," who are entitled to pursue their self-interest in the public domain. But the unbridled pursuit of selfish advantage produces a zero-sum game in which one person's gains truncate others' endeavors. Such a clash of rights and wills is incapable of achieving justice. It generates only intensive competition that leaves citizens mutually frustrated and morally depleted. According to Hegel, the remedy for such interest-driven politics is the creation of the "State as the Embodiment of the Ethical Idea"—a state that is able to inspire citizens to transcend their petty squabbles and unite in the pursuit of shared moral objectives. Hegel noted that war was particularly instrumental in achieving this end. The identification of a common enemy and the mobilization of patriotic sentiment contributed to a spirit of self-sacrifice and a willingness to work for a higher good. Thus Hegel theorized war as a stimulus to moral development, and to the attainment of a nationalist conception of a just order.

More recent political philosophy has taken the nation-state as its point of departure, situating distributive justice in relation to a state's obligations to its citizens, who are required to comply with, and accept responsibility for, the coercive laws that govern their lives (Nagel 2005). John Rawls (1921–2002) places particular emphasis on the importance of constitutional recognition of equal citizenship:

> The basis for self-esteem in a just society is not one's income share but the publicly affirmed distribution of fundamental rights and liberties. And this distribution being equal, everyone has a similar and secure status when they meet to conduct the common affairs of the wider society. No one is inclined to look beyond the constitutional affirmation of equality for further political ways to securing his status . . . In a well-ordered society, then, self-respect is secured by the public affirmation of the status of equal citizenship for all. (1971: 544–5)

In *A Theory of Justice*, Rawls identifies two principles of justice that recognize the importance of equality, yet allow some inequality if it serves to improve the condition of the worst-off. The principle of equal liberty stipulates that "Each person has an equal right to the most extensive liberties compatible with similar liberties for all." The difference principle requires that "Social and economic inequalities be arranged so that they are both (a) to the greatest benefit of the least advantaged persons, and (b) attached to offices and positions open to all under conditions of equality of opportunity" (60). Although these principles appear impressively egalitarian, critics have pointed out that the difference principle offers the same justification for inequality that has long been associated with capitalism. Economic inequality spurs growth, generating more wealth, which purportedly works to the benefit of the worst-off.

As an alternative to the inequities associated with capitalist markets, Michael Walzer (1983) suggested that the formal rights that lie at the heart of the liberal political order must be supplemented with substantive rights. Arguing that members of a polity have obligations to one another, Walzer claims that these obligations are grounded in the very definition of a social contract as an agreement to make decisions about what goods are necessary to common life, and then to provide those goods. Because the nature of need is not self-evident and resources are always limited, determinations about communal provision are political decisions that must be made by members of the political community. Walzer identifies two political principles that must guide these democratic determinations—a procedural principle of political justice and a substantive principle of fair shares. The principle of political justice requires that the processes of self-determination through which a democratic state shapes its internal life must not only be open, but *equally open* to all men and women who live within its territory, work in the local economy, and are subject to local law (thereby challenging the distinction between citizens, residents, and migrant or "guest" workers). The principle of fair shares requires that once the community undertakes to provide some needed good, they must provide it to all members who need it in proportion to their need. Taken in concert, these principles ensure that communal provision manifests a minimal respect for "our own," a recognition of the dignity and humanity of all citizens, and an assurance that the preconditions for citizens' participation in political life are met. Similarly, Ronald Dworkin (2000) argues that a principle of equal concern and respect for persons is fundamental to justice; hence, equal resources should be devoted to the life of each member of society.

Within the Western tradition of political philosophy, the state is envisioned as the embodiment of rationality, an enforcer of a rule of law applicable to all, an interpreter of natural law and a precondition for freedom, a protector of property relations and preserver of stability, the embodiment of the ethical idea, and as a collective mechanism through which a community administers justice. Across these diverse conceptualizations, the state allocates social roles and responsibilities, distributes burdens and benefits equitably, establishes impartial procedures to adjudicate disputes, provides compensation to those injured by acts of injustice, and imposes just and proportionate punishment on wrongdoers.

Critical race, feminist, Indigenous, postcolonial, queer, and trans* theorists have raised questions about these positive depictions of the state as a vehicle of justice. By drawing attention to the manifold ways that the state distributes inequality through the law, they theorize injustice beyond "juridically defined rights and wrongs," challenging accounts of the state as an apparatus of justice (Aultman and Currah 2017: 49).

State Injustice

Racialization

Colonial states are legendary for the cruelty with which they created and sustained racialized and gendered hierarchies. Following the abolition of slavery in the nineteenth century, for example, "colonial states and their agents used punishment of black bodies to demarcate social boundaries—boundaries that were crucial to the maintenance of white colonials' social, political, and economic dominance" (Harris 2017: 3). Gendered racialization in employment and punishment was routine, but, as Dawn Harris notes, "In many cases, colonial and imperial understandings about bodies, particularly female bodies, were inconstant and murky" (161). For employment purposes, black women were degendered, expected to do the same grueling field labor as black men. In the administration of punishment, however, the state equivocated. In some instances, black women and men were subjected to the same physical ordeals. For the crime of "obstinacy," for example, both women and men could be sentenced to the treadmill for 24 hours. The treadmill substituted human labor power for water power to keep a mill wheel turning. Deprived of food, water, and rest for the duration of the punishment, many died from this excruciating penal technique. Yet their deaths were attributed not to the brutal punishment, but to the very obstinacy that brought them before the colonial magistrates. "No deaths have ever occurred on the treadmill but those occasioned by the obstinacy of the parties themselves" (162). Harris reports that "barbarous punishments for black women appear to be based on the theory that the negro female does not possess the deep feelings and delicate sensibilities of her sex; or if she does possess them, they are incompatible with her servile condition and ought to be obliterated" (Sturge and Harvey 1837: 139, cited in Harris 2017: 165). The colonial state did, however, endorse sex-specific punishment for pregnant black women, allowing their pronatalist concerns about reproducing the labor force to off-set their efforts to inculcate subjectivities appropriate for those in servile positions. "Pregnant and nursing mothers were not to be whipped or placed in solitary confinement" (163). Under the 1877 criminal code implemented by the British in their colonies in the West Indies, pregnant women who were sentenced to death were given a stay of execution until the baby was born. Abortion was criminalized. Black women who sought to abort and black women who participated in rebellion were "particularly vilified for stepping outside the boundaries of femininity" and were sentenced to punishments "more brutal and more barbarous than the men" (167). Through employment and punishment practices, the colonial state artificially elevated white women as "the embodiment of modesty and respectability . . . as black women were unfairly debased" (163).

Progress narratives that circulate widely in the West convey the impression that the kind of racialized gendering associated with colonialism is a thing of the past. Yet critical race scholars illuminate manifold state policies that create and sustain racialized hierarchies among citizens. The United States, for example, has a dramatic history of racializing interventions at state and federal levels, despite the 14th Amendment guarantee of equal treatment and the government's insistence that its policies are colorblind. For the better part of the twentieth century, municipal ordinances mandated racial segregation in housing. In the 1960s, these were replaced by mortgage-lending practices that "redlined" certain neighborhoods as white only, reserving others for people of color. Since the 1990s, people of color were targeted for predatory loans by mortgage companies, whose lending practices contributed significantly to the 2008 economic crisis. As a consequence, foreclosures in their neighborhoods outpaced foreclosures in white neighborhoods. "Mostly Black and mostly Latino neighborhoods lost homes at rates approximately three times higher than white areas. Today Blacks are far less likely to own homes or have sizable retirement savings, two primary ways most families accumulate wealth" (Cohen 2015: B5).

> The U.S. racial wealth gap is substantial and is driven by public policy decisions . . . In 2011 the median white household had $111,146 in wealth holdings, compared to just $7,113 for the median Black household and $8,348 for the median Latino household. From the continuing impact of redlining on American homeownership to the retreat from desegregation in public education, public policy has shaped these disparities, leaving them impossible to overcome without racially-aware policy change. (Sullivan et al. 2015)

Racial disparities are equally pronounced with respect to "zero or negative wealth, which is the condition of 35 percent of Black households and 31 percent of Latino households, compared with 15 percent of white households" (King and Smith 2011).

Local, state, and federal governments have collaborated in highway construction, urban renewal projects, and the siting of public housing units to ensure the perpetuation of "ethnic enclaves"—more accurately characterized as ghettos. "Black urban poor communities are the product of a century's worth of systematic discrimination, spatial containment, and targeted disaccumulation of community resources" (Rose 2013). Residential segregation has had profound effects on the quality of public schools, which are funded by local property taxes. Sixty-five years after court-ordered school desegregation, more than 80 percent of black children remain in "minority-majority" schools, while more than 90 percent of white students remain in white-majority schools. The severely under-funded urban schools, which serve students of color whose family incomes fall below the poverty line, have been likened to "institutions of confinement whose primary mission is not to educate but to ensure 'custody and control' . . . children are herded into decaying and overcrowded facilities that resemble fortresses, complete with razor wire on outside fences, bricked up windows, heavy locks on iron doors, metal detectors at the gates, and hallways patrolled by armed guards" (Wacquant 2002).

Deindustrialization of cities is often discussed solely in terms of the profit-maximizing decisions of private corporations that relocate plants where they can find cheaper labor. But that is far from the whole story. US states and municipalities have offered large financial incentives and long-term tax abatement to lure industry to their jurisdictions. The federal government has negotiated treaties that facilitate the free flow of capital across national borders and encourage the establishment of free trade zones offshore. As stable blue-collar employment disappeared from northern cities, state and municipal governments offered considerable financial incentives for gentrification programs, a boon to white urban "homesteaders" who drive up the cost of real estate and rents in ways that further push low-income residents into dilapidated sectors of cities. Spatial containment contributes to overcrowding in poorly-constructed and poorly-maintained public housing and in increasingly deteriorating private rental units. In 1968, the National Advisory Commission on Civil Disorders, appointed by Lyndon Johnson to investigate the riots that had devastated twenty-three cities, linked the fundamental causes of racial unrest to white actions and behaviors that produced segregation and poverty in "the racial ghetto." "Segregation and poverty have created in the racial ghetto a destructive environment totally unknown to most white Americans. What white Americans have never fully understood—but what the Negro can never forget—is that white society is deeply implicated in the ghetto. White institutions created it, white institutions maintain it, and white society condones it" (NACCD 1968: 1).

Neoliberal cities use zoning regulations to "destroy public services, affordable housing, clinics, and community spaces for sake of corporate development" (Edelman 2014: 176). They have created "prostitution-free zones"—spaces of hyperpolicing that function to keep particular bodies out. Bodies that refuse to conform to binary gender and that turn to transactional sex to survive are subject to displacement and erasure, denied state protection, and constructed as a threat or danger. Transwomen of color, in particular, "experience an extraordinarily high incidence of violence from those they encounter on the street to those charged with protecting the public, such as the police" (176). Through such "zones of exclusion," the state deprives some citizens of the fundamental right to access and use specific kinds of public space. The "post justice city is based on social and racial containment, the purification of public spaces, subsidization of elite consumption, privatization of social reproduction, the normalization of economic insecurity, and pre-emptive crime control" (180).

Competition for the jobs that are available in urban centers is intense. In the US, black unemployment is typically twice the rate of white unemployment. In the aftermath of the 2008 economic crisis, the increase in black unemployment was seven times greater than that experienced by whites (Roberts 2011: 297). Neoliberal privatization has also had disproportionate negative effects on black workers.

> One in five black adults works for the government, teaching school, delivering mail, fighting fires, diving busses, processing criminal justice and managing large staffs. They are about 30 percent more likely to have a public sector job than whites, and twice as likely as Hispanics. Since 2007, half a million public sector jobs have been cut. When normal growth of population is factored in, there are 1.8 million

fewer jobs in the public sector for people to fill. Cuts in government employment disproportionately hurt black professionals, who lost their jobs at a higher rate than whites, concentrated in a shrinking sector of the economy. As schools shift to part-time positions without benefits, Blacks are particularly hard hit. (Cohen 2015: A1, B5)

Acting on its pledge to cut 200,000 public sector jobs, the Trump administration reduced nondefense agency spending by 30 percent in its first year, imposed a hiring freeze, and chose not to fill 220 of the 325 senior positions in cabinet-level departments, which require senate approval (Rein and Ba Tran 2017). Its proposed cuts for the 2019 fiscal year are even more draconian.

Racialized-gendering pervades public discourses concerning low-income communities of color and the policies devised to address them. Black and Latino youth are constructed as threats, subjected to hyper-surveillance, and disproportionately arrested and incarcerated (Isoke 2016; Cacho 2012; Alexander 2010). As legal scholar Ian Haney Lopez has pointed out, "Blacks are less likely than whites to commit crime, but are far more likely to be arrested and convicted" (2014: 50–1). The racial composition of police forces, changes in policing practices, new DNA technologies, and the "war on drugs" have all contributed to the "criminalization" of black and Latino youth (Cacho 2012; Roberts 2011). Although people of color and whites use illegal drugs at roughly the same rate (6.4 percent among whites compared to 6.4 percent among Blacks and 5.3 percent among Latinos), in some states black men are admitted to prison at twenty to fifty times greater than white men (Alexander 2011: 7). In 2010, a national survey on drug use indicated that young African Americans, aged eighteen to twenty-five, were less likely to use illegal drugs than the national average; yet young black men were twelve times more likely than white men to be sent to prison on drug charges (Roberts 2011: 279). Although ethnic patterns of criminal activity are similar, in 2014, one in every 106 white men over the age of eighteen had been in prison, compared to one in thirty-six Latinos, and one in fifteen black men (one in nine black men aged twenty to thirty-four) (Haney Lopez 2014: 53).

The consequences of incarceration are stark: African Americans who have been incarcerated face a 42 percent reduction in expected lifetime earnings, which constitutes a $300 billion loss of earnings for all offenders (Haney Lopez 2014: 53). State and federal laws deny welfare payments, veterans' benefits, and food stamps to anyone held in detention for more than sixty days. The Work Opportunity and Personal Responsibility Act of 1996 excludes most ex-convicts from Medicaid, public housing, rental vouchers for private housing, and related forms of assistance (Wacquant 2002). In addition,

> thirty-nine states forbid convicts placed on probation from exercising the right to vote; and thirty-two states disenfranchise parolees. In fourteen states, ex-felons are barred from voting even when they are no longer under criminal justice supervision—for life in ten of these states. The result is that nearly 4 million Americans have temporarily or permanently lost the ability to cast a ballot, including 1.47 million who are not behind bars and another 1.39 million who served their sentences in full. Despite the historic struggle for full voting rights, one black man in seven nationwide is banned from the electoral booth through penal disenfranchisement and seven states permanently deny the vote to more than one-fourth of their black male residents. (Wacquant 2002)

The US shift to mass incarceration occurred just as the National Advisory Commission on Criminal Justice Standards and Goals issued a report (1973) recommending that "no new carceral institutions for adults should be built and existing institutions for juveniles should be closed." The Commission asserted that, far from inhibiting crime, "the prison, the reformatory, and the jail have achieved only a shocking record of failure. There is overwhelming evidence that these institutions create crime rather than prevent it" (Alexander 2011: 8). The disproportionate number of black and Latino men in the prison population also has an unintended consequence. It contributes to the perception of African American and Latino men as dangerous "criminals"—a racialized-gendered depiction that haunts police as well as public perception. Indeed, investigation into the spate of deaths of young black men in police custody in 2014 indicated that "fear" of black and Latino youth is precisely what caused police officers to use their firearms or extreme force to "subdue" unruly suspects (Isoke 2016). The circularity is vicious indeed: policing practices subject black and Latino young men to excessive surveillance, increasingly negative encounters with police officers, and disproportionate arrest and incarceration for minor offenses, causing the prison population to soar. The soaring prison population contributes to the "criminalization" of black and Latino youth, who devise strategies for self-defense, including refusal to cooperate politely with stop and frisk policies, which the police perceive as unruly behavior that requires force to subdue, culminating in increasing numbers of suspicious deaths of "suspects" of color in police custody. Blacks and Latinos are overrepresented among those who die from police violence. Although African Americans comprise 12.6 percent of the US population, they comprised 32 percent of the victims of police homicides between 2003 and 2009 according to US Department of Justice. Latinos constitute 15 percent of the US population, but they made up 20 percent of those killed by the police while in custody between 2002 and 2009. These troubling statistics are evidence of systemic state injustice.

Gendered Exclusions and Insecurity

In *Sexism, Harassment and Violence against Women Parliamentarians* (2016), the Inter-Parliamentary Union (IPU) reported findings of a survey of fifty-five women MPs from thirty-nine nations. The data detailing job-related violence were chilling: 81.8 percent of the respondents reported that they had experienced psychological violence; 21.8 percent, sexual violence; 25.5 percent, physical violence; and 32.7 percent economic violence (IPU 2016: 3). Slightly more than half of the respondents (51.7 percent) reported these incidents to the parliamentary security services or the police, but they did not receive "unstinting support" (7). On the contrary, security officials and police did not follow up on the complaints, refused to provide security, and did nothing to investigate or prosecute those responsible—thereby affording the perpetrators impunity. Of those MPs who experienced violence, 61.5 percent recorded their belief that the intent was to dissuade them from continuing in politics (6). Similarly, UN Women has documented violence against women in politics in more than 100 nations (Salguero 2017). One study of South Asia found that 45 percent of women candidates in India faced physical violence and threats in comparison to 21 percent in Nepal and 16 percent in Pakistan (Centre for Social Research and UN Women, 2014).

"Psychological violence," the form of violence most frequently experienced by women MPs, is an encompassing category, ranging from verbal, visual, and virtual sexual harassment to death threats: 65.5 percent of the respondents noted that they had been subjected to "humiliating sexual or sexist remarks," 27.3 percent to "disre-spectful images" in traditional media, 41.8 percent to humiliating sexually-charged images on social media, 44.4 percent to "threats of death, rape, beatings or abduction," and 32.7 percent to quid pro quo "sexual harassment" (IPU 2016: 3). Characterized by Jennifer Piscopo as "institutionalized sexism," psychological violence may be "pernicious in its ability to undermine women's substantive exercise of their political rights, but it does not constitute a criminal act" (2016: 445). Typically conceptualized as a violation of a code of professional conduct or as a mode of sex discrimination subject to administrative censure, psychological violence trades on the invisibility of the harm done. Leaving "no visible signs on the body . . . physical invisibility allows political invisibility" (Schott 2011: 47–8).

In the progress narratives that circulate in the media about women in politics, emphasis is placed on the gains made by women in elective and appointive offices and on their substantive representation in policy arenas. Women, who comprise 49.6 percent of the global population, now hold 23.4 percent of the parliamentary seats on average in nations around the globe, up from 3 percent in the 1940s, 7 percent in the 1950s, 10 percent in the 1970s, and 14 percent in the 1980s (IPU 2018). Passage of quota laws and policies in more than 100 nations, new penal codes, and ratification of international conventions such as CEDAW (1979), Belém do Pará (1994), and the Istanbul Convention (2011) hold states responsible and accountable for securing gender equality by addressing violence against women in all its forms, taking measures to prevent such violence by protecting victims and prosecuting perpetrators. Yet recent feminist scholarship suggests a far more complicated tale. In many regions, increasingly rampant violence against women accompanies legal efforts to promote gender equality. Increasing numbers of elected women in National Assemblies coexist with the passage of legislation to restrict women's access to abortion and promote pronatalism. Women's increasing levels of education coexist with persistent pay inequities, job segregation by sex, and underrepresentation in positions of power in public and private sectors. Nationalist and fundamentalist discourses gaining ground in many regions of the world illuminate pervasive investments in "proper womanhood"—accredited modes of femininity, dress, and decorum—by states, political parties, and nonstate actors. And, as the data on violence against women in politics, and against human rights defenders, suggests, women in the contemporary era—including those at the pinnacle of public life—face physical and sexual violence, social and familial censure, marginalization and ostracism, as well as various forms of restriction, deprivation, and exclusion (Chawla et al. 2017).

To explain this paradox, some feminist scholars have suggested that it be understood as a form of "backlash—resistance of those in power to attempts to change the status quo," and the deployment of "coercive power to reinstate" established hierarchies (Mansbridge and Shames 2008: 625, 627). Mona Lena Krook and Juliana Restrepo characterize violence against women in politics as "patriarchal resistance to women's political participation . . . whose goal remains to intimidate, delegitimize, and exclude women as political actors" (2016: 472). The existence of this violence raises important questions about the impartial and inclusive character of contemporary states.

Toleration of violence against women in public and private life by liberal, social democratic, post-socialist, postcolonial, and post-conflict states challenges the seriousness of their commitment to the equality and security of all citizens. States routinely claim that their first priority is to provide order—to protect and secure the lives and livelihoods of their citizens. Feminist scholars have drawn attention to the gendered and racial patterns in states' failure to realize that goal: women, people of color, ethnic minorities, and LGBTQ citizens are routinely insecure in ways that privileged male citizens are not. Precarity is not an equal opportunity condition; failure to protect is not a universal phenomenon. Indeed, feminist scholars have argued that claims about "failure to protect" miss the mark in the face of so much evidence of state involvement in the perpetration of violence, whether through discriminatory practices, harassment in halls of government, abuses by the police, military, and security services, refusal to investigate and prosecute crimes, harmful speech circulated by the state such as political homophobia (rhetoric used by state leaders to publicly denigrate same-sex sexualities, non-heterosexual persons, gender variance, and sexual diversity activism) and political misogyny (public rhetoric of state leaders that denigrates, dehumanizes, insults and caricatures women), or rising trends in institutionalized sexism promoted by neoliberal, nationalist, and authoritarian political regimes.

States may claim that they do not have any direct role in violence against women. Neither legal codes nor official institutional practices permit it—indeed, most explicitly condemn it. Yet, states are involved through their incapacity or unwillingness to address violence against women and citizens whose lives are shrouded by precarity. Laws prohibiting gender- and race-based violence may be in place, but when they are not implemented, states afford impunity to the perpetrators of violence.

Feminist activists in Mexico coined the term "femicidal state" to conceptualize a state that actively or *through omission* creates a politico-legal environment that reaffirms and reproduces male power, thereby maximizing women's vulnerability (Olivera 2006; Fregoso and Bejarano 2010; Lagarde 2010). Demonstrating how violent modes of racialization and gendering are part of the daily operations of state power, feminist scholars in Latin America have suggested that states are ideologically and materially complicit in femicide (the murder of women with impunity), which they conceptualize as a "state crime." Accounts of femicidal states suggest an institutionalized gender regime characterized by a homosocial politics in which relations among men are mediated by and through the exclusion of women. Eve Sedgwick (1985) defined homosociality as a form of male bonding with a characteristic triangular structure. In this triangle, men have intense but predominantly nonsexual bonds with other men, yet women serve as conduits through which those bonds are expressed. Homosociality instrumentalizes women as the means to cement male social bonds, but it also tends to sexualize women as men's camaraderie is constructed through the sexual objectification of women—whether through jokes and sexual harassment in workplaces, frequenting strip clubs after work, hiring prostitutes for official functions, or participation in gang rape. Institutions and practices that segregate by sex encourage homosociality, thereby accrediting notions concerning inherent gender differences and suggesting that deep affection between men requires the exclusion of women.

Homosocial politics that contribute to femicidal policies are evident in liberal democratic, social democratic, revolutionary, and conservative regimes. The pervasiveness of homosocial politics suggests a more encompassing explanation of violence against women than accounts that attribute causality to remnants of patriarchy, pathological individuals, or misogynist cultures (Shalhoub-Kevorkian 2003: 590). "Femicide is all of the hegemonic masculine-social methods used to destroy females' rights, ability, potential, and power to live safely. It is a form of abuse, threat, invasion, and assault that degrades and subordinates women" (600–1). Rather than interpreting violence against women as the preserve of those in positions of entrenched power, the femicidal state encompasses many players, from street-level bureaucrats and human resources professionals, who are not typically considered particularly powerful, to the most powerful elected officials. Even minor players can contribute to the pervasive violence against women. In the words of Sita Ranchod-Nilsson, "imagined power may be more potent than actual possession of privilege" (2008: 649). Taking these complexities into account, Shalhoub-Kevorkian theorizes "femicide as part of a sociopolitical and economic legacy that reflects the hidden machinery of oppression . . . the central dynamic of the world that recreates, maintains, and justifies a pervasive, inhumane abuse" (2003: 581–2).

In *Working Law* (2016), Lauren Edelman demonstrates how a femicidal dynamic can operate through policies and programs that promise equal opportunity yet maintain practices that perpetuate the advantages of white males. She shows how ubiquitous equal opportunity laws not only mask discrimination and perpetuate inequality, but do so through institutional practices that operate beyond the level of individual intent. Through analysis of data gathered by the US Bureau of Labor Statistics tracking the racial and gender composition of the workforce over five decades, surveys of 350 organizations, interviews with hundreds of compliance professionals, content analyses of human resource journals, webinars, websites, Equal Employment Opportunity Commission (EEOC) Guidelines, and more than 1,000 judicial decisions, Edelman demonstrates that "managerialization of law tends to produce rules that are unenforced, procedures that are biased, programs that are ineffective, and ideologies that legitimate extant racial and gender inequality" (2016: 124). She identifies the precise mechanisms involved in the managerialization of law, such as the creation of equal opportunity policies that internalize dispute resolution, manage away legal risk, decouple legal rules from organizational activities, and rhetorically reframe legal ideals (125). Through these mechanisms, an abstract conception of "fair treatment" of everyone becomes the operative standard, overriding concern about disparate impact and disparate treatment. By these mechanisms equal employment opportunity is converted into "good management practice" by hollowing out its meaning.

The managerialization of law accomplishes an impressive sleight of hand: the careful creation of anti-discrimination and sexual harassment policies, publicly announced and displayed with clear guidelines for filing complaints, is taken as evidence of compliance with EEOC provisions against racial and gender discrimination. When discrimination cases are brought to the courts, judges infer lack of discrimination from the existence of formal policies even when those policies are ineffective and fail to protect employees' civil rights. Ironically, the existence of anti-discrimination policies and dispute-resolution mechanisms make employees less likely to complain or file suit when they experience discrimination because they believe it to be futile (161). Plaintiff's lawyers act as gate-keepers by reinforcing the belief that a plaintiff is unlikely to win a case. As a consequence, less than 1 percent of those who experience employment discrimination pursue litigation (158). Thus Edelman notes that carefully crafted anti-discrimination policies "ensure quiescent acceptance of chronic inequality, deprivation, and daily indignities" (5).

Working Law makes it clear that institutionalized sexism, economic marginalization, discrimination, sexual harassment, and symbolic violence do not disappear; they persist and may indeed increase, but are placed beyond redress through the very laws created to prohibit them. Pervasive and pernicious racial and gender hierarchies remain despite the global spread of equality norms. The very proliferation of national laws and international conventions affords cover to femicidal states, where homosociality has free reign. The guarantee of equal opportunity encourages women to exercise their talents, while subtly socializing them to accept as "normal" threats of rape and murder, and perpetual harassment on streets and in workplaces, government offices, and military barracks. As the proliferation of detailed anti-discrimination and sexual harassment policies ensures that attempts at redress are futile, institutionalized hierarchies become so naturalized that they become invisible. Another dimension of state injustice disappears from view.

Identity Invalidation and Reality Enforcement

State policies toward gender variant and sexually adventurous citizens expose unique dimensions of state injustice, ranging from denigration, dehumanization, and criminalization to "identity invalidation" and violent "reality enforcement." As discussed in the opening section of this chapter, state classifications of sex impose both a gender binary and a presumption of heterosexuality, "transforming social custom into legal control mechanisms, a sort of 'natural law' theory of gender" (Weiss 2001: 124). Those who fall afoul of heteronormative legal presumptions face the full force of the state's capacity to criminalize acts, behaviors, or even illness. The Center for HIV Law and Policy notes that in the United States between 2008 and 2013 there were over 200 prosecutions of people living with HIV for actions that are not linked scientifically with the transmission of the virus. Although HIV is not transmittable through saliva, an HIV-positive Texan was sentenced to thirty-five years in prison for spitting on a police officer. An Iowan was sentenced to twenty-five years in prison for failing to disclose his HIV status to his partner even though he had an undetectable viral load and used a condom (J. Price 2017: 63). These "crimes" have been prosecuted under various charges, ranging from "assault with a deadly weapon" and "attempted murder" to "possession of a biological weapon" under a Michigan anti-terrorism law (63). In ten states in the US, these convictions require subsequent registration as a sex offender. In many jurisdictions, MTF spouses have been denied the protections of civil law, when courts have refused to allow them to inherit their deceased spouse's estate despite explicit provisions in a will, or denied them the right to sue for their husband's wrongful death (Weiss 2001: 127).

Although the state is supposed to protect the privacy and physical security of children, intersex children often find themselves subjected to abusive genital scrutiny. As Cheryl Chase has noted, "This misplaced focus on gender distorts the perspective of clinicians in many ways that are harmful to patients. Intersex patients have frequently been subjected to repeated genital examinations, which create a feeling of freakishness and unacceptableness" (2003: 241–2). Given the non-consensual nature of surgery on intersex infants, some scholars consider these operations not only as a violation of physical integrity, but also as a kind of sexual violation. In the words of one intersex person, "I was forced to be surgically mutilated and medically raped at the age of fourteen" (Preves 2003: 73). The state is complicit in the exorbitant harm resulting from its failure to protect in such instances.

Trans and intersex citizens experience multiple harms as they are compelled to make themselves legible to the state. They are pressured to frame their existence in terms of a "wrong body problem," which forces them to endure pathologization (i.e., to be diagnosed as having a mental illness) and medicalization (i.e., to be subjected to hormonal and surgical intervention). They are also subjected to a form of identity invalidation. Neither the legal nor the medical system will acknowledge or accredit an account of their embodiment, self-understanding, or identity that deviates from the heteronormative script. Talia Mae Bettcher (2014, 2016) has noted that identity invalidation pervades the lives of trans people:

> Transsexuality is about having one's sex doubted, challenged, impugned in manifold daily transactions. It's about going out on a date and worrying about when to tell one's date that one is trans. It is about harassment by the police who treat trans prostitutes as "really men." It is about the risks of "being exposed as a man" in a commercial sexual encounter. It is about how pervasive identity-invalidation contributes to HIV-prevalence among trans women. (Bettcher 2016: 420)

It is also about being required by the state to deny one's embodied past and erase any trace of birth gender in order to fit in and reestablish normalized binary gender (Beauchamp 2009 [2013]). To make themselves legible to the state, trans citizens must incur insults, coercive and expensive medical treatments, and assaults on their memory and identity that cis-citizens never encounter. "Laws that require mandatory sex change as a condition for change in identity papers subject transgender people to legally-prescribed state-enforced sterilization" (Shrage 2012: 241, n. 40). Gender nonconforming citizens experience unique forms of state injustice.

Queer theorists and trans theorists have emphasized that gender and sexual variance have many manifestations. Although the "wrong body" narrative corresponds to the experiences of some, it systematically distorts the identities of many. When the state requires the adoption of a "wrong body" narrative as a condition for state recognition, it marginalizes and discredits all those who understand themselves as "beyond the gender binary." And it makes state recognition dependent on a degree of affluence that few trans and intersex people ever attain. Thus it forces the majority of gender nonconforming people who do not want or cannot afford surgical intervention into a liminal existence in which they quite literally possess erroneous state-issued identity documents. At a time when the "undocumented" are subjected to massive hostility and scrutiny, any gap between official papers and public gender presentation can be particularly hazardous, heightening the possibility that the individual will be subjected to "reality enforcement" by the police, employers, or members of the general public.

Bettcher defines reality enforcement as "one treacherous technology of identity invalidation, which turns 'appearance/reality' indeterminacy into a perceived misalignment between public gender presentation and private sexed body":

> It is not *merely* that a trans woman is called a man. It is that she is called "*really* a man who *appears* to be a woman," where *sartorial practices provide social content to such locutions*. This appearance-reality contrast is manifested in two ways, both to the detriment of trans identity. When a trans person passes as non-trans, the possibility of exposure as "really" a different gender is established; and if such an exposure occurs, the trans person is viewed as a deceiver. By contrast, when it's known that the trans person is trans, the trans person is often viewed as merely playing make-believe, a practice that again is said to involve deception. Exposure of trans people as deceivers is the point of "reality" enforcement, which is often accompanied by graphic genital verification: somebody physically exposes a trans person's genitals. Such practices are clearly abusive. (2016: 420; emphasis in the original)

Even in the absence of violent genital verification, trans citizens are subjected to unrelenting invasions of privacy, queried by police, airport security guards, airline personnel, medical professionals, potential employers, colleagues, transphobic bar patrons, and people on the street about the relation between their gender identity and their genitalia. State agencies themselves position trans and intersex people as "imposters." Since 1994, for example, the US Social Security Administration (SSA) has sent out "no match" letters to employers in cases where employees' hiring paperwork contradicts employee information on file with SSA, a policy that disproportionately affects trans people whose employers receive SSA notification of "no gender match" (Beauchamp 2009 [2013]: 49). The REAL ID Act passed by the US Congress in 2005 established a federal database that stores supporting documents used to create official ID (birth certificates, social security cards, court-ordered name changes) for seven to ten years. The purpose of the Act was to reveal "deception" (50). Due to the state classifications imposed on them, trans and intersex people are particularly liable to be identified as deceivers. This heightened vulnerability stems in part from "the impertinent assumption that the intimate details of trans bodies should be available for examination, diagnosis, judgment" (Heaney 2017: 237), and in part from the state's refusal to recognize the defects of classification schemes grounded in a gender binary. "Genders beyond the binary of male and female are neither fictive nor futural but are embodied and lived" (Salamon 2010: 95). Transwomen do not desire to be women; they are women; transmen are men. Gender variant and gender queer people are neither men nor women. That the state refuses to recognize that reality is another instance of state injustice.

Postcolonial and Imperial Interventions

Although Western nations typically depict the twenty-first century as "postracial" and "postcolonial," critics suggest that the form of equality associated with neoliberal multiculturalism bears little relation to material realities and class hierarchies (Duggan 2003). Despite their patent failures to realize meaningful equality for all citizens at home, nations in the North have taken the very existence of LGBTQI activism as evidence of their tolerance and progressiveness. By recognizing queer citizens' "right to have rights . . . 'enlightened' Western states" proclaim an obligation to "defend this new normalized sexual subject where he is oppressed" (Weber 2016: 111). Cynthia Weber has pointed out that the United States, in particular, has refigured itself as "the global champion of gay rights" and mapped the world "into normal and pathological states" with respect to their treatment of LGBTQI citizens. In December 2011, for example, US Secretary of State Hillary Clinton delivered an historic Human Rights Day speech at the UN Headquarters in Geneva. Declaring that "gay rights are human rights," Clinton insisted that states have a moral obligation to protect the human rights of sexual minorities, and called for an end to criminalization and violence against people because of their sexual orientation and gender identity (5). She also announced that President Obama had initiated

> the first U.S. government strategy dedicated to combating human rights abuses against LGBT persons abroad ... directing all U.S. Government agencies engaged overseas to combat the criminalization of LGBT status and conduct, to enhance efforts to protect vulnerable LGBT refugees and asylum seekers, to ensure that our foreign assistance promotes the protection of LGBT rights, to enlist international organizations in the fight against discrimination, and to respond swiftly to abuses against LGBT persons. (5)

Positioning itself as the world's policing arm committed to imposing democracy and equality on backward and cruel governments, the US took upon itself the task of monitoring other states and selectively intervening to correct and punish those deemed pathological, thereby enacting the principle of "white straights saving brown queers from brown straights" (Rao 2010: 139). In proposing to promote equality and democracy globally, the "West's defense of gay rights as human rights is a tool of empire" (Rao 2012).

The contradictions inherent in this mode of neo-imperialism are integral to the "illiberalism of liberalism" (Weber 2016: 109). Neville Hoad (2000) suggests that these contemporary practices replicate earlier constructions of colonized peoples as perverse—constructions that were used to legitimate subjection of the colonized to imperial rule. Claims concerning "deviant" sexuality figured prominently in imperial discourses about the "underdeveloped" and "undevelopable savages" who populated darker continents. Key tropes in Darwinian evolutionary theory positioned the male homosexual in relation to sexual and civilizational degeneracy. "Just as the 'female' was understood as the biologically degenerate sex in relation to the 'male', the 'homosexual' appeared in medical discourse as biologically degenerate in relation to the 'heterosexual'" (Hoad 2000: 136). In certain medical texts, the "'homosexual body' was equated with the retarded female fetus that developed more slowly than the male fetus and was described at a metabolic level as having inert, passive, anabolic cells rather than energetic, progressive, katabolic cells" (136). Characterized as primitive and promiscuous, "the not-properly civilized homosexual was placed on a racialized gender continuum, which described him as part male, part female, a sexual half-breed" (140).

Nael Bhanji suggests that the logic underlying contemporary deployments of trans bodies in international politics has not moved far beyond the perspectives of nineteenth- and early twentieth-century colonizers:

> Euro-American scholars often resort to comparative frameworks that naturalize and reproduce nationalist discourses of sexuality through fetishizing gestures that map racial difference as spectacle. Trans-identified people of color are frozen in anthropological taxonomy, which through a spatial and temporal sleight of hand renders them in another place, not here—premodern, precapitalist . . . Exotic transsexuality spans male transvestite shamans of West Africa to the shamans of Vietnamese countryside, to transsexual augurers and diviners of Angola to India's hijras . . . These accounts of transgender embodiment engage in a double move of universalizing transsexual difference while reproducing the body in excess . . . akin to a family of nations pageant in which a rotating chain of marginality is pitted against the unstated, white Western norm. (2013: 521)

Operating under the sign of progress, freedom, and tolerance, the state that upholds the white Western norm perpetuates the multiple injustices of settler colonialism—from environmental degradation and white supremacy to heteropatriarchal domination, class exploitation and consolidation of massive inequality (Coulthard 2014, 2018).

Limitations of State-Based Approaches to Justice

In addition to illuminating state injustices omitted from conventional political theory, feminist, critical race, Indigenous, postcolonial, queer, and trans* theorists have offered compelling accounts of the inadequacies of state-based approaches to justice. Positioning itself as the dispenser of justice and the guardian of liberty and equality, the state masks its own role in the creation and reproduction of racial, gender, and sexual inequalities. Indeed, the state's reliance on formal constitutional rights as the only meaningful form of equality camouflages its own failure to instantiate those rights. Morgan Bassichis and Dean Spade have pointed out that formal legal equality has not delivered material relief from racism: "Appeals to formal equality mistakenly assume that race consciousness on the part of white people and people of color, not intergenerational structures of white supremacy, is the problem that the law must eliminate" (2014: 200). Formal equality encourages "color blindness," which leaves in place ongoing discrimination, even as its proponents advocate dismantling programs such as affirmative action that seek to remedy racial disparities. Courts have shifted the criteria of evidence for discrimination from disparate treatment or disparate effects to "intent," which is notoriously difficult to prove in instances of hiring, promotion, or housing (201). As a consequence, "The broad conditions of extreme racial disparity in access to housing, employment, education, food, and health care, and the severe disproportionality in criminal punishment, environmental damage and immigration enforcement are cast as natural and inevitable by the discrimination principle" (201).

> When racist harm is framed as a problem of aberrant individuals who discriminate, and when intention must be proved to find a violation of the law, the background conditions of white supremacy are implicitly declared neutral . . . Critical race theorists have supplied the concept, "preservation through transformation," to describe the neat trick that civil rights law performed in this dynamic. In the face of significant

resistance to conditions of subjection, law reform tends to provide
just enough transformation to stabilize and preserve the status quo . . .
Explicit exclusion through policies and practices are officially forbid-
den, yet the unequal distribution of life chances remains the same or
worsens with the racialized concentration of wealth in the U.S., the
dismantling of social welfare, and the explosion of criminalization.
(201)

In her examination of gender-based violence, Laura Sjoberg
pointed out that "gender justice jurisprudence is about women as
victims, it therefore seeks to empower women, hold them equal
to men, and pay attention to women's special needs" (2016: 167).
Operating within the terms of a strict gender dichotomy, it assumes
that "justice means justice for women as they are positioned relative to men" (170). For this reason, it offers little assistance to those
marginalized or excluded by state reliance on a naturalized gender
binary. And it fails to recognize the harms of feminization—scripted
practices of subordination that have systemic effects well beyond
those assigned M/F at birth. Sjoberg also draws attention to prosecutorial discretion, which accords power to the state to define
who counts as worthy of state protection, a power that is routinely
exercised to grant legitimacy to some groups and not others. In
the context of international tribunals created to prosecute war
criminals, the "prosecutorial format relies on a distinction between
the civilized (those prosecuting) and the savage (those being
prosecuted and their victims) . . . which reifies sexist and racist-
essentialist assumptions about perpetrators and victims" (169). This
presumption is often replicated in criminal prosecutions within
nation-states. Even in instances of successful prosecution—where
the accused is held responsible for gendered violence, the law falls
far short of repairing injury, much less rectification. As victims'
voices are subordinated to inanimate forensic evidence, the trial
does not provide a venue for testimony, healing, or the vindication
of victims (168–9).

Because patterns of exclusion and exploitation do not count as
violations under the legal principle of nondiscrimination, many
forms of injustice are placed beyond redress. "Bodily terror, an

everyday aspect of a larger regime of structural racialized and gendered violence congealed within the practices of criminalization, immigration enforcement, poverty, and medicalization of black people at the population level—from before birth until after death"—remains untouched by legal remedies (Bassichis and Spade 2014: 196). To underscore this reality, Ruth Gilmore defines "racism as the state-sanctioned and/or extra-legal production and exploitation of group-differentiated vulnerability to premature death" (2007: 28). Trans* theorists have emphasized that bodily terror also characterizes the daily experience of those who refuse gender conformity.

In their efforts to find mechanisms of redress, some activists have lobbied for hate crimes legislation. Others have cautioned against positioning the neoliberal state as the guardian of oppressed racial and sexual citizens. Sarah Lamble has argued that "hate crimes legislation rests on the myth that the criminal justice system punishes those who deserve it . . . and denies the violent, racist nature of the carceral state" (2014: 155). The demand for such legislation suggests that state "recognition of the right to be free from identity-based harassment is best measured by the state's willingness to imprison those who harass. Such an approach collapses social justice into a promise of imprisonment . . . inaccurately conflating retribution and deterrence with prevention" (156). Moreover, the demand for hate crime legislation and enforcement asks activists to partner with police, which presumes that discrimination is simply a flaw in the system rather than intrinsic to the system itself. This presumption misconstrues the nature of punishment in the neoliberal carceral state. As Lamble notes, "Prisons are designed to insulate society from those who fall outside the proper functioning of the formal political economic order, as well as those who threaten the status quo or are marked as socially deviant" (159). Prisons are emblematic of a system in which the "enhancement and protection of life for some is predicated on the violent sequestering of others" (162). Thus Lamble cautions that it is a mistake to allow the police to "reinvent themselves as protector, patron, and sponsor of minorities at the very moment when they are targeting racialized populations and areas with new intensity . . . As the welfare state is abandoned, the carceral state claims the capacity to dole out justice . . . by reinventing the dangerous other who must be surveilled and contained" (163).

Following John Rawls, some political theorists have acknowledged the legitimacy of critics' indictments of existing states whose implementation of anti-discrimination and equality of opportunity policies falls far short of their normative potential. Yet they argue that Rawls theorized "fair equality of opportunity" as a principle that has transformative possibilities. In *A Theory of Justice*, Rawls stipulated that fair equality of opportunity requires the state to provide citizens with certain primary goods (rights and liberties, opportunities and powers, income and wealth, and a sense of self-worth) to enable them to achieve their aims. He designs a "transfer branch of government to take individual needs into account and assign them appropriate weight with respect to other claims" in the distribution of primary goods (1971: 276). To ensure fair equality of opportunity, the state would be obligated to transform educational and social welfare institutions to create a far more egalitarian society. By providing each citizen with whatever is necessary to develop fully, the guarantee of a social minimum of primary goods should counteract the negative effects of social class, race, gender, and family background.

Although it is possible that a state operating according to Rawls' principles of justice as fairness might be more egalitarian than existing social democratic and liberal democratic states, certain aspects of Rawls' account raise concern. He endorses a meritocracy that legitimates a hierarchy of social, economic and political roles. Fair equality of opportunity ensures that the "talented" will not be constrained by social barriers in their quest for upward mobility. But it does not guarantee that all social roles or individual aspirations will be equally valued in a just society. Indeed, Rawls' commitment to the

> priority of the right over the good sets constraints on individuals' choice of behaviors and life plans . . . sets bounds on what is good and what forms of character are morally worthy and so upon the kinds of persons men should be . . . The principles of right and so of justice put

limits on which satisfactions have value; they impose restrictions on what are reasonable conceptions of one's good. (31–2)

Rawls suggests that these restrictions are unproblematic because they derive from an impartial "way of reasoning such that all rational beings operating with relevantly similar and sufficient information will derive the same conclusions from the same premises" (263). But as many critics have pointed out, Rawls' conception of impartiality depends upon a form of disembodied rationality. An impartial decision is one made under a "veil of ignorance" that frees persons from knowledge of who they are, when and where they live, and what they desire—knowledge that might taint their stance with self-interest. Like many conceptualizations of universal reason, Rawls' notion of rationality assumes fungible minds unmarked by race, gender, sex, or sexuality. But that very fungibility is possible only when embodied knowledge concerning racialization, gendering, and heterosexualization is deemed morally irrelevant. It is difficult to imagine that states that deny the validity of embodied knowledge will avoid the modes of injustice associated with the kind of colorblind, genderblind and sexuality-blind policies discussed above. In the absence of an explicit theorization of intersectionality and conscious attention to the complex vectors of power that fuel injustice, state initiatives premised on fungible minds and impartial reasoning are likely to replicate the bias encoded in the unmarked norm that reflects elite white male experience.

Silvia Posocco has warned that in the context of late liberalism, "state recognition is neither benign nor transparently affirmative, but rather normative and disciplinary" (2014: 73). Within this horizon, justice is always paradoxical and at a loss, unable to remedy risk, expropriation, or deepening vulnerability and insecurity (73). Achille Mbembe's (2003: 40) account of "necropolitics"— the contemporary production of "death worlds" (new and unique forms of social existence in which vast populations are subjected to conditions of life that confer upon them the status of living dead)—seems far more insightful than Rawls' optimism about fair equality of opportunity. Replicating processes of depersonalization, exclusion, and expulsion associated with earlier eras of colonization and enslavement, "death making is constitutive of the polis, which connects everyday experience to slow death" (Berlant 2007: 755). "Letting die, abandonment, and differential belonging are central to forms of governance in late liberalism . . . the extreme and yet ordinary physical wearing out of a population and the deterioration of people in that population . . . heightens susceptibility to premature death" (Haritaworn, Kuntsman, and Posocco 2014: 7). Necropolitics repudiates the premise that "existing legal structures are generally fair and neutral" (Bassichis and Spade 2014: 199). It challenges the logic of neoliberalism, which insists that "there is no one to blame for the suffering . . . except for the responsible willing individual . . . to kill slowly via poverty exempts the state from responsibility for murderous laws and policies" (Shakhsari 2014: 93).

Envisioning Social Transformation

Despite many points of disagreement among them, critical race, feminist, Indigenous, postcolonial, queer, and trans* theorists tend to agree that current state practices are incapable of resolving pressing injustices because they fail to recognize that state action is responsible for continuing depredations. Critics also suggest that the Aristotelian framework of distributive and retributive justice is itself problematic. As a reparatory transaction, corrective justice presupposes the possibility of redress. Yet, as Saidiya Hartman has emphasized in the context of racial injustice, "given the magnitude of the breach" and the role of common law and statutory provision in perpetrating injury, "redress cannot restore or remedy loss" (1997: 76–7). By conceptualizing justice in relation to concrete distributions of goods and specific actions of individuals, the Aristotelian frame is incapable of capturing significant dimensions of injustice enacted by states that powerfully shape the subjectivity of those who live within and beyond the borders of those states.

Martha Ackelsberg has suggested that feminist, critical race, queer and trans* theories "add something different to our thinking about the workings of politics and power, expanding the definition of the political and challenging dominant paradigms and categories of analysis" (2017: 189). By asking new questions, they draw attention to inequalities and reveal how power structures even the most intimate of interpersonal relations. They demand a rethinking of kinship that also entails a rethinking of political life and all the inequities embedded in traditional presumptions about the public/private binary (Josephson and Marques 2017: 240).

José Muñoz has theorized *disidentification* as a means "to resist the oppressive and normalizing discourse of dominant ideology" (2013: 79). Refusing the benefits afforded by aligning with traditional theoretical accounts and existing state apparatus, disidentification can enable "subjects to imagine a way of breaking through the restraints of the social body" (83). B. Lee Aultman and Paisley Currah link disidentification to the prospects for "epistemic justice," the development of "new ways of understanding the self and the body as sites of democratic projects and a source of pluralism" (2017: 48).

As Glen Sean Coulthard (2014, 2018) has noted in the context of Indigenous Studies, breaking the power of Western political theory requires a critical rethinking of the modernist view of history with all its presumptions about Europe as the pinnacle of civilization. It requires an acknowledgement that settler colonialism is a structure of domination, predicated on the ongoing dispossession of Indigenous peoples' lands, and embedded in forms of political authority and jurisdiction that govern contemporary relationships to these lands. As Fanon recognized, epistemic justice also entails grappling with internalized violence, the means by which colonizers secure dominance over the colonized by warping the self-image of colonized subjects in ways that make dispossession and political subjugation appear to be an appropriate response to perceived cultural inferiority and backwardness (Adams 1989, 1999). Epistemic justice, then, involves "resurgence," a project that "calls on Indigenous people and communities to seek reprieve from the violent influence of colonial discursive formations and sites of non-Indigenous knowledge production through the revitalization of Indigenous epistemologies, political structures and land-connected economic practices" (Simpson 2017: 17). To decolonize their minds as well as their land, the Indigenous must act on their "own terms without the sanction, permission or engagement of the state, western theory, or the opinions of white settler colonialists" (17). According to Leanne Betasamosake Simpson, "resurgence" is akin to the Anishinaabe concept *biiskabiyang*, "the process of *returning* to ourselves, a *reengagement* with the things we have left behind . . . an unfolding *from the inside out*" (17).

Coulthard, Adams, and Simpson are concerned with Indigenous efforts to achieve meaningful decolonization, yet their theorization of resurgence resonates with arguments developed by queer and trans* theorists about the best means to resist assimilation to the injustices embedded in the existing order. Lisa Duggan called for resistance against "homonormativity, a politics that does not contest dominant heteronormative assumptions and institutions, but upholds and sustains them" by privatizing and depoliticizing gay culture, anchoring it in domesticity and consumption (2003: 50). Jasbir Puar called for disengagement from the racialized respectability politics of "homonationalism," which construes sexual identity politics in terms of coming out, public visibility, and legislative reform as the key to social progress, thereby affirming hegemonic cultural norms and marginalizing those critical of oppressive state practices (Puar 2007). Amy Lind and Christine Keating have cautioned against the seductions of "homoprotectionism," the deployment of the power of the state to protect LGBT people from persecution and domination, while obscuring the ways that the state simultaneously works to foment and mobilize discriminatory actions, attitudes or beliefs. As an example, Lind and Keating analyze Ecuador's 2008 Constitution, which forbids discrimination based on gender identity and redefines the family beyond blood kinship to encompass same-sex couples and transnational migrant households, while also stipulating that marriage exists only between a man and a woman and that adoption is possible only for couples of the opposite sex (2013: 522–4). Under the guise of homoprotectionism, states consolidate, extend, and centralize state authority as they shore up hierarchies among citizens. Like theorists of Indigenous resurgence, these scholars emphasize the difficulty involved in developing a critical relationship to hegemonic social norms and the painful estrangement that can accompany such efforts (Smith 2016: 968–9).

Talia Bettcher, for example, has analyzed the complexity associated with efforts to refuse "the representational relation between gender presentation and genitalia altogether" (2016: 421). As a set of naturalized assumptions about dichotomous sex and a system of visual communication tying dress to sexuality, the equation of gender presentation with genitalia has saturated public culture and private consciousness. To alter that equation, Bettcher suggests, would require a sophisticated resignification of the meaning of "man" and "woman" that avoids gender essentialism and biological determinism while also avoiding voluntarist accounts of gender identity (the view that one can simply "choose" a gender). Toward that end, Bettcher suggests, Emi Koyama's vision of "trans liberation" as "taking back the right of self-definition from medical, religious, and political authorities" (Koyama 2003: 250) must be supplemented with Cathy Cohen's recognition of the importance of social identity and communal ties to survival (2005: 34).

Bettcher's thoughtful prescription for inclusive "transfeminism" echoes aspects of Beauvoir's conceptualization of freedom as a struggle against the negative conditions of existence, which requires engagement with contingency, ambiguity, and potentiality. Beauvoir encouraged individuals to transcend fixed status restrictions imposed on bodies, to recognize that differences are relational and that otherness can be understood only in relation to a norm. Forms of human flourishing shaped by exercises in freedom "should not be taken as essential oppositions or ossified identities, but the way particularity develops in and through mediation of each subject's finite context and relations" (Beauvoir 1949 [1974]: 39). The challenge, however, is to avoid the tendency to conflate transcendence with an escape from the body, to devise a conception of freedom that prizes diverse modes of embodiment in order to institute new modes of reality, reorganize ways of seeing, transform oppressive aspects of past practices, and come together to constitute political collectivities in the service of freedom.

Critical race, feminist, Indigenous, postcolonial, queer, and trans* theory includes nuanced suggestions for "creating a democratic culture beyond dualism, ending colonizing relationships and finding a mutual, ethical basis for enriching coexistence with earth others," as well as creating "social formations built on radical democracy, co-operation and mutuality" (Plumwood 1994: 196). Responding to the manifold dimensions of injustice, "the social democratic wish goes beyond civil rights and identity politics to embrace a broader and more inclusive set of egalitarian and social justice goals" (Mucciaroni 2017: 540). Envisioning solidarity among oppressed groups, these theories seek to inspire broad coalitions of activism in order to disrupt the erasures enacted by racialized heteronormativity and devise strategies to address sexism, racism, homophobia, transphobia, poverty, criminalization, and cultural imperialism (Daum 2017: 364–5). To illuminate and subvert state injustices, Joseph Defilippis and Ben Anderson-Nathe have theorized "trickle-up social justice," grounded in intersectional activism that gives priority to the severe modes of violence and discrimination experienced by "those who rely on street economies, underground economies without a collective safety net—the undocumented, and the gender nonconforming" (2017: 115–16). Acknowledging the tensions between policy advocacy, service delivery, and organizing that activists confront, given the pervasiveness of contemporary injustice, Defilippis and Anderson-Nathe note that activists must "choose between working towards the world they envision and responding to the pain they see in the world that exists" (126). Yet in grappling with that difficult choice, they encourage social justice activists to refuse hierarchical organization and engage in direct democracy in an effort to transform power relations.

Since the earliest feminist works on gender and political theory, the terms of discourse have changed dramatically. Cressida Hayes has suggested that "feminists of all stripes share the political goal of weakening the grip of oppressive sex and gender dimorphisms in Western cultures, with their concomitant devaluing of the lesser terms 'female' and 'feminine'" (2013: 202). Over the past few decades, many feminist theorists have come to realize that the practical reach and power of racialized gender normativity extends well beyond the classical texts of Western philosophy and science, and have turned their attention to the practices of nation-states and imperial powers. In their commitment to struggle against coercive hierarchies linked to gender, race, sex, and sexuality, feminist scholars have used critique of the classic canon as a means to analyze and transform the practices of the living. In this endeavor, many have drawn important insights from critical race, Indigenous, postcolonial, queer, and trans* theory.

Despite diverse analytical approaches, contemporary feminist theory routinely involves disidentification from some of the guiding precepts of political theory, such as the norm of neutral, distanced, dispassionate analysis, and the quest for universal explanations. Attuned to ambiguity and indeterminacy, and committed to an ethics of freedom, they refuse to accredit essentialized gender oppositions or invariant modes of domination and subordination, analyzing instead the intersectional operations of power within particular institutions. By troubling false universals and confining stereotypes, this form of feminist theorizing seeks to enable new ways of thinking, thereby creating the conditions of possibility for new modes of social, political, and intellectual life.

Mary's Career Scope. —

Bibliography

Abu-Lughod, Lila. 2002. "Do Muslim Women Really Need Saving? Anthropological Reflections on Cultural Relativism and Its Others." *American Anthropologist* 104(3): 783–90.

Ackelsberg, Martha. 2017. "The Politics of LGBTQ Politics in APSA: A History (and its) Lesson(s)." In Marla Brettschneider, Susan Burgess, and Christine Keating, eds. *LGBTQ Politics*. New York: New York University Press, pp. 177–97.

Adams, Howard. 1989. *Prison of Grass: Canada from a Native Point of View*. Saskatoon: Fifth House Publishing.

Adams, Howard. 1999. *A Tortured People: The Politics of Colonization*. Penticton: Theytus Books.

Agamben, Giorgio. 2005. *State of Exception*. Kevin Attell, trans. Chicago: University of Chicago Press.

Alaimo, Stacy. 2016. "Nature." In Lisa Disch and Mary Hawkesworth, eds. *Oxford Handbook of Feminist Theory*. New York: Oxford University Press, pp. 530–50.

Alaimo, Stacy and Susan Hekman. 2008. *Material Feminisms*. Bloomington: University of Indiana Press.

Alexander, Claire. 2010. "Culturing Poverty? Ethnicity, Religion, Gender, and Social Disadvantage among South Asian Muslim Youth in the United Kingdom." In Sylvia Chant, ed. *The International Handbook of Gender and Poverty.* Cheltenham: Edward Elgar, pp. 272–7.

Alexander, Michelle. 2011. *The New Jim Crow: Mass Incarceration in the Age of Colorblindness.* New York: The New Press.

Alexander-Floyd, Nikol. 2012. "Disappearing Acts: Reclaiming Intersectionality in the Social Sciences in a Post-Black Feminist Era." *Feminist Formations* 24(1): 1–25.

Allen, Anita. 1988. *Uneasy Access: Privacy for Women in a Free Society.* Rowman and Littlefield.

Allison, Graham. 1971. *Essence of Decision.* Boston: Little Brown.

Anderson, Benedict. 1991. *Imagined Communities: Reflections on the Origin and Spread of Nationalism.* London: Verso.

Anderson, Bonnie. 2000. *Joyous Greetings: The First International Women's Movement, 1830–1860.* New York: Oxford University Press.

Anderson, Ellen Ann. 2017. "The State of Marriage? How Sociological Context Affects Why Some Same-Sex Couples Marry." In Marla Brettschneider, Susan Burgess, and Christine Keating, eds. *LGBTQ Politics.* New York: New York University Press, pp. 374–93.

Anzaldua, Gloria. 1987. *Borderlands/La Frontera: The New Mestiza.* San Francisco: Spinsters/Aunt Lute.

Arikha, Noga. 2007. *Passions and Tempers: A History of the Humours.* New York: Harpers.

Aristotle. 1987. *Nicomachean Ethics.* J.E.C. Weldon, trans. Buffalo: Prometheus Books.

Aultman, B. Lee and Paisley Currah. 2017. "Politics Outside the Law: Transgender Lives and the Challenge of Legibility." In Marla Brettschneider, Susan Burgess, and Christine Keating, eds. *LGBTQ Politics.* New York: New York University Press, pp. 34–53.

Bagemihl, Bruce. 1999. *Biological Exuberance: Animal Homosexuality and Natural Diversity.* New York: St. Martin's Press.

Banton, Michael. 1998. *Racial Theories.* Cambridge: Cambridge University Press.

Barrett, Michele. 1980. *Women's Oppression Today.* London: Verso.

Bassichis, Morgan and Dean Spade. 2014. "Queer Politics and Anti-Blackness." In Jin Haritaworn, Adi Kuntsman, and Silvia Posocco, eds. *Queer Necropolitics,* New York: Routledge, pp. 191–210.

Beauchamp, Toby. 2009 [2013]. "Artful Concealment and Strategic

Visibility: Transgender Bodies and State Surveillance after 9/11." *Surveillance & Society* 6(4): 105–36. Reprinted in Susan Stryker and Aren Aizura, eds. *The Transgender Studies Reader 2*. New York: Routledge, pp. 46–55.

Beauvoir, Simone de. 1949 [1974]. *The Second Sex*. H.M. Parshley, trans. New York: Vintage.

Beck, John and Beck, Theodric. 1863. *Elements of Medical Jurisprudence: Volume II*. Philadelphia: Desilver and Thomas.

Bentham, Jeremy. 1789 [1948]. *The Principles of Morals and Legislation*. Laurence Lafleur, ed. New York: Hafner Press.

Bergeron, Suzanne. 2006. *Fragments of Development: Nation, Gender, and the Space of Modernity*. Ann Arbor: University of Michigan Press.

Berlant, Lauren. 2007. "'Slow Death': Sovereignty, Obesity, Lateral Agency." *Critical Inquiry* 33(4): 754–80.

Berlant, Lauren. 2011. *Cruel Optimism*. Durham, NC: Duke University Press.

Bettcher, Talia Mae. 2007. "Evil Deceivers and Make-Believers: On Transphobic Violence and the Politics of Illusion." *Hypatia* 22(3): 43–65.

Bettcher, Talia Mae. 2014. "Trapped in the Wrong Theory: Rethinking Trans Oppression and Resistance." *Signs: Journal of Women in Culture and Society* 39(2): 383–406.

Bettcher, Talia Mae. 2016. "Intersexuality, Transgender, and Transsexuality." In Lisa Disch and Mary Hawkesworth, eds. *Oxford Handbook of Feminist Theory*. New York: Oxford University Press, pp. 407–27.

Bhabha, Homi K. 1994. *The Location of Culture*. London: Routledge.

Bhanji, Nael. 2013. "Trans/Scriptions: Homing Desires, (Trans)sexual Citizenship and Racialized Bodies." In Susan Stryker and Aren Aizura, eds. *The Transgender Studies Reader 2*. New York: Routledge, pp. 512–26.

Bordo, Susan. 1993. *Unbearable Weight: Feminism, Western Culture and the Body*. Berkeley: University of California Press.

Braidotti, Rosi. 2016. "Posthuman Feminist Theory." In Lisa Disch and Mary Hawkesworth, eds. *Oxford Handbook of Feminist Theory*. New York: Oxford University Press, pp. 671–98.

Brownmiller, Susan. 1975. *Against Our Will: Men, Women, and Rape*. New York: Ballantine.

Buff, Ian. 2013. "The Body in Capitalist Conditions of Existence: A Foundational Materialist Approach." In Angus Cameron, Jen Dickenson and Nikola Smith, eds. *Body/State*. Abingdon: Ashgate, pp. 67–83.

Bunch, Charlotte. 1972. "Lesbians in Revolt." *The Furies* [January]: 8–9.

Burgess, Susan and Kate Leeman. 2016. *CQ Press Guide to Radical Politics in the United States*. Thousand Oaks, CA: CQ/Sage.

Burke, Edmund. 1790 [1993]. *Reflections on the Revolution in France*. L.G. Mitchell, ed. Oxford: Oxford University Press.

Butler, Judith. 1990. *Gender Trouble*. New York: Routledge.

Butler, Judith. 1993. *Bodies that Matter*. New York: Routledge.

Cacho, Lisa Marie. 2012. *Social Death: Racialized Rightlessness and the Criminalization of the Unprotected*. New York: New York University Press.

Calhoun, Cheshire. 1994. "Separating Lesbian Theory from Feminist Theory." *Ethics* 104(3): 558–81.

Cameron, Angus, Jen Dickenson and Nikola Smith, eds. 2013. *Body/ State*. Abingdon: Ashgate.

Capers, I. Bennett. 2008. "Cross Dressing and the Criminal." *Yale Journal of Law and Humanities* 20(1): 1–30.

Carbado, Devon. 2013. "Colorblind Intersectionality." *Signs: Journal of Women in Culture and Society* 38(4): 811–45.

Carter, Julian. 2013. "Embracing Transition, or Dancing in the Folds of Time." In Susan Stryker and Aren Azira, eds. *The Transgender Studies Reader 2*. New York: Routledge, pp. 130–44.

Centre for Social Research and UN Women. 2014. "Violence Against Women in Politics: A Study of India, Nepal, and Pakistan." New Delhi, India: UN Women's Office for India, Bhutan, Maldives, and Sri Lanka.

Chambers, Clare. 2013. "The Marriage-Free State." *Proceedings of the Aristotelian Society* 113 (2): 123–43.

Chase, Cheryl. 2003. "What is the Agenda of the Intersex Patient Advocacy Movement?" *Endocrinologist* 13(3): 240–2.

Chawla, Swati, Dannah Dennis, Vanessa Ochs, Paromita Sen, Catalina Vellejo and Denise Walsh. 2017. "Increasing the Civic and Political Participation of Women: Understanding the Risk of Strong

Resistance." Research and Innovative Grants Working Papers Series. Washington, DC: USAID.

Chen, Mel. 2013. "Animals Without Genitals: Race and Transsubstantiation." In Susan Stryker and Aren Azira, eds. *The Transgender Studies Reader 2.* New York: Routledge, pp. 168–77.

Clare, Eli. 2013. "Body Shame, Body Pride: Lessons from the Disability Rights Movement." In Susan Stryker and Aren Azira, eds. *The Transgender Studies Reader 2.* New York: Routledge, pp. 261–5.

Clinton, Hillary. 2011. "On Gay Rights Abroad: Secretary of State Delivers Historic LGBT Speech in Geneva." *Huffington Post*, December 6, https://www.huffingtonpost.com/2011/12/06/hillary-clinton-gay-rights-speech-geneva_n_1132392.html.

Cody, Lisa Forman. 2001. "Sex, Civility, and the Self: Du Coudray, D'Eon, and Eighteenth-century Conceptions of Gendered, National and Psychological Identity." *French Historical Studies* 24(3): 379–407.

Cody, Lisa Forman. 2005. *Birthing the Nation: Sex, Science, and the Conception of Eighteenth-Century Britons.* Oxford: Oxford University Press.

Cohen, Cathy. 2005. "Punks, Bulldaggers, and Welfare Queens: The Radical Potential of Queer Politics?" In Patrick Johnson and Mae Henderson, eds. *Black Queer Studies.* Durham, NC: Duke University Press, pp. 21–51.

Cohen, Patricia. 2015. "Public-Sector Jobs Vanish, and Blacks Take Blow." *New York Times*, May 25, A1, B5.

Cohen, Simon Baron. 2004. *The Essential Difference.* London: Penguin.

Colebrook, Claire. 2012. "Not Symbiosis, Not Now: Why Anthropogenic Climate Change Is Not Really Human." *The Oxford Literary Review* 34(2): 185–209.

Collins, Patricia Hill. 2004. *Black Sexual Politics: African Americans, Gender, and the New Racism.* New York: Routledge.

Comaroff, Jean. 1985. *Body of Power, Spirit of Resistance: The Culture and History of a South African People.* Chicago: University of Chicago Press.

Connell, R.W. 1987. *Gender and Power.* Palo Alto: Stanford University Press.

Cooper, Brittney. 2016. "Intersectionality." In Lisa Disch and Mary Hawkesworth, eds. *The Oxford Handbook of Feminist Theory,* New York: Oxford University Press, pp. 385–406.

Corbett, Greville. 1991. *Gender*. Cambridge: Cambridge University Press.

Cott, Nancy. 2000. *Public Vows: A History of Marriage and the Nation.* Cambridge, MA: Harvard University Press.

Coulthard, Glen Sean. 2014. *Red Skin, White Masks: Rejecting the Colonial Politics of Recognition*. Minneapolis: University of Minnesota Press.

Coulthard, Glen Sean. 2018. "Global Red Power: A Theoretical History." Paper presented at the Political Theory Forum, University of Pennsylvania. February 22.

Crenshaw, Kimberlé. 1989. "Demarginalizing the Intersection of Race and Sex: A Black Feminist Critique of Antidiscrimination Doctrine, Feminist Theory and Antiracist Politics." *University of Chicago Legal Forum* 4: 139–67.

Crenshaw, Kimberlé. 1991. "Mapping the Margins: Intersectionality, Identity Politics, and Violence against Women of Color." *Stanford Law Review* 43: 1241–99.

Currah, Paisley and Lisa Jean Moore. 2013. "'We Won't Know Who You Are': Contesting Sex Designations in New York City Birth Certificates." In Susan Stryker and Aren Aizura, eds. *The Transgender Studies Reader 2*. New York: Routledge, pp. 607–22.

Daum, Courtenay. 2017. "Marriage Equality: Assimilationist Victory or Pluralist Defeat?" In Marla Brettschneider, Susan Burgess, and Christine Keating, eds. *LGBTQ Politics*. New York: New York University Press, pp. 353–73.

Davidoff, Leonore. 1998. "Regarding Some 'Old Husbands' Tales: Public and Private in Feminist History." In Joan Landes, ed. *Feminism, the Public and the Private*. New York: Oxford University Press, pp. 164–94.

Defilippis, Joseph Nicholas and Ben Anderson-Nathe. 2017. "Embodying Margin to Center: Intersectional Activism among Queer Liberation Organizations." In Marla Brettschneider, Susan Burgess, and Christine Keating, eds. *LGBTQ Politics*. New York: New York University Press, pp. 110–33.

Deleuze, Gilles and Félix Guattari. 1987. *A Thousand Plateaus*. Brian Massumi, trans. Minneapolis: University of Minnesota Press.

Delphy, Christine. 1993. "Rethinking Sex and Gender." *Women's Studies International Forum* 16(4): 1–9.

Descartes, René. 1637 [1998]. *Discourse on the Method of Rightly Conducting*

One's Reason and Seeking Truth in the Sciences. Indianapolis: Hackett Publishing Company.

Devor, Holly. 1989. *Gender Blending: Confronting the Limits of Duality*. Bloomington: Indiana University Press.

Dietz, Mary. 1985. "Citizenship with a Feminist Face: The Problem of Maternal Thinking." *Political Theory* 13(1): 19–37.

Doulin, Tim. 2001. "Some Judges Fashion Punishment to Fit Crime." *Columbus Dispatch*, November 28, C13.

Duggan, Lisa. 2003. *The Twilight of Equality? Neoliberalism, Cultural Politics, and the Attack on Democracy*. Boston: Beacon Press.

Duncan, Pamela. 2017. "Gay Relationships Are Still Criminalized in 72 Countries, Report Finds." *Guardian*, July 27, https://www.the guardian.com/world/2017/jul/27/gay-relationships-still-criminalised-countries-report.

Dworkin, Andrea and Catharine MacKinnon. 1988. *Pornography and Civil Rights: A New Day for Women's Equality*. Minneapolis: Organizing Against Pornography.

Dworkin, Ronald. 2000. *Sovereign Virtue: The Theory and Practice of Equality*. Cambridge, MA: Harvard University Press.

Edelman, Elijah Adiv. 2014. "'Walking While Transgender': Necropolitical Regulations of Trans Feminine Bodies of Color in the Nation's Capital." In Jin Haritaworn, Adi Kuntsman, and Silvia Posocco, eds. *Queer Necropolitics*. New York: Routledge, pp. 172–90.

Edelman, Lauren. 2016. *Working Law*. Chicago: University of Chicago Press.

Elshtain, Jean Bethke. 1981. *Public Man, Private Woman*. Princeton: Princeton University Press.

Enke, A. Finn. 2012. *Transfeminist Perspectives in and Beyond Transgender and Gender Studies*. Philadelphia: Temple University Press.

Enke, A. Finn. 2013. "The Education of Little Cis: Cisgender and the Discipline of Opposing Bodies." In Susan Stryker and Aren Aizura, eds. *Transgender Studies 2*. New York: Routledge, pp. 234–47.

Evans, Peter, Dietrich Rueschmeyer, and Theda Skocpol. 1985. *Bringing the State Back In*. Cambridge: Cambridge University Press.

Fanon, Frantz. 1952 [1967]. *Black Skin, White Masks*. New York: Grove Press.

Farris, Sara. 2017. *In the Name of Women's Rights: The Rise of Femonationalism*. Durham, NC: Duke University Press.

Fausto-Sterling, Anne. 1985. *Myths of Gender*. New York: Basic Books.

Fausto-Sterling, Anne. 1993. "The Five Sexes: Why Male and Female Are Not Enough." *The Sciences* (March/April): 20–4.

Fausto-Sterling, Anne. 2000. *Sexing the Body: Gender Politics and the Construction of Sexuality*. New York: Basic Books.

Fedigan, Linda M. 1992. *Primate Paradigms*. Chicago: University of Chicago Press.

Ferguson. Kathy E. 2017. "Feminist Theory Today." *Annual Review of Political Science* 20: 269–86.

Fichte Johann Gottlieb. 1796 [1889]. *The Science of Rights*. A.E. Kroeger, trans. Philadelphia: J.B. Lippincott & Co.

Fichte, Johann Gottlieb. 1807 [2013]. *Addresses to the German Nation*. Isaac Nakhimovsky, Béla Kapossy, and Keith Tribe, trans. Indianapolis: Hackett Publishing Company.

Firestone, Shulamith. 1970. *The Dialectic of Sex*. New York: William Morrow.

Flemming, Roy. 2004. *Tournament of Appeals: Granting Judicial Review in Canada*. Vancouver: University of British Columbia Press.

Ford, Andrea. 2015. "Sex Biology Redefined: Genes Don't Indicate Binary Sexes." *Stanford Medicine: Scope*. February 24, https://scopeblog.stanford.edu/2015/02/24/sex-biology-redefined-genes-dont-indicate-binary-sexes.

Foucault, Michel. 1977. *Discipline and Punish: The Birth of the Prison*. Alan Sheridan, trans. New York: Vintage Books.

Foucault, Michel. 1978. *The History of Sexuality, Vol. 1*. Robert Hurley, trans. New York: Vintage Books.

Foucault. Michel. 1994. *Dits et écrits IV*. Paris: Gallimard.

Fregoso, Rosa Linda and Cynthia Bejarano. 2010. *Terrorizing Women: Feminicide in the Americas*. Durham, NC: Duke University Press.

Freud, Sigmund. 1924. *Collected Works*, vol. 5. London: Pergamon Media.

Friedman, Susan Stanford. 1998. *Mappings: Feminism and the Cultural Geographies of Encounter*. Princeton: Princeton University Press.

Garfinkel, Harold. 1967. *Studies in Ethnomethodology*. Englewood Cliffs: Prentice Hall.

Germon, Jennifer. 2009. *Gender: A Genealogy of an Idea*. New York: Palgrave Macmillan.

Gilmore, Ruth Wilson. 2007. *Golden Gulag: Prisons, Surplus, Crisis, and Opposition in Globalizing California*. Berkeley: University of California Press.

Global Network of Sex Work Projects. 2017. *Policy Brief: Sex Work and Gender Equality*. Edinburgh, Scotland, http://www.nswp.org/sites/nswp.org/files/policy_brief_sex_work_and_gender_equality_nswp_-_2017.pdf.

Gould, Stephen J. 1980. "Sociobiology and the Theory of Natural Selection." In G.W. Barlow and J. Silverberg, eds. *Sociobiology: Beyond Nature/Nurture*. Boulder: Westview Press, pp. 257–69.

Grant, Judith. 2016. "Experience." In Lisa Disch and Mary Hawkesworth, eds. *Oxford Handbook of Feminist Theory*. New York: Oxford University Press, pp. 227–46.

Grosz, Elizabeth. 1994. *Volatile Bodies: Toward a Corporeal Feminism*. Bloomington: Indiana University Press.

Grosz, Elizabeth. 1999. "Thinking the New: Of Futures Yet Unthought." In Elizabeth Grosz, ed. *Becomings: Explorations in Time, Memory, and Futures*. Ithaca: Cornell University Press, pp. 15–28.

Grosz, Elizabeth. 2004. *The Nick of Time*. Durham, NC: Duke University Press.

Grosz, Elizabeth. 2011. *Becoming Undone*. Durham, NC: Duke University Press.

Guattari, Félix. 2000. *Three Ecologies*. London: The Athlone Press.

Gullette, Margaret. 2004. "The New Case for Marriage." *The American Prospect*, March 5, http://prospect.org/article/new-case-marriage.

Habermas, Jürgen. 1962 [1989]. *The Structural Transformation of the Public Sphere: An Inquiry into a Category of Bourgeois Society*. Thomas Berger and Frederick Lawrence, trans. Cambridge, MA: MIT Press.

Hall, Stuart. 1980a. "Cultural Studies: Two Paradigms." *Media, Culture, and Society* 2(1): 57–72.

Hall, Stuart. 1980b. "Encoding/Decoding." In S. Hall, D. Hobson, A. Lowe, and P. Willis, eds. *Culture, Media, Language*. London: Hutchinson, pp. 128–40.

Hamilton, Alexander, James Madison, and John Jay. 1787 [1980]. *The Federalist Papers*. Toronto: Bantam Books.

Hancock, Ange-Marie. 2007a. "Intersectionality as a Normative and Empirical Paradigm." *Politics & Gender* 3(2): 248–54.

Hancock, Ange-Marie. 2007b. "When Multiplication Doesn't Equal Quick Addition: Examining Intersectionality as a Research Paradigm." *Perspectives on Politics* 5(1): 63–79.

Hancock, Ange-Marie. 2011. *Solidarity Politics for Millennials: A Guide to Ending the Oppression Olympics*. New York: Palgrave Macmillan.

Hancock, Ange-Marie. 2016. *Intersectionality: An Intellectual History*. Oxford: Oxford University Press.

Haney Lopez, Ian. 1996. *White by Law*. New York: New York University Press.

Haney Lopez, Ian. 2014. *Dog Whistle Politics: How Coded Racial Appeals Have Reinvented Racism and Wrecked the Middle Class*. New York: Oxford University Press.

Haraway, Donna. 1991a. "The Promise of Monsters: A Regenerated Politics for Inappropriate/d Others." In Lawrence Grossberg, Cary Nelson, and Paula Treichler, eds. *Cultural Studies*. New York: Routledge, pp. 295–337.

Haraway, Donna. 1991b. "Gender for a Marxist Dictionary: The Sexual Politics of a Word." In *Simians, Cyborgs and Women*. New York: Routledge, pp. 127–48.

Haritaworn, Jin, Adi Kuntsman, and Silvia Posocco, eds. 2014. *Queer Necropolitics*, New York: Routledge.

Harrington, Carol. 2010. *Politicization of Sexual Violence: From Abolitionism to Peacekeeping*. Burlington: Ashgate.

Harris, Dawn. 2017. *Punishing the Black Body: Marking Social and Racial Structures in Barbados and Jamaica*. Athens: University of Georgia Press.

Hartman, Saidiya. 1997. *Scenes of Subjection: Terror, Slavery, and Self-Making in Nineteenth-Century America*. Oxford: Oxford University Press.

Hausman, Bernice L. 1995. *Changing Sex: Transsexualism, Technology, and the Idea of Gender*. Durham, NC: Duke University Press.

Hawkesworth, Mary. 1997. "Confounding Gender." *Signs: Journal of Women in Culture and Society* 22(3): 649–85.

Hawkesworth, Mary. 2006. *Feminist Inquiry*. New Brunswick: Rutgers University Press.

Hawkesworth, Mary. 2012. *Political Worlds of Women: Activism, Advocacy, and Governance in the 21st Century*. Boulder: Westview Press.

Hayes, Cressida. 2013. "Feminist Solidarity after Queer Theory: The Case of Transgender." In Susan Stryker and Aren Aizura, eds. *The Transgender Studies Reader 2*. New York: Routledge, pp. 201–12.

Heaney, Emma. 2017. *The New Woman: Literary Modernism, Queer Theory, and the Trans Feminine Allegory*. Evanston: Northwestern University Press.

 Heberle, Renee. 2016. "The Personal Is Political." In Lisa Disch and Mary Hawkesworth, eds. *Oxford Handbook of Feminist Theory*. New York: Oxford University Press, pp. 593–609.

Hegel, Georg Wilhelm Friedrich. 1820 [1967]. *The Philosophy of Right*. T.M. Knox, trans. Oxford: Oxford University Press.

Hegel, Georg Wilhelm Friedrich. 1830 [1971]. *Encyclopaedia of the Philosophical Sciences*, Part III. Oxford: Clarendon Press.

Hegel, Georg Wilhelm Friedrich. 1837 [1975]. *Lectures on the Philosophy of World History*, H.B. Nisbet, trans. Cambridge: Cambridge University Press.

Higginbotham, Evelyn Brooks. 1992. "African-American Women's History and the Metalanguage of Race." *Signs: Journal of Women in Culture and Society* 17(2): 251–74.

 Hird, Myra. 2004. "Naturally Queer." *Feminist Theory* 5(1): 85–9.

Hird, Myra. 2013. "Animal Trans." In Susan Stryker and Aren Aizura, eds. *The Transgender Studies Reader 2*. New York: Routledge, pp. 156–67.

Hird, Myra and Noreen Giffney. 2008. *Queering the Nonhuman*. Farnham: Ashgate.

Hoad, Neville. 2000. "Arrested Development or the Queerness of Savages." *Postcolonial Studies* 3(2): 133–58.

Hobbes, Thomas. 1651 [1994]. *Leviathan*. Indianapolis: Hackett Publishing.

Hume, David. 1738 [1987]. *A Treatise of Human Nature*. London: Penguin Books.

Hume, David. 1753. "Of National Character." *Essays and Treatises on Several Subjects*, https://archive.org/details/essaysandtreati24humeg oog.

Hunter, Nan and Sylvia Law. 1987. "Brief Amici Curiae of Feminist Anti-Censorship Taskforce, et al., in *American Booksellers* v. *Hudnut*." *University of Michigan Journal of Law Reform* 21: 69–136.

IPU (Inter-Parliamentary Union). 2016. *Sexism, Harassment and Violence against Women Parliamentarians*, http://www.ipu.org/pdf/publications/issuesbrief-e.pdf.

IPU (Inter-Parliamentary Union). 2018. *Women in National Parliaments: Statistical Archives*, http://archive.ipu.org/wmn-e/classif-arc.htm.

Irving, Dan. 2013. "Normalized Transgressions: Legitimizing the Transsexual Body as Productive." In Susan Stryker and Aren Aizura, eds. *The Transgender Studies Reader 2*. New York: Routledge, pp. 15–29.

Isoke, Zenzele. 2016. "Race and Racialization." In Lisa Disch and Mary Hawkesworth, eds. *Oxford Handbook of Feminist Theory*. New York: Oxford University Press, pp. 741–60.

Jaggar, Alison and Paula Rothenberg. 1993. *Feminist Frameworks: Alternative Theoretical Accounts of the Relations between Women and Men*, 3rd edition. New York: McGraw Hill.

Jordan-Young, Rebecca. 2010. *Brain Storm: The Flaws in the Science of Sex Differences*. Cambridge, MA: Harvard University Press.

Josephson, Jyl and Thais Marques. 2017. "Unfulfilled Promises: How Queer Feminist Political Theory Could Transform Political Science." In Marla Brettschneider, Susan Burgess, and Christine Keating, eds. *LGBTQ Politics*. New York: New York University Press, pp. 234–48.

Kant, Immanuel. 1764 [1964]. *Observations on the Feeling of the Beautiful and the Sublime*. Berkeley: University of California Press.

Kant, Immanuel. 1775 [2000]. *Of the Different Human Races*. In Robert Bernasconi and Tommy Lott, eds. *The Idea of Race*. Indianapolis: Hackett Publishing Company, pp. 8–22.

Keating, Christine. 2017. "LGBTQ Politics in Global Context." In Marla Brettschneider, Susan Burgess, and Christine Keating, eds. *LGBTQ Politics*. New York: New York University Press, pp. 437–8.

Kessler, Suzanne J. 1990. "The Medical Construction of Gender: Case Management of Intersexed Infants." *Signs: Journal of Women in Culture and Society* 16(1): 3–26.

Kessler, Suzanne J. 1998. *Lessons from the Intersexed*. New Brunswick: Rutgers University Press.

Kessler, Suzanne and Wendy McKenna. 1978. *Gender: An Ethnomethodological Approach*. New York: John Wiley.

King, Deborah. 1988. "Multiple Jeopardy, Multiple Consciousness: The

Context of Black Feminist Ideology." *Signs: Journal of Women in Culture and Society* 14(1): 42–72.

King, Desmond and Rogers Smith. 2011. "On Race, the Silence is Bipartisan." *New York Times*, September 2.

Koedt, Anne. 1970. "The Myth of the Vaginal Orgasm." *Notes from the First Year*. New York: New York Radical Women, http://www.uic.edu/orgs/cwluherstory/CWLUArchive/vaginalmyth.html.

Koyama, Emi. 2003. "The Transfeminist Manifesto." In Rory Dicker and Alison Piepmeier, eds. *Catching a Wave: Reclaiming Feminism for the 21st Century*. Boston: Northeastern University Press, pp. 244–59.

Kretsedemas, Philip. 2008. "Immigration Enforcement and the Complication of National Sovereignty: Understanding Local Enforcement as an Exercise in Neoliberal Governance." *American Quarterly* 60(3): 553–73.

Krook, Mona Lena and Julia Restrepo Sanin. 2016. "Violence against Women in Politics: A Defense of the Concept." *Política y gobierno* 23(2): 459–90.

Lagarde y de los Ríos, Marcela. 2010. "Preface: Feminist Keys for Understanding Feminicide: Theoretical, Political and Legal Construction." In Rosa Linda Fregoso and Cynthia Bejarano, eds. *Terrorizing Women: Feminicide in the Americas*. Durham, NC: Duke University Press, pp. xi–xxv.

Lamble, Sarah. 2013. "Retelling Racialized Violence, Remaking White Innocence: The Politics of Interlocking Oppressions in Transgender Day of Remembrance." In Susan Stryker and Aren Aizura, eds. *The Transgender Studies Reader 2*. New York: Routledge, pp. 30–45.

Lamble, Sarah. 2014. "Queer Investments in Punitiveness: Sexual Citizenship, Social Movements, and the Expanding Carceral State." In Jin Haritaworn, Adi Kuntsman, and Silvia Posocco, eds. *Queer Necropolitics*. New York: Routledge, pp. 151–71.

Landes, Joan. 1988. *Women and the Public Sphere in the Age of the French Revolution*. Ithaca: Cornell University Press.

Landes, Joan, ed. 1998. *Feminism, the Public and the Private*. New York: Oxford University Press.

Laqueur, Thomas. 1990. *Making Sex: Body and Gender from the Greeks to Freud*. Cambridge, MA: Harvard University Press.

Laqueur, Thomas. 2012. "The Rise of Sex in the Eighteenth Century:

Historical Context and Historiographical Implications." *Signs: Journal of Women in Culture and Society*, 37(4): 802–13.

Ledingham, Katie. 2013, "Bodies of the State: On the Legal Entrenchment of (Dis)Ability." In Angus Cameron, Jen Dickenson, and Nikola Smith, eds. *Body/State*. Abingdon: Ashgate, pp. 133–44.

Lévi-Strauss, Claude. 1969. *The Elementary Structures of Kinship*. Boston: Beacon Press.

Lévi-Strauss, Claude. 1971. "The Family." In H. Shapire, ed. *Man, Culture and Society*. Oxford: Oxford University Press, pp. 261–85.

Lewis, Vek. 2013. "Thinking Figurations Otherwise: Reframing Dominant Knowledge of Sex and Gender Variance in Latin America." In Susan Stryker and Aren Aizura, eds. *The Transgender Studies Reader 2*. New York: Routledge, pp. 457–70.

Lind, Amy and Christine Keating. 2013. "Navigating the Left Turn: Sexual Justice and the Citizen Revolution in Ecuador." *International Feminist Journal of Politics* 15(4): 515–33.

Lindblom, Charles. 1965. *The Intelligence of Democracy*. New York: Free Press.

Locke, John. 1689 [1997]. *An Essay Concerning Human Understanding*. London: Penguin Classics.

Locke, John. 1690 [1980]. *Second Treatise on Government*. Indianapolis: Hackett Publishing.

Lorde, Audre. 1985. *I Am Your Sister: Black Women Organizing Across Sexualities*. New York: Women of Color Press.

Lovejoy, Arthur O. 1936. *The Great Chain of Being: A Study of the History of an Idea*. Cambridge, MA: Harvard University Press.

Lugones, Maria. 2007. "Heterosexualism and the Colonial Modern Gender System." *Hypatia* 22(1): 186–209.

Lugones, Maria. 2010. "Towards a Decolonial Feminism." *Hypatia* 25(4): 742–59.

McCall, Leslie. 2005. "The Complexity of Intersectionality." *Signs: Journal of Women in Culture and Society* 30(3): 1771–800.

McCann, Carole and Seung-Kyung Kim. 2003. *Feminist Theory Reader: Local and Global Perspectives*. New York: Routledge.

McClintock, Anne. 1997. "No Longer a Future in Heaven: Gender, Race, Nationalism." In Anne McClintock, Aamir Mufti, and Ella Shohat, eds. *Dangerous Liaisons: Gender, Nation, and Postcolonial*

Perspectives. Minneapolis: University of Minnesota Press, pp. 89–112.

MacKinnon, Catharine. 1983. "Feminism, Marxism, Method, and the State: Toward Feminist Jurisprudence." *Signs: Journal of Women in Culture and Society* 8(4): 635–58.

MacKinnon, Catharine. 1987. *Feminism Unmodified.* Cambridge, MA: Harvard University Press.

MacKinnon, Catharine. 1989. *Towards a Feminist Theory of the State.* Cambridge, MA: Harvard University Press.

Magubane, Zine. 2014. "Spectacles and Scholarship: Caster Semenya, Intersex Studies, and the Problem of Race in Feminist Theory." *Signs: Journal of Women in Culture and Society* 39(3): 761–85.

Mahmood, Saba. 2005. *The Politics of Piety: The Islamic Revival and the Feminist Subject.* Princeton: Princeton University Press.

Mansbridge, Jane and Shuana Shames. 2008. "Toward a Theory of Backlash: Dynamic Resistance and the Central Role of Power." *Politics & Gender* 4(4): 623–34.

Markowitz, Sally. 2001. "Pelvic Politics: Sexual Dimorphism and Racial Difference." *Signs: Journal of Women in Culture and Society* 26(2): 389–414.

Marx, Karl and Friedrich Engels. 1848 [2004]. *The Communist Manifesto.* L. M. Findlay, trans. London: Broadview Press.

Matta, Christine. 2005. "Ambiguous Bodies and Deviant Sexualities: Hermaphrodites, Homosexuality, and Surgery in the United States, 1850–1904." *Perspectives in Biology and Medicine* 48(1): 74–83.

May, Vivian. 2015. *Pursuing Intersectionality, Unsettling Dominant Imaginaries.* New York: Routledge.

Mbembe, Achille. 2003. "Necropolitics." *Public Culture* 15(1): 11–40.

Mehrhof, Barbara and Pamela Kearan. 1971 [1973]. "Rape: An Act of Terror." *Notes from the Third Year.* Reprinted in Anne Koedt, Ellen Levine, and Anita Rapone, *Radical Feminism*, New York: Quadrangle, pp. 228–33.

Mehta, Uday. 1997. "Liberal Strategies of Exclusion." In Frederick Cooper and Ann Laura Stoler, eds. *Tensions of Empire: Colonial Cultures in a Bourgeois World.* Berkeley: University of California Press, pp. 59–86.

Mendoza, Breny. 2016. "Coloniality of Gender and Power: From Postcoloniality to Decoloniality." In Lisa Disch and Mary Hawkesworth, eds. *Oxford Handbook of Feminist Theory*. New York: Oxford University Press, pp. 100–21.

Metz, Tamara. 2010. *Untying the Knot: Marriage, the State, and the Case for their Divorce*. Princeton: Princeton University Press.

Mill, James. 1813. "Report on the Negotiation Between the Honorable East India Company and the Public, Respecting the Renewal of the Company's Exclusive Privileges of Trade for Twenty Years from 1794." *The Monthly Review* 70 (January): 20–37.

Mill, John Stuart. 1869 [1970]. *The Subjection of Women*. London: Longmans, Green, Reader, and Dyer.

Miller, Ruth. 2007. "Rights, Reproduction, Sexuality and Citizenship in the Ottoman Empire and Turkey." *Signs: Journal of Women in Culture and Society* 32(2): 347–74.

Millett, Kate. 1969 [2000]. *Sexual Politics*. Champaign: University of Illinois Press.

Miranda, Deborah. 2013. "Extermination of the Joyas: Gendering in Spanish California." In Susan Stryker and Aren Aizura, eds. *The Transgender Studies Reader 2*. New York: Routledge, pp. 350–63.

Mohanty, Chandra. 2003. "Under Western Eyes Revisited." *Signs: Journal of Women in Culture and Society* 28(2): 499–535.

Money, John. 1995. "Lexical History and Constructionist Ideology of Gender." *Gendermaps: Social Constructionism, Feminism, and Sexosophical History*. New York: Continuum, pp. 15–32.

Money, John and Anke E. Ehrhardt. 1972. *Man and Woman, Boy and Girl: The Differentiation and Dimorphism of Gender Identity from Conception to Maturity*. Baltimore: Johns Hopkins University Press.

Money, John, Joan G. Hampson, and John L. Hampson. 1955. "An Examination of Some Basic Sexual Concepts: The Evidence of Human Hermaphroditism." *Bulletin of the Johns Hopkins Hospital* 97(4): 301–19.

Morgan, Jennifer. 2004. *Laboring Women: Reproduction and Gender in New World Slavery*. Philadelphia: University of Pennsylvania Press.

Moses, Claire. 1984. *French Feminism in the Nineteenth Century*. Albany: SUNY Press.

Mucciaroni, Gary. 2017. "Whither the LGBTQ Movement in the Post-Civil Rights Era?" In Marla Brettschneider, Susan Burgess, and Christine Keating, eds. *LGBTQ Politics*. New York: New York University Press, pp. 525–44.

Muñoz, José Esteban. 2009. *Cruising Utopia: The Then and There of Queer Futurity*. New York: New York University Press.

Muñoz, José Esteban. 2013. "The White to Be Angry." In Susan Stryker and Aren Aizura, eds. *The Transgender Studies Reader 2*. New York: Routledge, pp. 79–90.

NACCD (National Advisory Commission on Civil Disorders). 1968. *Report of the National Advisory Commission on Civil Disorders*. Washington, DC: National Institute of Justice, US Department of Justice.

Nadler, Steven. 2016. "Baruch Spinoza." *The Stanford Encyclopedia of Philosophy*. Edward N. Zalta, ed., https://plato.stanford.edu/archives/fall2016/entries/spinoza.

Nagel, Thomas. 2005. "The Problem of Global Justice." *Philosophy and Public Affairs* 33: 113–47.

Najmabadi, Afsaneh. 2005. *Women with Mustaches, Men without Beards: Gender and Sexual Anxiety of Iranian Modernity*. Berkeley: University of California Press.

Najmabadi, Afsaneh. 2013. "Reading Transsexuality in 'Gay' Tehran (around 1979)." In Susan Stryker and Aren Aizura, eds. *The Transgender Studies Reader 2*. New York: Routledge, pp. 380–400.

Namaste, Viviane and Georgia Sitara. 2013. "Inclusive Pedagogy in the Women's Studies Classroom: Teaching the Kimberly Nixon Case." In Susan Stryker and Aren Aizura, eds. *The Transgender Studies Reader 2*. New York: Routledge, pp. 213–25.

Narayan, Uma. 1997. "Cross-Cultural Connections, Border-Crossings, and '*Death by Culture*': Thinking about Dowry-Murders in India and Domestic-Violence Murders in the United States." *Dislocating Cultures: Identities, Traditions and Third World Feminisms*. London: Taylor & Francis, pp. 81–118.

Nath, Dipika. 2008. "Discourses of Liberation or the Master's Tools?" https://www.academia.edu/4439534/Discourses_of_Liberation_or_the_Masters_Tools.

Nicholson, Linda. 1994. "Interpreting Gender." *Signs: Journal of Women in Culture and Society* 20 (1): 79–105.

Noble, Bobby Jean. 2013. "Our Bodies Are Not Ourselves: Tranny Guys and the Racialized Class Politics of Incoherence." In Susan Stryker and Aren Azira, eds. *The Transgender Studies Reader 2*. New York: Routledge, pp. 248–58.

Norton, Laura H. 2013. "Neutering the Transgendered: Human Rights and Japan's Law No. 111." In Susan Stryker and Aren Aizura, eds. *The Transgender Studies Reader 2*. New York: Routledge, pp. 591–603.

Novas, Carlos and Nikolas Rose. 2000. "Genetic Risk and the Birth of the Somatic Individual." *Economy and Society* 29(4): 485–513.

Nuti, Alasia. 2016. "How Should Marriage Be Theorized?" *Feminist Theory* 17(3): 285–303.

Oakley, Ann. 1972. *Sex, Gender and Society*. London: Temple Smith.

Offen, Karen. 2000. *European Feminisms, 1700–1950*. Stanford: Stanford University Press.

Okin, Susan Moller. 1979. *Women in Western Political Thought*. Princeton: Princeton University Press.

Okin, Susan Moller. 1989. *Justice, Gender and the Family*. New York: Basic Books.

Okin, Susan Moller. 1999. "Is Multiculturalism Bad for Women?" In Joshua Cohen, Matthew Howard, and Marth Nussbaum, eds. *Is Multiculturalism Bad for Women*. Princeton: Princeton University Press, pp. 7–26.

Okonjo, Kamene. 1994. "Women and the Evolution of a Ghanaian Political Synthesis." In Barbara Nelson and Najma Chowdhury, eds. *Women and Politics Worldwide*. New Haven: Yale University Press, pp. 285–97.

Olivera, Mercedes. 2006. "Violencia Feminicida: Violence against Women and Mexico's Structural Crisis." *Latin American Perspectives* 33(2): 104–14.

Osborne, Martha. 1979. *Women in Western Thought*. New York: Random House.

Oyewumi, Oyeronke. 1997. *The Invention of Women: Making an African Sense of Western Gender Discourses*. Minneapolis: University of Minnesota Press.

Pateman, Carole. 1988. *The Sexual Contract*. Cambridge: Polity Press.

Pateman, Carole. 1989. "Feminist Critiques of the Public/Private Dichotomy." *The Disorder of Women: Democracy, Feminism, and Political Theory*. Stanford: Stanford University Press, pp. 118–40.

Pateman, Carol. 1998. "The Patriarchal Welfare State." In Joan Landes, ed. *Feminism, the Public and the Private*. New York: Oxford University Press, pp. 241–74.

Pew Research Center for Religion and Public Life. 2017. "Gay Marriage Around the World." http://www.pewforum.org/2017/08/08/gay-marriage-around-the-world-2013.

Pharr, Suzanne. 1997. *Homophobia: Weapon of Sexism*. Berkeley: Chardon Press.

Phelan, Shane. 2001. *Sexual Strangers: Gays, Lesbians, and Dilemmas of Citizenship*. Philadelphia: Temple University Press.

Pinker, Steven. 2002. *The Blank Slate: The Modern Denial of Human Nature*. New York: Penguin Books.

Piscopo, Jennifer. 2016. "State Capacity, Criminal Justice, and Political Rights: Rethinking Violence Against Women in Politics." *Política y gobierno* 23(2): 437–58.

Plato. 1961. *Republic*. E. Hamilton and H. Cairns, eds. *Plato: The Collected Dialogues*. Princeton: Princeton University Press.

Plumwood, Val. 1994. *Feminism and the Mastery of Nature*. New York: Routledge.

Pocock, J.G.A. 1973. *Politics, Language, and Time*. New York: Atheneum.

Poole, Kristen. 1995. "'The Fittest Closet for All Goodness': Authorial Strategies of Jacobean Mothers' Manuals." *Studies in English Literature* 35(1): 69–89.

Posocco, Silvia. 2014. "On the Queer Necropolitics of Transnational Adoption." In Jin Haritaworn, Adi Kuntsman, and Silvia Posocco, eds. *Queer Necropolitics*. New York: Routledge, pp. 72–90.

Preciado, Beatriz. 2013. "The Pharmaco-Pornographic Regime: Sex, Gender and Subjectivity in the Age of Punk Capitalism." In Susan Stryker and Aren Azira, eds. *The Transgender Studies Reader 2*. New York: Routledge, pp. 266–77.

Preves, Sharon. 2003. *Intersex and Identity: The Contested Self*. New Brunswick: Rutgers University Press.

Price, J. Ricky. 2017. "The Treatment and Prevention of HIV Bodies: The Contemporary Politics and Science of a Thirty-Year-Old Epidemic." In Marla Brettschneider, Susan Burgess, and Christine Keating, eds. *LGBTQ Politics*. New York: New York University Press, pp. 54–71.

Price, Kimala. 2017. "Queering Reproductive Justice: Toward a Theory and Practice for Building Intersectional Political Alliances." In Marla Brettschneider, Susan Burgess, and Christine Keating, eds. *LGBTQ Politics*. New York: New York University Press, pp. 72–88.

Puar, Jasbir. 2007. *Terrorist Assemblage: Homonationalism in Queer Times.* Durham, NC: Duke University Press.

Puar, Jasbir. 2017. *The Right to Maim: Debility, Capacity, Disability.* Durham, NC: Duke University Press.

Quijano, Anibal. 2000. "Coloniality of Power, Eurocentrism, and Latin America." *Nepantla: Views from South* 1(3): 533–80.

Rabinow, Paul and Nikolas Rose. 2003. "Thoughts on the Concept of Biopower Today." Paper presented at the Conference on Vital Politics: Health, Medicine, and Bioeconomics in the 21st Century. London School of Economics. September 5–7.

Ranchod-Nilsson, Sita. 2008. "Gender Politics and Gender Backlash in Zimbabwe." *Politics & Gender* 4(4): 642–52.

Rao, Rahul. 2010. *Third World Protest: Between Home and the World.* Oxford: Oxford University Press.

Rao, Rahul. 2012. "On Gay 'Conditionality,' Imperial Power and Queer Liberation." *Kafila,* January 1, https://kafila.online/2012/01/01/on-gay-conditionality-imperial-power-and-queer-liberation-rahul-rao.

Rawls, John. 1971. *A Theory of Justice.* Cambridge, MA: Harvard University Press.

Reich, Robert B. 1991. "Secession of the Successful." *New York Times Magazine.* January 20, http://www.nytimes.com/1991/01/20/magazine/secession-of-the-successful.html?pagewanted=1.

Rein, Lisa and Andrew Ba Tran. 2017. "How the Trump Era is Changing the Federal Bureaucracy." *The Washington Post.* December 30, https://www.washingtonpost.com/politics/how-the-trump-era-is-changing-the-federal-bureaucracy/2017/12/30/8d5149c6-daa7-11e7-b859-fb0995360725_story.html?utm_term=.1c70bdca7bfe.

Reis, Elizabeth. 2009. *Bodies in Doubt: An American History of Intersex.* Baltimore: Johns Hopkins.

Rich, Adrienne. 1980. "Compulsory Heterosexuality and Lesbian Existence." *Signs: Journal of Women in Culture and Society* 5(4): 631–60.

Richardson, Sara. 2012. "Sexing the X: How the X Became the 'Female Chromosome'." *Signs: Journal of Women in Culture and Society* 37(4): 909–33.

Rivera Cusicanqui, Silvia. 2004. "La noción de 'derecho' o las paradojas de la modernidad postcolonial: indígenas y mujeres en Bolivia." *Revista Aportes Andinos* 11: 1–15. Ecuador: Universidad Andina Simon

Bolivar, http://repositorio.uasb.edu.ec/bitstream/10644/678/1/RAA -11-Rivera-La%20noci%C3%B3n%20de%20derecho%20o%20las%20 paradojas%20de%20la%20modernidad.pdf.

Roberts, Dorothy. 1997. *Killing the Black Body: Race, Reproduction, and the Meaning of Liberty.* New York: Vintage Books.

Roberts, Dorothy. 2011. *Fatal Invention: How Science, Politics, and Big Business Re-create Race in the 21st Century.* New York: The New Press.

Rosario, Vernon A. 2007. "The History of Aphallia and the Intersexual Challenge to Sex/Gender." In George E. Haggerty and Molly McGarry, eds. *A Companion to Lesbian, Gay, Bisexual, Transgender, and Queer Studies.* London: Blackwell, pp. 262–81.

Rose, Nikolas. 2000. "The Politics of Life Itself." *Theory, Culture, and Society* 18(6): 1–30.

Rose, Nikolas and Peter Miller. 1992. "Political Power Beyond the State: Problematics of Government." *British Journal of Sociology* 43(2): 172–205.

Rose, Tricia. 2013. "Public Tales Wag the Dog: Telling Stories about Structural Racism in the Post-Civil Rights Era." *Du Bois Review* 10(2): 447–69.

Rosen, Hannah. 2009. *Terror in the Heart of Freedom: Citizenship, Sexual Violence, and the Meaning of Race in the Postemancipation South.* Chapel Hill: University of North Carolina Press.

Roughgarden, Joan. 2004. *Evolution's Rainbow: Diversity, Gender, and Sexuality in Nature and People.* Berkeley: University of California Press.

Rousseau, Jean Jacques. 1762 [1950]. *The Social Contract.* G.D.H. Cole, trans. New York: E.P. Dutton.

Rousseau, Jean Jacques. 1762 [1955]. *Emile.* Barbara Foxley, trans. New York: E.P. Dutton.

Rubin, David A. 2012. "'An Unnamed Blank that Craved a Name': A Genealogy of Intersex and Gender." *Signs: Journal of Women in Culture and Society* 37(4): 883–908.

Rubin, David A. 2017. *Intersex Matters: Biomedical Embodiment, Gender Regulation, and Transnational Activism.* Albany: SUNY Press.

Rubin, Gayle. 1975. "The Traffic in Women: Notes on the Political Economy of Sex." In Rayner Reiter, ed. *Toward an Anthropology of Women.* New York: Monthly Review Press, pp. 157–210.

Rubin, Gayle. 1984. "Thinking Sex: Notes for a Radical Theory of the

Politics of Sexuality." In Carol Vance, ed. *Pleasure and Danger: Exploring Female Sexuality.* Boston: Routledge and Kegan Paul, pp. 143–78.

Rubin, Gayle. 2011. *Deviations: A Gayle Rubin Reader.* Durham, NC: Duke University Press.

Rubin, Lillian. 1993. "The Sexual Dilemma." In Alison Jaggar and Paula Rothenberg, eds. *Feminist Frameworks*, 3rd edition. New York: McGraw Hill, pp. 461–8.

Rupp, Leila and Carly Thomsen. 2016. "Sexualities." In Lisa Disch and Mary Hawkesworth, eds. *Oxford Handbook of Feminist Theory.* New York: Oxford University Press, pp. 894–914.

Salamon, Gayle. 2010. *Assuming a Body: Transgender and Rhetorics of Materiality.* New York: Columbia University Press.

Salguero, Elizabeth. 2017. "Tackling Violence against Women in Political Life: Insights from UN Women." Conference on Resisting Women's Political Leadership: Theories, Data, Solutions. Rutgers University, New Brunswick, May 24.

Scheman, Naomi. 1997. "Queering the Center by Centering the Queer." In Diana Meyers, ed. *Feminists Rethink the Self.* Boulder: Westview Press, pp. 124–62.

Schott, Robin May. 2011. "War Rape, Social Death and Political Evil." *Development Dialogue* 55 (March): 47–62.

Scott, James. 1998. *Seeing Like a State: How Certain Schemes to Improve the Human Condition Have Failed.* New Haven: Yale University Press.

Scott, Joan. 1986. "Gender: A Useful Category for Historical Analysis." *American Historical Review* 91: 1053–75.

Sears, Clare. 2013. "Electric Brilliancy: Cross Dressing Laws and Freak Show Displays in Nineteenth Century San Francisco." In Susan Stryker and Aren Aizura, eds. *The Transgender Reader 2.* New York: Routledge, pp. 554–64.

Sedgwick, Eve. 1985. *Between Men: English Literature and Male Homosocial Desire.* New York: Columbia University Press.

Sedgwick, Eve. 1990. *Epistemology of the Closet.* Berkeley: University of California Press.

Sedgwick, Eve. 2003. *Touching Feeling: Affect, Pedagogy, Performativity.* Durham, NC: Duke University Press.

Segato, Rita. 2011. "Género y colonialidad: en busca de claves delectura y de un vocabulario estratégico descolonial." In Karina Bidaseca y

Vanesa Vazquez Laba, eds. *Feminismos y poscolonialidad. Descolonizando el feminismo desde y en América Latina*. Buenos Aires: Godot, pp. 17–48.

Shakhsari, Sima. 2014. "Killing Me Softly With Your Rights: Queer Death and the Politics of Rightful Killing." In Jin Haritaworn, Adi Kuntsman, and Silvia Posocco, eds. *Queer Necropolitics*. New York: Routledge, pp. 93–110.

Shalhoub-Kevorkian, Nadera. 2003. "Reexamining Femicide: Breaking the Silence and Crossing 'Scientific' Borders." *Signs: Journal of Women in Culture and Society* 28(2): 581–608.

Sheffield, Carole. 1984. "Sexual Terrorism." In Jo Freeman, ed. *Women: A Feminist Perspective*, 3rd edition. Mountain View: Mayfield Publishing Co, pp. 1–20.

Shrage, Laurie. 2012. "Does Government Need to Know Your Sex?" *The Journal of Political Philosophy* 20(2): 225–47.

Simien, Evelyn. 2007. "Doing Intersectionality Research: From Conceptual Issues to Practical Examples." *Politics & Gender* 3(2): 264–71.

Simpson, Leanne Betasamosake. 2017. *As We Have Always Done: Indigenous Freedom Through Radical Resistance*. Minneapolis: University of Minnesota Press.

Singh, Nikhil Pal. 2004. *Black is a Country: Race and the Unfinished Struggle for Democracy*. Cambridge, MA: Harvard University Press.

Sjoberg, Laura. 2016. *Women as Wartime Rapists: Beyond Sensation and Stereotyping*. New York: New York University Press.

Skocpol, Theda. 1979. *State and Revolutions*. Cambridge: Cambridge University Press.

Smith, Alison A. 1998. "Gender, Ownership and Domestic Space: Inventories and Family Archives in Renaissance Verona." *Renaissance Studies* 12(3): 375–91.

Smith, Anna Marie. 2016. "Subjectivity and Subjectivation." In Lisa Disch and Mary Hawkesworth, eds. *Oxford Handbook of Feminist Theory*. New York: Oxford University Press, pp. 955–72.

Smith, Steven G. 1992. *Gender Thinking*. Philadelphia: Temple University Press.

Spade, Dean and Craig Willse. 2016. "Norms and Normalization." In Lisa Disch and Mary Hawkesworth, eds. *Oxford Handbook of Feminist Theory*. New York: Oxford University Press, pp. 551–71.

Spelman, Elizabeth. 1988. *Inessential Woman*. Boston: Beacon Press.

Spinoza, Baruch. 1677 [1994]. *The Ethics and Other Works*. E. Curley, trans. and ed. Princeton: Princeton University Press.

Stevens, Jacqueline. 1999. *Reproducing the State*. Princeton: Princeton University Press.

Stoler, Ann Laura, 1995. *Race and the Education of Desire*. Durham, NC: Duke University Press.

Stoller, Robert. 1985. *Presentations of Gender*. New Haven: Yale University Press.

Strossen, Nadine. 1993. "Preface: Fighting Big Sister for Liberty and Equality." *New York Law School Review* 37: 1–8.

Strossen, Nadine. 1995. *Defending Pornography: Free Speech, Sex, and the Fight for Women's Rights*. New York: Scribner.

Stryker, Susan. 1994. "My Words to Victor Frankenstein above the Village of Chamounix: Performing Transgender Rage." *GLQ* 1(3): 237–54.

Stryker, Susan. 2013. "Kaming Mga Talyada (We Who Are Sexy): The Transsexual Whiteness of Christine Jorgensen in the (Post)colonial Philippines." In Susan Stryker and Aren Aizura, eds. *The Transgender Studies Reader 2*. New York: Routledge, pp. 543–53.

Stryker, Susan and Aren Aizura, eds. 2013. *The Transgender Studies Reader 2*. New York: Routledge.

Sturge, Joseph and Thomas Harvey. 1837 [1968]. *The West Indies in 1837*. London: Dawsons of Pall Mall.

Sullivan, Laura, Tatjana Meschede, Lars Dietrich, Thomas Shapiro, Amy Traub, Catherine Ruetschlin, and Tamara Draut. 2015. *The Racial Wealth Gap: Why Policy Matters*. New York: Demos, http://www.demos.org/sites/default/files/publications/RacialWealthGap_1.pdf.

Tang-Martinez, Zuleyma. 1997. "The Curious Courtship of Sociobiology and Feminism: A Case of Irreconcilable Differences." In Patricia Adair Gawaty, ed. *Feminism and Evolutionary Biology*. New York: Chapman Hall, pp. 116–50.

Thomas, Jerry D. 2017. "Queer Sensibilities and Other Fagchild Tools." In Marla Brettschneider, Susan Burgess, and Christine Keating, eds. *LGBTQ Politics*. New York: New York University Press, pp. 394–413.

Thomas, Kylie. 2013. *Homophobia, Injustice, and Corrective Rape in Post-Apartheid South Africa*. Centre for the Study of Violence and Reconciliation and Centre for the Humanities. University of the

Western Cape, South Africa. https://www.files.ethz.ch/isn/16 6656/k_thomas_homophobia_injustice_and_corrective%20rape_in_ post_apartheid_sa.pdf.

Tillyard, Stella B. 1995. *Aristocrats: Caroline, Emily, Louisa and Sarah Lennox, 1750–1832*. London: Chatto and Windus.

Tong, Rosemarie. 2014. *Feminist Thought: A More Comprehensive Introduction*, 4th edition. Boulder: Westview Press.

Towns, Ann. 2009. "The Status of Women as a Standard of 'Civilization'." *European Journal of International Relations* 15(4): 681–706.

Towns, Ann. 2010. *Women and States: Norms and Hierarchies in International Society*. Cambridge: Cambridge University Press.

Tuana, Nancy. 1997. "Fleshing Gender, Sexing the Body: Refiguring the Sex-Gender Distinction." *Southern Journal of Philosophy* 35(1): 53–71.

Vaccaro, Jeanne. 2013. "Felt Matters." In Susan Stryker and Aren Aizura, eds. *The Transgender Studies Reader 2*. New York: Routledge, pp. 91–100.

Vickery, Amanda. 1998. *The Gentleman's Daughter: Women's Lives in Georgian England*. New Haven: Yale University Press.

Vincent, Andrew. 2004. "Conceptions of the State." In Mary Hawkesworth and Maurice Kogan, eds. *Encyclopedia of Government and Politics*, 2nd edition. London: Routledge, pp. 39–53.

Wacquant, Loïc. 2002. "Deadly Symbiosis: Rethinking Race and Imprisonment in Twenty-First-Century America." *Boston Review* (April/May), http://bostonreview.net/BR27.2/wacquant.html.

Wacquant, Loïc. 2008. "The Body, the Ghetto, and the Penal State." *Qualitative Sociology* 32(1): 101–29.

Wall, Corey. 2007. "Application Denied: Kimberly Nixon v. Vancouver Rape Relief Society." The Court.CA. February 7, http://www. thecourt.ca/application-denied-kimberly-nixon-v-vancouver-rape-relief-society.

Walzer, Michael. 1983. *Spheres of Justice*. New York: Basic Books.

Ward, Julie K. 2016. "Roots of Modern Racism: Early Modern Philosophers on Race." *The Critique*, Special Issue, The Bright Continent: Illuminating the Challenges, Opportunities & Promises of a Rising Africa (September–October): 1–22.

Warner, Michael. 1991. "Introduction: Fear of a Queer Planet." *Social Text* 9(4): 3–17.

Warner, Michael. 1993. *Fear of a Queer Planet*. Minneapolis: University of Minnesota Press.

Weber, Cynthia, 2016. *Queer International Relations: Sovereignty, Sexuality, and the Will to Knowledge*. Oxford: Oxford University Press.

Weber, Max. 1919 [1946]. "Politics as a Vocation." *From Max Weber: Essays in Sociology*. Hans Gerth and C. Wright Mills, trans. and eds. New York: Oxford University Press, pp. 77–128.

Weinrich, James. 1982. "Is Homosexuality Biologically Natural?" In William Paul, James Weinrich, John Gonsiorek and Mary E. Hodveldt, eds. *Homosexuality: Social Psychological, and Biological Issues*. Beverly Hills: Sage Publications, pp. 197–211.

Weismantel, Mary. 2013. "Towards a Transgender Archaeology: A Queer Rampage through Prehistory." In Susan Stryker and Aren Azira, eds. *The Transgender Studies Reader 2*. New York: Routledge, pp. 319–34.

Weiss, Jillian Todd. 2001. "The Gender Caste System: Identity, Privacy, and Heteronormativity." *Law and Sexuality* 10(1): 123–86.

West, Candace and Zimmerman, Don. 1987. "Doing Gender." *Gender and Society* 1(2): 125–51.

Willen, Diane. 1989. "Women and Religion in Early Medieval England." In Sherrin Marshall, ed. *Women in Reformation and Counter-Reformation Europe: Public and Private Worlds*. Bloomington: Indiana University Press, pp. 140–88.

Wilson, Edward O. 1975. *Sociobiology: The New Synthesis*. Cambridge, MA: Harvard University Press.

Wilson, Edward O. 1978. *On Human Nature*. Cambridge, MA: Harvard University Press.

Wimmer, Andreas and Nina Glick Schiller. 2003. "Methodological Nationalism, the Social Sciences, and the Study of Migration: An Essay in Historical Epistemology." *The International Migration Review* 37(3): 576–610.

Wingrove, Elizabeth. 2016. "Materialisms." In Lisa Disch and Mary Hawkesworth, ed. *Oxford Handbook of Feminist Theory*. New York: Oxford University Press, pp. 454–71.

Wittig, Monique. 1979. "One Is Not Born a Woman." *Proceedings of the Second Sex Conference*. New York: Institute for the Humanities.

Wittig, Monique. 1992. *The Straight Mind and Other Essays*. Boston: Beacon Press.

Wollstonecraft, Mary. 1792 [1975]. *Vindication of the Rights of Woman.* Carol H. Poston, ed. New York: W.W. Norton.

Young, Iris. 1990. *Justice and the Politics of Difference.* Princeton: Princeton University Press.

Young, Iris. 1994. "Gender as Seriality: Thinking about Women as a Social Collective." *Signs: Journal of Women in Culture and Society* 19(3): 713–38.

Yuval Davis, Nira. 1997. *Gender and Nation.* London: Sage Publications.

Yuval Davis, Nira. 2006. "Belonging and the Politics of Belonging." *Patterns of Prejudice* 40(3): 197–214.

Index

Index

racialization 16–17
  colonialism and 70, 72–7, 134, 163–5
  embodiment and 62, 66–72
  parallels with feminization 23
  as political process 16
  public/private spheres and 88–117
  state employment of 135–44
  state injustice 163–70
Ranchod-Nilsson, Sita 174
rape 107–10
  of enslaved women 100
  gang rape 108–9, 174
  LGBTQ people, attacks on 109
  male-on-male rape 108
  marital rape 103
  patriarchal framing 109
  politicizing 109
  racial dynamics 108–9
  relations of domination 107, 108
  sexual terrorism 107–8
rationality 12, 63, 64, 65–6, 72, 95, 160, 163, 187
Rawls, John 98, 161–2, 186–7
reality enforcement 176, 179
reproduction
  heterornormative ideology of procreation 46
  politicized 128
  privileged as heterosexual domain 40
  pronatalist legislation 128
  risks and opportunities 45
  sexual differentiation and 45–6, 55
republicanism 96, 97, 98
residential segregation 165–6
Restrepo, Juliana 172
Rich, Adrienne 39
rights-bearers 160–1
Roberts, Dorothy 66, 67
Rose, Nikolas 77
Rosen, Hannah 108–9
Roughgarden, Joan 78
Rousseau, Jean-Jacques 13
Rubin, David 24, 31, 33

Sartre, Jean-Paul 55, 56
Scala Natura 63
Scheman, Naomi 152
Schiller, Nina Glick 129
Scott, James 134–5, 140
Sears, Clare 137
secondary sex characteristics 35
Sedgwick, Eve 39, 57, 174
Segato, Rita 75
self-identification 6
seriality 55, 56
servitude 64, 65, 74
sex
  binary constructions 5, 14
  biological sex 35, 41, 42
  canonical conceptions of 12–14, 65, 71–2
  chromosomal sex 35, 36
  denaturalizing 14–21
  natural attitude 11–12, 15, 42–3, 47, 50, 52, 56
  proliferating diversity in nature 36, 78–9
sex confirmation surgery 2, 3, 4, 119, 149
sex radical feminists 115
sex-specific sexual practices 43–4
sex/gender distinction 26, 59
  base/superstructure model of 28
sexual difference 13, 14, 18, 22, 23, 44
  Aristotle on 12
  attitudinal and behavioral differences 37
  brain and 44–5
  erotic pleasure and 57
  naturalization of 15
sexual dimorphism 16, 18, 31, 33–8, 43, 46, 47, 71, 79, 86
  and politics of modernity 34
sexual harassment policies 175, 176
sexual objectification of women 174
sexuality 106–10
  denaturalizing 38–41
  domination and 38
  "mature sexuality" 38–9
  normalization of 19

how she constructed this bk —

17th c colour~~geter~~ concepts —

2 sexes
& etc
5 races,

← (in rel to colonization proje
forwarding

using trans / queer to
show this

Laqueur - History of the
Body

think about how to think about
the LGBTQ text

This entire bk is a repudiation of dominance, not only in word — though that would be a remarkable feat in & of itself, but in deed / in form by taking on an authoritative, ___ voice that challenges what we are "supposed" to be.

No small feat b/c so much of political science asks us, or compels us, to perform subservience.

So many, but
Mary & Shane

what is yr + theory?

111 FS bk

86 for bk ~~por~~ 102 105